D1601050

MANAGEMENT EDUCATION AND COMPETITIVENESS

Globally two processes are striking about modern management education. First, management education is changing rapidly to meet new challenges from business and governments and to improve competitiveness. Second, management education has become one of the fastest growing areas in higher education.

These developments ask for comparative research of the progress and function of different systems of management education. *Management Education and Competitiveness* provides a wide overview, including studies by scholars in nine countries in Europe, Japan and the United States. It examines how countries have developed different national systems in spite of strong influence from the American system of management education. It also examines the links between education and business. Understanding the processes through which each country has arrived at its present style of management education indicates the direction for further development. This collection of essays will be invaluable to managers and professionals in educational research and business administration.

Rolv Petter Amdam is Associate Professor of Business History at the Norwegian School of Management in Oslo. He developed this book whilst a Visiting Research Fellow at the University of Reading. He is the co-author of *Wealth of Contrasts: Nyegaard & Co – A Norwegian Pharmaceutical Company* and co-editor of *Crossing the Borders: Studies in Norwegian Business History*

ROUTLEDGE INTERNATIONAL STUDIES IN
BUSINESS HISTORY
Series editor: Geoffrey Jones

1 MANAGEMENT, EDUCATION AND COMPETITIVENESS
Edited by Rolv Petter Amdam

MANAGEMENT EDUCATION AND COMPETITIVENESS

Europe, Japan and the United States

Edited by

Rolv Petter Amdam

London and New York

First published 1996
by Routledge
11 New Fetter Lane, London EC4P 4EE

Simultaneously published in the USA and Canada
by Routledge
29 West 35th Street, New York, NY 10001

© 1996 Rolv Petter Amdam

Typeset in Garamond by LaserScript, Mitcham, Surrey
Printed and bound in Great Britain by
Mackays of Chatham PLC, Chatham, Kent

British Library Cataloguing in Publication Data
A catalogue record for this book is available from the British Library

Library of Congress Cataloging in Publication Data
A catalogue record for this book has been requested

ISBN 0–415–12092–6

CONTENTS

List of illustrations   vii
Notes on contributors   ix
Preface   xiii

1 INTRODUCTION   1
   Rolv Petter Amdam

Part I Different systems of management education

2 NATIONAL SYSTEMS VERSUS FOREIGN MODELS
   IN MANAGEMENT EDUCATION – THE
   NORWEGIAN CASE   19
   Rolv Petter Amdam

3 AMERICAN INFLUENCE ON EUROPEAN
   MANAGEMENT EDUCATION – THE ROLE OF
   THE FORD FOUNDATION   38
   Giuliana Gemelli

4 CONTINUITIES IN DUTCH BUSINESS EDUCATION –
   ENGINEERING, ECONOMICS, AND THE BUSINESS
   SCHOOL   69
   Huibert de Man

5 BUSINESS STUDIES AND MANAGEMENT EDUCATION
   IN JAPAN'S ECONOMIC DEVELOPMENT – AN
   INSTITUTIONAL PERSPECTIVE   96
   Tamotsu Nishizawa

6 MANAGEMENT EDUCATION IN A COUNTRY IN
   TRANSITION – THE CASE OF SLOVENIA   111
   Marjan Svetličič and Andreja Čibron

CONTENTS

Part II Management education and business

7 MANAGEMENT EDUCATION IN BRITAIN –
   A COMPROMISE BETWEEN CULTURE AND
   NECESSITY   133
   John F. Wilson

8 DO THEY MEAN BUSINESS? AN INVESTIGATION
   OF THE PURPOSE OF THE 'NEW UNIVERSITY'
   BUSINESS SCHOOLS IN BRITAIN   150
   Reva Berman Brown, Sean McCartney, and Jeff Clowes

9 THE INSTITUTIONALIZATION OF INDUSTRIAL
   ADMINISTRATION IN NORWAY 1950–90 –
   CONSEQUENCES FOR EDUCATION IN BUSINESS
   ADMINISTRATION OF DOMINATION BY
   ENGINEERING   171
   Haldor Byrkjeflot and Tor Halvorsen

10 MERCURY'S MESSENGERS – SWEDISH BUSINESS
    GRADUATES IN PRACTICE   194
    Lars Engwall, Elving Gunnarsson, and Eva Wallerstedt

11 DINOSAURS IN THE GLOBAL ECONOMY?
    AMERICAN GRADUATE BUSINESS SCHOOLS IN
    THE 1980s AND 1990s   212
    Susan Aaronson

12 MANAGING MANAGEMENT TEAMS – A
    CHALLENGE FOR MANAGEMENT EDUCATION   227
    Ove Bjarnar and Hallgeir Gammelsæter

13 BETWEEN ACADEMIA AND BUSINESS – NEW
    CHALLENGES FOR TODAY'S MODERN BUSINESS
    SCHOOLS   246
    Peter Lorange

    Index   259

LIST OF ILLUSTRATIONS

FIGURES

7.1	MBS income shares	140
7.2	MBA intake, 1965–6 to 1989–90	141
7.3	Income and surplus or deficit	141
12.1	The combination of type of knowledge and object of education and the resulting paradigms	235

TABLES

3.1	The American contribution to INSEAD 1971–2	44
4.1	Major dichotomies in management education	78
4.2	Hierarchy of applied sciences according to Goudriaan	81
6.1	Evaluation of the quality of teachers	116
6.2	MBA graduates according to the size and ownership of the company	118
6.3	What motives decisively influenced your decision to start studying for an MBA?	120
6.4	If asked, would you again select the same MBA programme?	121
6.5	Were expectations regarding MBA studies realized?	123
6.6	What would be the advantages of studying for an MBA abroad?	124
6.7	Which type of knowledge do you consider as the most useful?	124
6.8	Have you utilized your knowledge?	125
8.1	The model of university business schools	161
8.2	Research in university business schools	163
8.3	Teaching in university business schools	164
8.4	Education and training in the university business school	165
10.1	Five epochs in Swedish business administration	198
10.2	Background of top managers in Sweden	203
10.3	Educational background of top managers in different industry sectors	204

10.4 Proportion of top managers making their career in a single
      company   204
10.5 Proportion of Swedish top managers with business, engineering,
      and law degrees   205
10.6 Relative success of graduates in top management   206
10.7 Relative success in top management for business, engineering,
      and law graduates in two sectors of Swedish private enterprise   207
12.1 Number of articles or responses to articles focusing on top
      management team(s) in three US-based academic journals on
      management in the period 1974–94   240

NOTES ON CONTRIBUTORS

Susan Aaronson is Assistant Professor of History at the University of North Texas and Guest Scholar, Economics, The Brookings Institute. She has taught at the George Washington University. Her recent research focuses on how policy makers communicate and the public understands trade policy, and her publications include *Trade is Everybody's Business* (Close-Up Publisher, 1995).

Rolv Petter Amdam is Associate Professor of Business History at the Centre for Business History, Norwegian School of Management in Oslo. In 1993–4, he was a Visiting Research Fellow at the University of Reading. He is co-author of *Wealth of Contrasts: Nyegaard & Co. – A Norwegian Pharmaceutical Company* (Oslo: Ad Notam, 1994), and co-editor of *Crossing the Borders: Studies in Norwegian Business History* (Scandinavian University Press, 1994). He has also published widely on the development of management ideas and institutions for management education.

Ove Bjarnar is Research Fellow at Møre Research Centre, Molde College, in Norway. His main research areas are business history and organizational history. He is also a Visiting Research Fellow at the Centre for Business History, Norwegian School of Management, and University of Reading. His publications include books on educational history as well as on the development of regional business communities.

Reva Berman Brown is Research Reader in Management at Nene College, Northampton. She completed her PhD, entitled 'The Business of Knowledge and the Knowledge of Business', an investigation of the knowledge strategies of British university business school academics, at the University of Bradford, in 1991. From 1991 to 1995, she was a Lecturer in Management at the University of Essex, and Director of the MBA Programme. Her research interests range from the exploration of time as an organizational variable, through competence and capability as managerial attributes, to professionalism in the National Health Service, management education, and business history.

Haldor Byrkjeflot is Research Fellow at the Norwegian Research Centre in Organization and Management in Bergen. His main research areas are economic sociology, political economy and historical comparative studies of capitalism. Among his publications are papers on technological change and human resources in the service sector and on management education in the United States and Germany.

Andreja Čibron is a Master of Science (Sociology), and works as chief editor of an internal newspaper at the Ravne Iron Works, Slovenia. She has published several articles, on self-managed enterprises in particular.

Jeff Clowes is Senior Lecturer in Marketing at Coventry Business School at Coventry University. He joined the University in 1989 after working in management and marketing positions for several companies in the United States. His main research interests are in the marketing of services, particularly education and leisure. He is currently investigating the sponsorship of sport by major firms.

Lars Engwall is Professor of Business Administration at Uppsala University, Sweden. He holds a PhD from Stockholm University and has devoted his research primarily towards the analysis of organizational strategy and the diffusion of management ideas. Among his publications are *Newspapers as Organizations* (Saxon House, 1978) and *Mercury Meets Minerva: Business Studies and Higher Education* (Pergamon Press, 1992).

Hallgeir Gammelsæter is Senior Research Fellow at Møre Research Centre, Molde College, in Norway. His main research area is management and organizational change. He obtained his PhD degree in administration and organizational theory from the University of Bergen on the basis of a dissertation on organizational change through generations of managers. His publications include articles on divisionalization and on small and middle-sized enterprises.

Giuliana Gemelli is Professor of French Contemporary History at the University of Bologna, Italy. Her main field of research is on the history of science and scientific institutions, especially in the fields of social sciences and economics. Her recent publications include the editing of *Big Culture: Intellectual Cooperation in Large-Scale Cultural and Technical Systems* (CLUEB, Bologna, 1994).

Elving Gunnarsson is Lecturer in the Department of Business Studies at Uppsala University, Sweden. He gained a PhD for a dissertation on the development of business education in Sweden in the nineteenth century. His present research interests focus on management education as an academic discipline, and together with Lars Engwall he has edited *Management Studies in an Academic Context* (Acta Universitatis Upsaliensis, 1994).

Tor Halvorsen is Associate Professor in the Department of Administration and Organizational Science, University of Bergen, Norway. He is also attached to Christian Michelsen's Institute for the Studies of Development and Human Rights. His main research interest is on the relationship between education and work organization in Europe and South Asia.

Peter Lorange has been President of IMD in Lausanne since 1993. He is Professor of Strategy and holds the Maucher Nestlé Chair. He was affiliated with The Wharton School at the University of Pennsylvania for a decade, and had various assignments, including being Professor of Multinational Management. From 1989 to 1993 he was President of the Norwegian School of Management. His areas of special interest are business policy, strategic planning, global strategic management, strategic alliances, and strategic control. His publications include *Strategic Alliances: Formation, Implementation and Evolution* (Blackwell, 1992) with Johan Roos, and *Strategic Planning and Control* (Blackwell, 1993).

Sean McCartney is Lecturer in Accounting at the University of Essex. His research interests include accounting and management education, professionalism in the National Health Service, auditing, and business and accounting history. He has published articles on accounting education.

Huibert de Man is Senior Lecturer at the Open University of the Netherlands, where he is responsible for the development of courses in the field of organization and research methodology. In 1988, he obtained his PhD degree on the basis of a dissertation on organizational change. In the last few years, his research interests have focused on the history and function of the management sciences and on management educational institutions.

Tamotsu Nishizawa is Professor at the Institute of Economic Research, Hitotsubashi University, in Japan. His current research area is the development of economics and business studies in British and Japanese colleges and universities. He has recently published a study of Birmingham Economists in the Early Nineteenth Century, and a chapter on Tokyo University of Commerce in T. Yuzawa (ed.) *Japanese Business Success* (Routledge, 1994).

Marjan Svetličič is Professor and Head of the Centre for International Relations at the Faculty of Sciences, University of Ljubljana, Slovenia. He has published widely on foreign direct investment, and he is co-author of *Foreign Investment in Central and Eastern Europe* (St Martin's Press, 1993).

Eva Wallerstedt is Lecturer in the Department of Business Studies at Uppsala University, Sweden. She gained a PhD from Uppsala for a thesis on the development of business studies in Sweden. Her present research interest focuses on the professionalization of auditors in Sweden.

John F. Wilson is Lecturer in Economic History at the University of Manchester. His main research interests are the development, management, and finance of British and Japanese business since the eighteenth century. Among his publications are *'The Manchester Experiment': A History of Manchester Business School, 1965–1990* (Paul Chapman, 1991) and *British Business History, 1720–1994* (Manchester University Press, 1995).

PREFACE

In the 1980s and 1990s, management education has been one of the fastest-growing areas within the educational systems of many countries. However, surprisingly few scholars devote their time to studying the development and function of institutions for management education. Like many other new fields of research, papers are published in different kinds of journals within different disciplines. Several small research networks are emerging, but unfortunately with very little contact between them. It may therefore be hard to get an overview of research in the field.

This book is a result of one attempt to develop an interdisciplinary and international research network on the development and function of institutions for management education. In 1991, Lars Engwall of Uppsala University invited some scholars to a symposium there to celebrate the 250th anniversary of the appointment of the first Swedish professor of economics and business, Anders Berch. What came out of that symposium was a comparative analysis of management education, with contributors from seven countries (see L. Engwall and E. Gunnarsson (eds) *Management Studies in an Academic Context*, Uppsala: Acta Universitatis Upsaliensis, 1994). In May 1994, some of the participants who met in Uppsala were invited, with other scholars, to a conference at the University of Reading in Britain. This book, which contains thirteen papers from scholars in nine countries, has emerged out of the Reading conference.

I want to thank all the participants who accepted the invitation to come to Reading, wrote a paper, and after the conference supported the editing with new drafts and listened patiently to comments and suggestions. I also want to thank Peter Lorange of IMD, Lausanne, and Tamotsu Nishizawa of Hitotsubashi University, Tokyo, for responding to an invitation to write papers even though they were not able to participate in the conference. Most of the comments came during discussions at this conference. Besides comments from those who are represented in this book, we have also received critical and useful comments from Frances Bostock, Lisa Bud-Frierman, Keith Burgess, Mark Casson, T.A.B. Corley, Andrew Godley, Peter Hart, Geoffrey Jones, and Alan Roberts.

The conference was a result of the year I spent as Visiting Research Fellow in the Department of Economics at the University of Reading. My grateful thanks go to the Head of the Department, Professor Mark Casson, and to the Professor of Business History, Geoffrey Jones, who invited me to Reading and allowed me to organize the conference. I also want to thank the Norwegian Research Council, which provided me with money to stay overseas for a period, and accepted an application for an additional grant to finance the conference. The Business History Research Foundation at the Norwegian School of Management has also been very helpful in financially supporting the publication of this book.

During my stay at Reading, I was attached to the Business History Group. I discovered there some of the secrets behind what creates an exciting research milieu. One of the key factors, I found out, is linked to the enthusiasm and quality of the person at the head of this environment. Geoffrey Jones is a very supportive host, with a deep belief in interdisciplinary and comparative studies. Besides encouraging me to organize the conference, he also stimulated me to produce this book for the Routledge Studies in International Business History, for which he is the editor. Another key factor is the quality of the administrative staff, which here means the Business History Group's secretary, Lynn Cornell. She helped me with a lot of the practical details, which made the task of preparing the conference a pleasant one. Back in Norway, Lisa Moi Reime and Gro Simonsen helped me in preparing the manuscript. A third key factor is the quality of the researchers who are attached to the research milieu. The Business History Group at Reading not only includes some hard-working and bright scholars, but also a Visiting Fellow, Frances Bostock, who turned out to be a perfect initial copy editor – especially in making bad English readable. Without the support of all these people, this book would have been different, if published at all.

Rolv Petter Amdam

1

INTRODUCTION

Rolv Petter Amdam

INTRODUCTION

Globally, two processes are striking about management education in the mid 1990s. First, since management is regarded as a key source of success in business, modern management education methods are changing rapidly in order to meet new challenges from business and governments. They all seem to aspire to the same aim, namely to develop educational systems and institutions which will have a positive effect on the formation of managerial skills, and by these means contribute to improved competitiveness. Second, management education represents one of the fastest-growing areas within higher education. Moreover, management and business studies are also among the youngest buds of the tree of academic disciplines. The strong growth in management education has thus taken place at the same time as the discipline has been striving to define its own identity.

The dynamic of these processes is underlined by the fact that business, whose demand this kind of education is intended to meet, is also changing rapidly. This means that expectations of the output of management educational and training institutions are altering all the time. As a result, some of the fundamental questions about management education's *raison d'être* are still causing – or at least should cause – much discussion. Questions such as 'Can management education and training really contribute to the formation of managerial skills in a way that improves competitiveness?' and 'If so, what kind of management education does this best?' need to be addressed.

Bearing these questions in mind, the book focuses on two main themes which are fundamental for a discussion of management education's function in the economic process. The first theme is linked to how and why systems of management education have developed differently within disparate business systems, and the second to the relationship between education and business.

DIFFERENT SYSTEMS OF MANAGEMENT EDUCATION

A hundred years ago, academic management education hardly existed anywhere. Towards the end of the twentieth century, however, the question of how to develop managerial skills so that business can meet new challenges and countries improve their competitiveness has emerged as one of the most important topics of the international educational debate. This shift of emphasis has been accompanied by the strong growth of management education within educational systems. In many countries this rise has been especially potent from the mid 1970s. In about 1990, for instance, one-quarter of all undergraduate students in the United States, and a quarter of all postgraduates, studied business. Twenty-five years ago, only one-eighth of all undergraduate students studied business (Handy *et al.* 1987: 8; McKenna 1989: 37). Similarly, in Britain, the number of different MBA programmes has increased from twenty-six in 1985 to about 100 in 1994 (Amdam 1994). In Eastern Europe, the fall of communism, which was accompanied by the introduction of a market economy, has widened the geographical area in which the development of organizations for management education and training is given priority (Woodall 1994). In China too, there has been, since the 1980s, a new interest in developing courses and programmes in management education. Some of these programmes have been developed in collaboration with foreign business schools, and from 1991 the government has allowed even universities to offer MBA programmes (Borgonjon and Vanhonacker 1994).

This global expansion of management education has been caused by various changes, some of which are common to a great number of countries.

First, the expansion of management education is linked to the transformation of higher education from an elite system to a system of mass education. Obviously it is true that there are still some business schools in existence which may be described as elite institutions – Harvard Business School in the United States, for example, and the London Business School in Britain, INSEAD in France, and IMD in Switzerland. However, the expansion of management education primarily reflects a broadening of the educational system in management to include larger groups of people.

Second, the increase in institutions for management education is connected to changes in the relationship between the state and the market for higher education. The role of the state versus the private sector in higher education differs from country to country (Geiger 1986). However, during the 1980s in particular, there was a general tendency to increase the role of the market (OECD 1990). In order to finance the expansion of the higher educational systems, governments have tried to raise funds from sources other than the state. Educational institutions have found a source of finance for parts of this expansion in the business community, and new programmes in management education have been a means to increase the share paid for by the private sector.

Third, the mobilization of financial resources from the business community also reflects an increase in the demand from business for management education. Organizational changes, like globalization (e.g. Dunning 1993) and divisionalization (e.g. Chandler 1990), which have led to new opportunities for employees with an educational background in management and business, have taken place. Greater emphasis has been placed on competence and human resources as the most critical factors for developing enterprises, as Peter Lorange discusses in Chapter 13. One result of these changes is that managerial skills have been felt as an increasingly critical bottleneck in many enterprises, and businesspeople have therefore turned to the educational system to solve their problems.

However, despite the similar explanations for the growth of management education, which can be found in most developed countries, differences between national systems of management education still exist. Nor is it obvious that these systems will develop towards one – or even a few – standardized systems. Recent comparative studies of business systems (Whitley 1992a), management styles (Lane 1989), organizational changes (Kogut 1993), and human resource management (Kirkbride 1994) have challenged theories on convergence. Comparative studies on management education have also led to an interest in the differences between countries, even though the question of convergence or divergence has not been the main topic of discussion (Byrt 1989a; Engwall and Gunnarsson 1994a; Locke 1984, 1989; Whitley et al. 1981).

The question of national styles of management and management education may have an impact on competitiveness. Given the fact that differences exist between business systems, and that different business systems show great strength in resisting tendencies of convergence, developing a unique style of management and management education may be necessary if education is to give support to competitiveness. This argument is based on an assumption that the style of management education will complement business activities, and there are historical examples to support the argument. According to Robert Locke (1984), what characterized Germany in the period of economic growth during the Second Industrial Revolution, was that Germany – unlike France and Britain – developed a system of management education which complemented entrepreneurial activities.

In the rest of this chapter, some of the differences between national systems of management education will be discussed. The focus will be on the roots of modern management education in the countries represented by contributions to this book.

The United States and Germany: two models of management education and training

In addition to Britain, where the birth of industrialism took place, the United States and Germany have a special position in the history of modern capitalism. Both Germany and the United States were successful followers of the British Industrial Revolution. They were not only able to catch up with the British advantage during the Second Industrial Revolution but also to take over as leaders in the world economy. Of these two countries, the United States first established herself as a world-leading economic nation. When American economic power began to decline, however, Germany was in a better position to face new challenges, and, together with Japan, to show strength in the face of international economic downturns. Whereas Britain continued to rely on social recruitment combined with the Oxbridge system, and neglected the development of special institutions for educating and training managers, until after the Second World War, both the United States and Germany gave priority to the development of such institutions when they entered the period of the Second Industrial Revolution. Nonetheless, the two systems were very different.

In the United States, the business schools played a dominant position in the system of management education (Cheit 1991). The Wharton School of Finance and Economy in Philadelphia was founded in 1881 as the first academic business school, not only in the United States, but in the world (Sass 1982). From the beginning of the twentieth century the number of business schools increased, and it is this fact which has contributed to their strength as key institutions in American management education. The first MBA (Master of Business Administration) programme was set up, and this two-year postgraduate programme soon became a symbol of American management education. Even though undergraduate programmes in business existed at American universities, it was this MBA programme that was defined as the very core of American management education.

At American business schools the MBA courses have developed in several directions, and the essence of the programme, as Susan Aaronson shows (Chapter 11), can vary from one business school to another. But even though business schools have put different emphases on case methods in teaching, on theory, and on quantitative or qualitative methods, to mention just a few examples, the aim of the MBA programmes has been to develop managerial skills. The importance of the MBA degree is reflected in the fact that one-third of the chief executive officers (CEOs) of the 500 largest companies in the United States in 1990 had an MBA degree from one of the twenty leading American business schools (*Economist*, 2 March 1991).

Germany began to set up her business schools (*Handelshochschulen*) at about the same time as the Americans did. Between 1898 and 1910, the first business schools were established in Aachen, Leipzig, Cologne, and Berlin, amongst other cities (Engwall 1992: 5), and their development reflected a deeply rooted scientific tradition within the German university system. The system of management education was very different from the American one (Locke 1984, 1989), however. Most importantly, German business schools did not achieve, as did their American counterparts, the position of providing a widely shared educational background for managers. There were several reasons for this. First, engineering education, which took place at the technical *Hochschulen* from the 1820s, developed a strong reputation for the education and training of managers in German manufacturing companies. Second, the content of the business schools was primarily focused on business economics (*Betriebswirtschaftslehre*), rather than on management like the American MBA programmes. Graduates of German business schools were, therefore, trained in administration techniques and to work on accounting, financial and other specialized tasks, not primarily as managers. On the other hand, German companies have had a strong tradition of training managers themselves. Within the German business schools, the educational programmes were organized differently from the American business schools. A German business school was organized as a *Hochschule*. Its programme lasted for four – in the postwar period five – years, after which graduates were awarded the *Diplom Kaufmann* degree. Thus the German system was not based, as was its American counterpart, on the division between undergraduate and postgraduate programmes.

The historical function of German business schools demonstrates that business education in Germany, unlike that in the United States, has not generally been equated with management education. The chapters by Haldor Byrkjeflot and Tor Halvorsen on Norway (Chapter 9) and by Lars Engwall, Elving Gunnarsson and Eva Wallerstedt on Sweden (Chapter 10) show that within other countries also engineers and lawyers have had an historically strong position as managers.

The dissimilarities in the structure and function of the American and German systems of business education must be seen in the light of differences in the national style of management. As shown by Byrkjeflot and Halvorsen (Chapter 9), American management has combined the functions of leadership and administration in the idea of general management. This means that persons in a position of formal authority are responsible for leadership as well as administration. In contrast, the German tradition puts less emphasis on leadership and more on administration in lower managerial positions. The leadership dimension is taken more for granted. In the career system, most emphasis is put on administration, and therefore on education in appropriate administrative techniques or in engineering. The logic of the American model is supported by a system of industrial relationships which draws a sharp distinction between managers and workers, and the Americans have developed an educational system which separates education for manual and for management functions. In general, therefore, and in contrast to Germany, engineers cannot hold major positions as managers.

International models and national systems of management education

In countries other than the United States and Germany, the system of management education has very often developed in a melting pot of national traditions and ideas from other countries – both as to the style of management and the system of education in general. In some countries, Germany played the part of ideal model in the development of national systems of management education from 1880 to the Second World War. Since that war, however, the role of ideal model has been primarily linked to the United States. In different ways, foreign ideas have been moulded with national traditions in several of the countries which are examined in this book.

In the Scandinavian countries, as discussed by Rolv Petter Amdam with regard to Norway (Chapter 2) and Lars Engwall *et al.* with regard to Sweden (Chapter 10), German influence was strong before the Second World War. The Scandinavian university systems were in general strongly inspired by German universities, and the Scandinavian countries decided to establish their own technical universities based on the German model, before they founded their first business schools. This has resulted, as shown by Byrkjeflot and Halvorsen so far as Norway is concerned (Chapter 9) and Engwall *et al.* with regard to Sweden (Chapter 10), in engineers having had – as in Germany – a traditionally strong position among Scandinavian managers. The first business schools, which appeared between 1909 (Sweden) and 1936 (Norway), had striking similarities to the German *Hochschule* model as well as to the curricula in the German business schools, with an emphasis on accounting and finance as core subjects in business economics. After the Second World War, however, the American system of business education took over from the German one as the main source of inspiration. Despite close contacts with the United States, which have included numerous study visits and the employment of staff members with American PhD degrees, this influence has been limited to the content of the education. With regard to the structure, the *Hochschule* system was able to resist Americanization until the 1980s, when the first MBA programmes were introduced, albeit on a very small scale. One result of this is that the *Hochschule* system – leading to the degree *siviløkonom* after some four years – has had an equivalent function on the labour market to the MBA degree in the United States (Engwall and Gunnarsson 1994b: 20). Further evidence of the disparity between the Scandinavian and American models is provided by the fact that engineers have maintained their strong position among Scandinavian managers.

6

The development of business education in the Netherlands has shown some similarities to that in the Scandinavian countries. As Huibert de Man demonstrates (Chapter 4), the structure of business education still reflects the originally strong influence of the German *Handelshochschule* tradition. After the Second World War, American ideas were widely introduced, and contributed to important changes in what the business schools taught. Nevertheless, the MBA system – as in the Scandinavian countries – has on the whole had a very marginal influence. The most striking difference between the Netherlands and the Scandinavian countries is linked to the relationship between foreign ideas and players at the national level in the formative period of business education before the Second World War. While the Scandinavian countries followed the German model very closely at that time, the founding fathers of the movement for business education in the Netherlands were very influential in its formative period, which gave the Dutch system a unique character from the very beginning. Owing to the different university traditions in Rotterdam and Amsterdam and the different background and interests of two of its founding fathers – J. Goudriaan and Th. Limperg Jr – business education developed in two different directions. In Rotterdam, *bedrijfsleer* – later *bedijfskunde*, which de Man translates as business studies – evolved. *Bedrijfsleer* emphasized organizational theory, and was the more ready to take on ideas from the United States after the war. The other direction – *bedrijfseconomie* (business economics), which had its roots in Amsterdam – was essentially linked to accounting, and was more typical of the German tradition.

While the Scandinavian countries and the Netherlands all belong to a cluster of nations which were originally strongly influenced by German business schools, France and Italy, which Giuliana Gemelli discusses (Chapter 3), and Britain, as examined by John F. Wilson (Chapter 7), did not. They faced the American challenge after the Second World War from a different background. Indeed, one may consider, as did Jean-Pierre Nioche (1992), that there was a traditional Latin model including France, Italy and Spain as opposed to the German one. In this Latin model, management education was established through the disciplines of law and economics. Far from being a copy of the German one, the French system of management education was a unique system, rooted in the *grandes écoles*, which first appeared in the eighteenth century. In addition, the universities have also offered business degrees. The *grandes écoles*, of which the technical variety were older and more numerous than the commercial ones, were – and to some extent still are – elite schools that produced graduates for top jobs in the private as well as public sector. The emphasis on mathematics as a core subject in the curricula represented another characteristic of the French system. After the war, great efforts were made to transfer American ideas on management education to both Italy and France. With regard to France, these efforts were successful insofar as, for

7

example, INSEAD was established in 1958 as a European business school of the American type, which soon developed into one of the most influential business schools in Europe. Some of the *grandes écoles* also adopted American educational ideas. But the essential *grandes écoles* system remained intact (Barsoux 1989: 124). Efforts to introduce the American model were thus mainly directed towards the creation of new institutions rather than towards the transformation of the old *grandes écoles* system.

While most West European countries developed institutions for higher management and business education in the period from the 1880s to 1940, Britain did not take part in this process, as John F. Wilson demonstrates (Chapter 7). Attempts, from the beginning of the twentieth century, to establish such institutions within the university structure failed, and the British system of management education may be described as a 'non-system' (Aldcroft 1992: 109). Traditionally, there were two principles which governed the recruitment of managers to jobs within industry. First, managers – or future managers – were recruited on the basis of their social position rather than on formal skills. This reflected what is known as the 'gentleman ideal' within British business: namely, that social status is more important than formal knowledge and degrees. Second, managers were trained in a practical fashion, within the company which recruited them. It should also be mentioned that accounting was held to be an ideal qualification for top management positions (Lane 1989: 92). Customarily, however, the education of British accountants did not take place predominantly within academic institutions but was an apprenticeship-based system with strong involvement from professional associations (Locke 1984: 138–9). One consequence of the British neglect of management education was that, when the American model was being strongly promoted after the Second World War, Britain appeared to lack some of the preconditions, possessed by some other countries, for the creation of a melting pot. Britain had in fact developed few national institutions into which new ideas could be absorbed. Thus it is probably no coincidence that, when the first two business schools were finally established in London and Manchester in the mid 1960s, the result was a system which was strongly influenced by the American model, with the MBA degree as its main programme.

Japan's economic success during the last decades has attracted much attention. This has also included the way Japanese business trains its managers. A situation of an almost total absence of business schools with MBA programmes, or with programmes which last for several years like the German system, illustrates the differences between the Japanese and the American and German systems of business education. In particular, Japan has developed a system of in-firm management training that is deeply rooted in cultural tradition, and is of a completely different quality and dimension to its British equivalent (Lorriman and Kenjo 1994). But, as

Tamotsu Nishizawa shows (Chapter 5), Japan has, despite her ability to develop unique institutions, been actively looking overseas for the know-how to develop her own special system of management education. In the formative years from the late nineteenth century, she looked towards Europe. As well as transferring ideas from Germany, Japan also learnt from other European countries like Britain and Belgium. After the Second World War, however, American influence was very strong, and American advisers played an important role in the reconstruction of the educational system. Japan showed great skill in absorbing new know-how, and what came out of the melting pot was a system of management education which still manifested traditional values and methods of training (Warner 1994: 528).

From the late 1980s, political changes in Eastern Europe opened a new market for management education. Slovenia, according to Marjan Svetličič and Andreja Čibron (Chapter 6), is one of the countries that is presently transforming its institutions for management education in order to support the change from a planned to a market economy and strengthen national independence. In the process, she has been looking abroad for new ideas and for ways to increase her capacity and skills in management education. By these means, Slovenia – like many other East European countries – has recently entered the crucible in which national traditions and foreign influences are mixed. For such countries, the experiences of others that have preceded them should be of great interest.

Diffusion of educational ideas and models

In a number of recent studies, the differences between national systems of management education have been highlighted (e.g. Byrt 1989b; Engwall and Gunnarsson 1994a; Lane 1989; Locke 1984, 1989). The diffusion of ideas and models of management education from Germany to parts of Europe before the Second World War, in particular, and, on a broader spectrum, from the United States after the war, has also been studied at national levels (e.g. Engwall 1992; Kogut and Parkinson 1993; de Man and Karsten 1994). However, there are few studies that systematically discuss the factors which have influenced the spread of ideas and models of management education in a comparative perspective. In his study on the development of management education (Byrt 1989b), William Byrt characterizes the process of transferring the American model to Australia as 'educational imperialism' (Byrt 1989a: 80). The concept of 'imperialism' implies that the transmitters have had an especially important function in the process of diffusion. However, the use of this concept may underestimate the dynamics between the transmitter and the receiver, and also the conditions of the host country. Since, in some cases, countries have received more or less the same know-how in management education but have absorbed it differently, conditions in these host countries should be of importance. What, then, decides the diffusion of management ideas and models? This book does not attempt to give any general answer to the question. It will, however, give pointers to some of the specific issues that should be taken into consideration when studying the question.

First, it is necessary to differentiate between those countries which provide the models for management education, those which contain the institutions and people that carry the ideas and models of management education across borders, and the receiving countries. With regard to model countries, Germany's role as a model before the Second World War has already been mentioned, as has the fact that the United States, which was also to some extent a model before the war, strengthened its position as the main model after the war. In addition, certain other countries became models on a smaller scale: Belgium, for instance, for Japan (Chapter 5). Moreover, the manner in which Japanese scholars turned to Britain from the end of the nineteenth century for ideas on how to educate managers, illustrates the fact that even those countries perceived to be backward in management education could, in certain circumstances, be models. In this case, the general admiration for British culture and elite universities (Oxbridge) seems to have been the important factor. Among the Scandinavian countries, Sweden, which established her first business school in 1909, was, in addition to Germany, a model for the Norwegians in their efforts to establish their first business school in 1936 (Amdam and Norstrøm 1994).

Second, the question needs to be asked: 'Who is playing the most active role in the diffusion process – the transmitter or the receiver?' This question is linked to the character of the channels through which the diffusion takes place, and also to the carriers of ideas. These carriers may be closely connected to the country that serves as a model. After the Second World War, the European Productivity Agency (EPA) and Ford Foundation were examples of American-dominated institutions, as Giuliana Gemelli shows in her study of Italy and France (Chapter 3). The EPA also contributed to the transfer of management ideas to a number of other countries, such as Norway (Chapter 2). In Japan, scholars from model countries – especially Britain in the last quarter of the nineteenth century, and the United States, after the Second World War – stayed on for some years to transfer their knowledge to Japanese business and the educational system. In Slovenia (Chapter 6), this process is taking place today, with foreign scholars staying at Slovene business schools as visiting professors. However, in some countries, such as Japan and Norway, the active role of host has been striking. Carriers representing such receiving countries have initially been students and academic scholars who have visited the model countries for a time. There is, in short, a dialectic relationship between the exporter and the importer. This makes it possible to test Parker's thesis (Parker 1989: 25), based on studies of transfers of accounting theory and practice, that such transfers are likely to take place most quickly and effectively when an active exporter is faced with an active importer.

Third, it is also necessary to focus on what the factors are that influence the way in which foreign ideas and educational models are adapted in the receiving country. Since imported ideas are absorbed differently in different national contexts, the role of institutional constraints and opportunities within the national system should be examined. According to recent comparative studies of business systems, these differences are the results of particular national institutional environments (Whitley 1992b: 5; Zysman 1994).

The origins of these institutions very often predate modern capitalism (Dornseifer and Kocka 1993; Zysman 1994), and their strength counterbalances any tendencies they may have of developing towards congruency. The important factors behind changes in management education would seem to be the strength of the national system of management education, as well as of the educational system in general; styles of management; and such cultural elements as how a country has developed traditions of learning across borders. According to Robert Locke, the way in which France, Germany, and Britain developed systems for the education and training of managers before the Second World War had a decisive influence on how these countries reacted towards and absorbed American ideas after the war (Locke 1989: 123–38, 164–211). As far as cultural factors are concerned, Amdam (Chapter 2) refers to the differences between Japan and Britain. While Japan has a long tradition of combining an active approach towards learning from other countries with developing its own institutions, Britain has been suffering from the attitudes and values developed when she was the world's leading economy and has not felt the need to learn from other cultures (see also Lorriman and Kenjo 1994). Britain's shift from being a latecomer, with almost no interest in developing higher institutions for management education before the 1960s, to becoming one of the European countries that adopted the American MBA system most directly, is striking, and contrasts with the Japanese case.

MANAGEMENT EDUCATION AND BUSINESS

The second main theme focused on by the book concerns the relationship between management education and competitiveness: namely, how educational institutions can serve business. The activities of business schools, which despite the existence of national differences are, from an international perspective, key institutions in management education, are judged by two bodies, business and the academic community (Cheit 1991: 208). Lars Engwall and his colleagues describe this as a dualism between Mercury and Minerva (Chapter 10). From an academic point of view, business schools should attain a certain scientific standard. This means,

11

amongst other things, that staff members should qualify for appointments and promotions by publishing, writing papers for refereed journals, and so forth. From the point of view of business, they should provide graduates who have the potential to help firms to add value. Historically there are several examples which demonstrate that handling this dualism can be a difficult task.

Since the beginning of the 1980s, business schools in the United States have been criticized for having moved away from a close relationship with business (e.g. Aaronson 1992; Cheit 1985). After being attacked by the Ford Foundation, the Carnegie Corporation and other institutions in the late 1950s for neglecting scientific work, American business schools changed and placed greater emphasis on scientific work. This improved their status in the university community and contributed to the establishment of business studies as an academic discipline. The critics of the 1980s must be seen as a reaction to this development – a reaction that was exacerbated by the downturn of the United States from being the world's leading economy. The question being asked was: 'Did American business schools bear any responsibility for the economic decline of the United States?'

A similar question has been asked about Britain's loss of competitiveness. John F. Wilson shows (Chapter 7) how the lack of interest at best, and positive hostility, at worst, towards the business school idea, by both the university and business community, hampered the development of British business education. He concludes his examination of Britain by saying that 'failure at the most fundamental level of training has been among the most damaging obstacle to growth'. In the 1990s, business schools still suffer from the criticism of those companies which prefer to train managers themselves instead rather than support a specialized institution. Comparative studies by Locke (1984, 1989) and Charles Handy et al. (1987) lend support to this analysis.

Typically, comparative studies which criticize Britain and the United States for mistakes in their management education highlight Germany and Japan as examples of how educational systems have had a positive function vis-à-vis business (e.g. Handy et al. 1987; Locke 1984, 1994). Based on the one hand on the institutional stability of the German and Japanese methods of training managers, and on the other on the economic success of these two countries, the results of the comparisons seem reasonable. However, it remains to be seen if the Japanese and German models are resistant to strong criticism if the two countries meet with severe economic crisis.

The methods which the United States, Britain, Japan, and Germany have used to train and educate business managers have reflected – in their different ways – a sort of stability in what may be thought of as the typical management style of these countries. In other countries, however, the management style has changed. Referring to Sweden, Engwall et al. (Chapter 10) relate the way in which graduates from business schools have replaced lawyers and, to some extent, engineers as top executives in Swedish companies. This transformation seems to represent a change in the style of management. The same transformation has, according to Rolv Petter Amdam (Chapter 2), also taken place in Norway. It may be that the ability to make radical changes in the style of management is important in explaining how the system of management education can respond to changes in business. Even though the belief of Haldor Byrkjeflot and Tor Halvorsen (Chapter 9) in the ability of Norwegian engineers to resist attack and retain their leading position as managers might seem to raise critical questions about Amdam's analysis, the importance of radical changes in the style of management may have been underestimated in the existing comparative literature, which is primarily based on studies of large economies.

Some challenges

Institutions for management education are faced with enormous challenges. On the one hand, business is changing rapidly. On the other, the unclarified position between business and academia may limit the possibility of these institutions being able to develop in a way that serves business but does no damage to their relationship with the academic community. Susan Aaronson's discussion of seven different patterns in the response of American business schools to these challenges (Chapter 11) illustrates the difficulties they are facing.

Reva Brown, Sean McCartney, and Jeff Clowes examine how deans of British business schools look upon the relationship between business and academia (Chapter 8). Their study shows that deans of the new university business schools, which emerged out of the British polytechnic system, have a more positive attitude towards cooperating with business than deans from traditional university business schools. By asking if, in the 1960s, it might have been a better idea to establish the first business schools at two of the polytechnics instead of at the Universities of London and Manchester, they touch on the question of whether academic business schools are really necessary. This question is also examined by Ove Bjarnar and Hallgeir Gammelsæter (Chapter 12). In particular, they focus on the necessity of developing the skills necessary to manage teams of managers. Typically, the predominance of a top executive as manager, representing one influential professional group, will, they believe, be replaced by the predominance of teams of managers from different professions. In their view, traditional business schools are not suitable for developing these kinds of skills, and they ask for alternative institutions for the education of management teams.

In the final chapter, Peter Lorange – President of IMD – discusses the further development of the relationship between business schools and business. Like Bjarnar and Gammelsæter he emphasizes the importance of management teams for the future but regards this development as a challenge, which modern business schools should respond to and be able to handle. His main theme is how business and business schools can develop partnerships. By establishing different kinds of partnership, business and business schools may be able to help each other in a way that surmounts the boundaries between them. If this model is shown to be successful, it may help to answer one question that Brown *et al.* (Chapter 8) do not discuss, and that is: 'In considering what the educational system can contribute to the improvement of competitiveness, what is the role of the production of scientific knowledge?' If institutions for management education respond directly to the demand from business, hopefully business may get what it wants, but will it get anything else? The danger of neglecting the development of science-based knowledge is obvious in a period in which the establishment of close links with business matters more than anything else. The partnership concept may be one way to solve this problem.

REFERENCES

Aaronson, S. (1992) 'Serving America's Business? Graduate Business Schools and American Business, 1945–60', *Business History* 34(2): 160–82.

Aldcroft, D.H. (1992) *Education, Training and Economic Performance 1944 to 1990*, Manchester: Manchester University Press.

Amdam, R.P. (1994) 'Business Schools as Business Enterprises: Market, Institutions and Organisations in Management Education', *Working Paper* No. 64, Norwegian School of Management.

—— and Norstrøm, C.J. (1994) 'Business Administration in Norway 1936–1990', in L. Engwall and E. Gunnarsson (eds) *Management Education in an Academic Context*, Uppsala: Acta Universitatis Upsaliensis, Studia Oeconemiae Negotiorum 35: 66–83.

Barsoux, J.-L. (1989) 'Management Education in France', in W. Byrt (ed.) *Management Education: An International Survey*, London: Routledge, 120–50.

Borgonjon, J. and Vanhonacker, W.R. (1994) 'Management Training and Education in the People's Republic of China', *International Journal of Human Resource Management* 5(2): 327–56.

Byrt, W. (1989a) 'Management Education in Australia', in W. Byrt (ed.) *Management Education: An International Survey*, London: Routledge, 78–103.

—— (ed.) (1989b) *Management Education: An International Survey*, London: Routledge.

Chandler, A.D., Jr (1990) *Scale and Scope: The Dynamics of Industrial Capitalism*, Cambridge, MA: Harvard University Press.

Cheit, E.F. (1985) 'Business Schools and Their Critics', *California Management Review* XXVII(3): 43–62.

—— (1991) 'The Shaping of Business Management Thought', in D. Easton and C.S. Schelling (eds) *Divided Knowledge*, London: Sage, 195–218.

Dornseifer, B. and Kocka, J. (1993) 'The Impact of the Preindustrial Heritage. Reconsiderations on the German Pattern of Corporate Development in the Late 19th and Early 20th Centuries', *Industrial and Corporative Change* 2(2): 233–48.

Dunning, J.H. (1993) *The Globalization of Business: The Challenge of the 1990s*, London: Routledge.

Engwall, L. (1992) *Mercury Meets Minerva: Business Studies and Higher Education The Swedish Case*, Oxford: Pergamon Press.

—— and Gunnarsson, E. (eds) (1994a) *Management Studies in an Academic Context*, Uppsala: Acta Universitatis Upsaliensis, Studia Oeconemiae Negotiorum 35.

—— (1994b) 'Perspectives on Management Studies', in L. Engwall and E. Gunnarsson (eds) *Management Studies in an Academic Context*, Uppsala: Acta Universitatis Upsaliensis, Studia Oeconomiae Negotiorum 35: 13–32.

Geiger, R.L. (1986) *Private Sectors in Higher Education: Structure, Function, and Change in Eight Countries*, Ann Arbor, MI: University of Michigan Press.

Handy, C. *et al.* (1987) *The Making of Managers: A Report on Management Education, Training and Development in the USA, West Germany, France, Japan and the UK*, London: National Economic Development Council.

Kirkbride, P.S. (ed.) (1994) *Human Resource Management in Europe: Perspectives for the 1990s*, London: Routledge.

Kogut, B. (ed.) (1993) *Country Competitiveness: Technology and the Organizing of Work*, Oxford: Oxford University Press.

—— and Parkinson, D. (1993) 'The Diffusion of American Organizing Principles to Europe', in B. Kogut (ed.) *Country Competitiveness: Technology and the Organizing of Work*, Oxford: Oxford University Press, 179–202.

Lane, C. (1989) *Management and Labour in Europe: The Industrial Enterprise in Germany, Britain and France*, Aldershot: Edward Elgar.

Locke, R.R. (1984) *The End of the Practical Man: Entrepreneurship and Higher Education in Germany, France, and Great Britain, 1880–1940*, Greenwich, CT.: JAI Press.

—— (1989) *Management and Higher Education since 1940: The Influence of America and Japan on West Germany, Great Britain, and France*, Cambridge: Cambridge University Press.

—— (1994) 'Management Education and Higher Education since 1940', in L. Engwall and E. Gunnarsson (eds) *Management Studies in an Academic Context*, Uppsala: Acta Universitatis Upsaliensis, Studia Oeconomiae Negotiorum 35: 155–66.

Lorriman, J. and Kenjo, T. (1994) *Japan's Winning Margins: Management, Training and Education*, Oxford: Oxford University Press.

Man, H. de and Karsten, L. (1994) 'Academic Management Education in the Netherlands', in L. Engwall and E. Gunnarsson (eds) *Management Studies in an Academic Context*, Uppsala: Acta Universitatis Upsaliensis, Studia Oeconomiae Negotiorum 35: 84–115.

McKenna, J.F. (1989) 'Management Education in the United States', in W. Byrt (ed.) *Management Education: An International Survey*, London: Routledge, 18–55.

Nioche, J.-P. (1992) 'The War of Degrees in European Management Education', *EFMD Forum* 1: 21–4.

OECD (1990) *Financing Higher Education: Current Patterns*, Paris: OECD.

Parker, R.H. (1989) 'Importing and Exporting Accounting: The British Experience', in A.G. Hopwood (ed.) *International Pressures for Accounting Change*, Hemel Hempstead: Prentice Hall, 7–29.

Sass, S.A. (1982) *The Pragmatic Imagination: A History of The Wharton School 1881–1981*, Philadelphia: University of Pennsylvania Press.

Warner, M. (1994) 'Japanese Culture, Western Management: Taylorism and Human Resources in Japan', *Organizational Studies* 15(4): 509–33.

Whitley, R. (1992a) 'The Comparative Study of Business Systems in Europe: Issues and Choices', in R. Whitley (ed.) *European Business Systems: Firms and Markets in their National Contexts*, London: Sage, 267–84.

—— (ed.) (1992b) *European Business Systems: Firms and Markets in their National Contexts*, London: Sage.

—— Thomas, A., and Marceau, J. (1981) *Master of Business: The Making of a New Elite?*, London: Tavistock.

Woodall, J. (1994) 'The Transfer of Managerial Knowledge to Eastern Europe', in P.S. Kirkbride (ed.) *Human Resource Management in Europe: Perspectives for the 1990s*, London: Routledge, 164–77.

Zysman, J. (1994) 'How Institutions Create Historically Rooted Trajectories of Growth', *Industrial and Corporate Change* 3(1): 243–83.

Part I

DIFFERENT SYSTEMS OF MANAGEMENT EDUCATION

2

NATIONAL SYSTEMS VERSUS FOREIGN MODELS IN MANAGEMENT EDUCATION

The Norwegian case

Rolv Petter Amdam

INTRODUCTION

A central issue in the study of management education is the question of international standards versus national styles of management and systems of management education. While the general opinion in the decades following the Second World War was that management style and education in different countries developed towards the American model, many scholars today stress the differences between various national systems, and their ability to survive (Byrkjeflot 1993; Byrt 1989: 210; Handy *et al.* 1987; Lane 1989; Locke 1989; Nioche 1992).

The fact that neither Japan nor Germany adopted the American system of management education has attracted great attention (Lawrence 1989; Locke 1988: 93, 1989: ch. 5). Since these countries have been seen as successful with regard to economic development, their methods of educating and training managers have created new interest in the relationship between educational systems and competitiveness. It has also been argued that the adoption of the American pattern of management education in some countries has been an expression of weakness; and that the MBA degree has been imported in a major way only by those European countries that lack a strong tradition of training future elites in which their corporations have confidence (Nioche 1992: 23). Britain, which has not been among the most successful of countries with regard to its recent economic development, has been mentioned as one of these. She is said to have looked in the wrong direction – somewhere halfway between France and the United States – and that one of her mistakes has been to turn to the American model of postgraduate and post-experience business schools (Handy *et al.* 1987: 11–12).

It appears, therefore, that the relationship between national systems and foreign influences in management education is important to competitiveness insofar as those countries which have stuck to and developed their own national patterns, rather than uncritically adopting the American system of management education, have been the most successful.

However, to explain failure by alluding merely to the introduction of the American model of management education is too simple. When the first English business schools were established in London and Manchester in the mid 1960s, the founders chose a pattern that, in comparison with other European countries, was more like the American business school model (Barnes 1989; Wilson 1992). On the other hand, what characterizes Britain is not that it is a clone of the American system. Britain has been criticized for having neglected management education (Barry 1989: 56–8; Locke 1989), and it has been argued that it is this neglect that has had a bad influence upon economic performance (Aldcroft 1992; Porter 1990: 497–8). The British system is therefore different from the American one because Britain developed management education late and on a small scale. In an historical perspective, moreover, Britain developed her own style – as characterized by a combination of on-the-job training of managers, a strong belief in the Oxbridge system, and the 'gentleman ideal', which says that no formal education in management is needed for managers (Aldcroft 1992: 108–9; Lane 1989: Ch. 4).

The British case contradicts the hypothesis which states that isolationism towards foreign influences in management education is a good thing. Britain's refusal to develop organizations for higher management education until 1965 may be interpreted as an expression of isolationism to defend the traditional way of preparing managers. Japan also misrepresents the hypothesis. What characterizes Japan is not her refusal to entertain foreign ideas in management education, but her ability to make the most of them and to mould foreign ideas and expertise in such a way that her educational system is not changed fundamentally (Lorriman and Kenjo 1994).

Under the Meiji regime of the second half of the nineteenth century, Japan must have been one of the most intensive consumers of foreign expertise in education in the world. To mention just one example, the cost of supporting 330 students abroad in 1871 represented a third of the total budget of the Ministry of Education (Yasumuro 1993: 88). After the Second World War, the Japanese educational system changed radically, based on directives from the United States (Geiger 1986; Keeble 1992: 34–5), and numerous scholars visited the United States (Collins 1989: 176–81). But despite the attempt to recreate her educational pattern, based on the American system, Japan was able to stick to some of her basic traditions. While some foreign ideas were adopted, others were not. And, as regards management education, Japan preferred to strengthen the tradition of training managers within the firm rather than develop a system of American-style MBA programmes.

Based on this overview of different interpretations of the balance between national systems and foreign influence in management education, an alternative hypothesis will be suggested. It is that a country's ability to use foreign expertise critically; to adopt what is needed, and refuse what is not needed; and to mould these foreign influences with national traditions is what matters for business performance. To be able to act in this way, the country needs (a) an open attitude towards foreign ideas, (b) a system of transferring those foreign ideas, (c) the skills to examine foreign ideas critically, and (d) strong national traditions in education which enable it to resist pressure from outside.

This hypothesis may be tested comparatively on different countries. With regard to Britain, management education is criticized for two failures: that the first business schools were established too late, and that when they were eventually established, they followed the American pattern instead of developing a national style (Aldcroft 1992: 109). In other words, for a long period Britain did not have either an open attitude towards different systems or the ability to adopt foreign ideas critically. And when she did, her own tradition of management education was too weak to be able to resist foreign pressure. The result was too great an emphasis on copying the United States rather than on developing her own pattern. The United States, herself, undoubtedly had strong national traditions of management education. On the other hand, she had weakly developed skills in absorbing foreign influences, and her modern business education has been criticized for not having learned from European and Japanese management education (Cheit 1985).

The purpose of this chapter is to discuss the above hypothesis in the Norwegian context. First, the way in which the Norwegian system of management education changed from a pattern strongly inspired by the German educational model before the Second World War to one influenced by the American model after the war will be examined. Then the issue of whether Norway was able to combine foreign ideas with national traditions will be discussed.

The chapter will focus on two periods of change – 1945 to 1965, and the 1980s. Furthermore, these will be considered from two aspects. First, the development of business schools and other institutions for management education will be looked at; and this will include a discussion of the structure as well as the content of the degree offered. Second, the educational background of Norwegian managers will be examined.

THE GERMAN CONNECTION

During the first four decades of the twentieth century, a Norwegian system of management education strongly influenced by Germany was established (Amdam 1993a, 1994). To begin with, Norway adopted the German *Hochschule* pattern for higher technical as well as business education. Then, in 1910, the Norwegian Institute of Technology (NTH) was established in Trondheim, and in 1936 the Norwegian School of Economics and Business

Administration (NSEBA) in Bergen. Both schools were based on German models. Moreover, the similarities between Germany and Norway were not limited to the structure of these institutions, but were also striking in the content of their curricula. So far as NSEBA was concerned, German business economics (*Betriebswirtschaftslehre*) was the main subject, with economics coming next (Amdam and Norstrøm 1994). Textbooks by Eugen Schmalenbach, the founder of German business economics, and other German scholars dominated the study of business economics. Close ties between business economics and national economics were typical of the German business schools. However, owing to the influence of a new generation of economists at the University of Oslo – with Ragnar Frisch, who was awarded the Nobel Prize for Economics in 1973, and Ingvar Wedervang, who became the president of the business school in Bergen in 1937, as the most influential scholars – the teaching of economics was less directly influenced by German scholars than was business economics (Amdam 1994).

Germany and Norway were also similar in the strong position that engineers held among business managers in manufacturing industry. A study of 100 top managers in manufacturing industry in 1939 shows that forty-two of them had a technical education at secondary or university level, while only twelve had a secondary commercial school background (Amdam 1994).[1]

The main difference, however, between the German and Norwegian systems of management education was the use of foreign institutions in educating and training Norwegian managers. During the interwar years most Norwegian managers in manufacturing and commercial companies seem to have had some educational background in, or had been trained by, other nations. The Norwegian system was not, therefore, an exact blueprint of the German system. What characterized it before the Second World War was the combination of German educational models with an extensive use of foreign educational institutions. The use of the latter compensated for the lack of domestic institutions. Several studies have argued that this combined system had a positive effect on business performance in the 1930s (Amdam 1994; Lange 1989).

THE AMERICAN CONNECTION

In the decades following the Second World War, the Norwegian educational authorities did not attempt to change the German *Hochschule* system in higher technical and business education (Amdam 1993a; Hanisch and Lange 1985). The system was strongly regulated and controlled by the government. Indeed, until the 1980s, NTH in Trondheim had the exclusive monopoly of conferring the degree of *sivilingeniør* (civil engineer), and NSEBA in Bergen had a similar monopoly over the degree of *siviløkonom* (civil economist).[2] With 250 students graduating from NTH, and only fifty from the business school in Bergen each year until the 1960s (NOS Utdanningsstatistikk), the two institutions established an exclusive position within the Norwegian educational system. Although the number of graduates increased to over 600 in technology and over 300 in business during the 1970s, the regulation of student numbers resulted in a high degree of competency on entrance. This situation strengthened the position of these schools as elite institutions in the Norwegian context. It also made them relevant to the education not only of skilled professional specialists but also of managers.

However, even though Norway did not change the German structure of higher business and technical education, the decades after 1945 were characterized by a strong American influence. What was the basis of this influence, and what were its channels? One channel was, as in many other countries, the transfer of ideas through scholars and managers visiting the United States just after the war. In addition to individual travellers, several professors from NTH in Trondheim and some from NSEBA in Bergen, alternative study groups were set up consisting of scholars, managers, and workers to study American productivity. A general tendency in the reports of these groups was the feeling that Norway was not behind American industry with regard to technical questions. On the other hand, American firms were far better organized and managed than their Norwegian counterparts (Amdam 1993a: 101).

A second channel of transfer was through the different American companies that had subsidiaries or branches in Norway, of which IBM seems to have been especially important. In addition to its role as an intermediate body for the transfer of office machines and punch-card machines, which were an integral part of practical American management (Nerheim and Nordvik 1986), IBM's Norwegian subsidiary contributed to changes in business education at a more concrete level. In 1956, it financed a three-month visit to the United States for Finn Øien, the owner and director of a small business school in Oslo, later known as the Norwegian School of Management (NSM).

NSM was founded in 1943 as a private consultancy. The firm also offered short courses in business administration, and during the first two postwar years it transformed itself into a higher business school offering a two-year programme in business administration. However, it only produced fifteen to twenty-five graduates a year during the 1950s, in addition to the twenty-five to thirty evening students who got a lower degree. The school was not approved by the government, and it developed independently from the rest of the educational system until it received some state funding after 1969. In 1985, it was finally given the right to award the degree of *siviløkonom*, on terms of equality with NSEBA in Bergen (Amdam 1993a).

Although German business economics was the core of its programme,

NSM was more influenced by American ideals and methods than NSEBA.[3] The contribution from IBM, which enabled the director of the school to visit the United States, strengthened its impulse to evolve along American lines. During Øien's visit in 1956, and again in 1958, he met James March, and other scholars within American management research, who were interested in organizational behaviour. Most of all, however, Øien was inspired by the new quantitative direction in American management education known as operational research. His positive impression was further strengthened by what he saw at such large American companies as Standard Oil and AT&T, which had introduced operational research methods into practical management.[4]

In 1956, NSM was one of the first institutions in Norway to establish a course in operational research methods. It also began teaching data processing. And, because computers were too expensive for the school to buy, IBM in Stockholm helped NSM to run some tests on one of its own machines. By adopting operational research as part of its programme, the school, which originally had no intention of developing into a research-based business school, discovered that it was, in fact, in the forefront – at least from a Norwegian perspective – of the development of a new scientific discipline. The contact with the international research community inspired the school to introduce research – to begin with, on a very small scale – and to recruit academic teachers with research experience (Amdam 1993a: ch. 6).

A third channel for the transfer of American ideas on management was through the Norwegian Productivity Institute (NPI). NPI was established in 1953 by the Norwegian government and the main associations representing Norwegian industry, employers, and employees. However, following the Marshall Aid programme, NPI was also actively supported by some American organizations. From 1950, the Economic Cooperation Administration (ECA), Special Mission to Norway, worked hard to encourage the Ministry for Industry and associations within industry to establish the Institute (Steiro 1974). NPI received money from the European Productivity Agency, an independent organization linked to OEEC, and a grant of US$1.5 million through the Benton–Moody Amendment (NPI 1963). This latter grant financed most of the Institute's activity during the 1950s.[5] The degree of American financial help might have proved to be an inhibition: before making any decision on which project it should support, NPI's director had to inform the American Foreign Operation Administration (FOA), which was allowed to suggest whether the project should be supported or not.[6] However, it does not seem that the FOA interfered in NPI's activity. On the contrary, the FOA criticized NPI for supporting too few projects, and several times asked NPI to use more money, not less, on productivity projects. Thus, the FOA contributed to the speed of the productivity work being carried out in Norway (Amdam 1993a: 102).

The purpose of NPI was to support different kinds of productivity projects. These included the education and training of managers; and issues related to management, such as the improvement of accounting practice, budgeting, marketing, and the use of managerial techniques to improve financial control. NPI encouraged Norwegian managers to give priority to topics related to human relations and personnel administration, and to organize training-within-industry (TWI) courses. It also contributed to an extended use of long-term planning among managers.[7]

Supported by American money and expertise, NPI diffused American ideas in management through three different channels: namely, directly to managers, through consultant firms, and through educational institutions. With regard to the work among managers, NPI organized several seminars at which American professors and consultants lectured. These experts were also sent to various industrial companies to give advice on how to improve management. However, the problem was that most of them only remained in Norway for a short time and had to return to the United States before they were able to develop good relationships with the firms they were meant to advise.[8] However, among those who stayed for more than a couple of months was George Kenning – a consultant with experience of General Motors. Up until the 1980s, he visited Norway several times, and organized a number of the top managers of some of Norway's largest companies into a group called 'the Kenning Circle', which met on a regular basis. Strongly influenced by Peter Drucker, he emphasized that the authority of managers should be based on skill in general management rather than in a technical field. In the late 1980s, members of this group were dominant among the top managers of Norway's ten largest companies (Kalleberg 1991).

So far as the transfer of American ideas through consultant firms was concerned, NPI contributed heavily to the growth of such firms in management. While the Association for Consultant Firms in Management (*Bedriftsøkonomiske Konsulenters Forening*) had only seven members in 1951, the number had grown to twenty three by 1960 (Amdam 1993a: 104). NPI's ambition was to professionalize management consultants, so that they 'could contribute more heavily to the increase of productivity'.[9] The Institute, together with the EPA, also financed several visits by consultants to the United States, and trained them in how to teach business managers the methods of operational research and the basic principles of long-term planning (Gundhus 1960; Nordby 1956).

Regarding the transfer of American ideas through educational institutions, in 1953, NPI, the Ministry of Education, and the Ministry for Industry invited the President of the Carnegie Institute of Technology, E. Dunlap Smith, to evaluate the Norwegian system of management and technical education. In his report, Dunlap Smith stated that as Norway was dominated by small firms the great proportion of graduates from NTH in Trondheim and NSEBA in Bergen would be recruited to managerial positions within a few years. In order to prepare their students for managerial work, therefore, both institutions had to improve their teaching of management disciplines. As a result of this report, NPI began to support changes in the educational system at all levels. New commercial schools, specializing in the retail trade at a secondary level, were established, and the Institute financed a chair in industrial organization at NTH. NPI's main contribution to the improvement of management education, however, was primarily directed towards NSEBA, the business school in Bergen. It financed chairs in marketing and management for the school, and provided money for a visiting professor in management from Yale, E. Wight Bakke (Amdam 1993a: 105).

This financial support helped to broaden NSEBA's perspective from its rather narrow focus on German-inspired business economics, which nevertheless remained the core of its programme. However, in 1950, the school established a chair in organizational psychology. The new professor, Rolf Waaler, who received financial support from NPI, was strongly influenced by the Harvard Business School, and, especially, by the attempt to introduce post-experience management education based on the American pattern at Henley in the United Kingdom. Waaler soon organized an institute attached to NSEBA – the Administration Research Foundation (ARF) – to offer Norwegian managers short courses in management. Through ARF, which turned out to be a success, the business school at Bergen developed, in the 1950s, into the most important centre for management training in Norway (Askvik 1983; Bakke 1959).

TOWARDS THE AMERICAN MODEL?

The 1960s were known as the golden decade of Norwegian industry (Hanisch and Lange 1986). During this decade, American desiderata in management education were introduced on a broad scale. Each year, forty or fifty Norwegian managers went through a training programme at ARF (NSEBA) in Bergen – the so-called *Solstrand* programme – which was heavily influenced by American ideals. While between 1953 and 1962 19 per cent of the participants had been top managers within Norwegian business, from 1963 to 1972 the ratio rose to 27 per cent (Askvik 1983: 7). In cooperation with the training institute of the insurance companies, staff members at ARF also regularly ran seminars in management and organizational psychology for managers of the Norwegian insurance companies (Amdam 1993b). Furthermore, NTH began to organize regular training programmes in management for engineers, and business journals routinely published articles on American management, marketing, long-term planning, and human relations. Moreover, when the leading glass company, Christiania Glasmagasin, one of the ten largest manufacturing companies in Norway, appointed a new top manager in 1965, he was not an engineer but had a commercial education, had been trained in management, and had actively defended the American way of training managers (Amdam *et al.* 1989).

However, the Norwegian system of management education and training during the 1960s was not a copy of the American system. Even though the business school in Oslo was strongly influenced by American management ideals, it was still a small school with no academic reputation. At Bergen's business school, NSEBA, neither the introduction of organizational disciplines nor the founding of ARF had succeeded in turning it into a business school of the American type. It remained essentially a *Hochschule*, strongly dominated by economics and the quantitative approach. The American influence had transformed NSEBA, but, instead of copying the American business school model wholesale, it developed its own style, combining American influences with its German traditions (Jensen and Strømme Svendsen 1986).

Nor was the experience of Christiana Glasmagasin typical of Norwegian industry as a whole. Engineers were still to the fore amongst Norwegian managers. When Nyegaard & Co., the leading Norwegian pharmaceutical company, appointed three new directors around 1965, they were all engineers or chemists (Amdam and Sogner 1994). However, two of them had got PhDs from British universities that were internationally well known for their research into vitamins. And as this was the core of the company's research activities as well, the appointment of these directors illustrates, in this respect, the strong tradition in Norway of qualifying for managerial work by studying abroad. Even though no general study exists of the background of Norwegian managers in the 1960s, individual case studies of the largest Norwegian manufacturing companies show that engineers predominated among managers (Gammelsæter 1991). Most of the top managers in Norwegian insurance companies were actuaries or lawyers who had worked in the insurance industry since graduation (Amdam 1993b). In other words, it was still expected that a manager would qualify for a managerial position by becoming a specialist, through relevant education combined with practical experience from the industry itself. Education in general management was not a sufficient qualification for managerial work, but was in some cases regarded as a good additional qualification to specialist training.

CONTEMPORARY MANAGEMENT EDUCATION

A major difference between contemporary management education in the United States and Germany is that in the former a business school educational background is preferred, whereas in the latter a background in technical education still predominates (Lawrence 1989; Locke 1989). In Norway, there was a radical change in this regard during the 1980s.

First of all, the number of students in business schools expanded. And in

1985, NSEBA, the business school in Bergen, lost its exclusive right to produce graduates with the degree of *siviløkonom* after a four-year programme in business administration. In that year, NSM in Oslo and Bodø Graduate School in northern Norway were given the right, by government, to grant degrees of *siviløkonom*. The number of business schools able to confer these degrees was extended to four in 1991. The expansion meant that the number of graduate *siviløkonomer* increased from 200 to almost 1,000 in ten years (Annual Reports).

The main growth area, however, was in conjunction with several shorter programmes. Within the private educational sector, NSM in Oslo had tremendous success with its one-year undergraduate programme in business administration, which was offered at its thirteen regional colleges. Between 1980 and 1986 the number of new students entering the school increased from 1,000 to 6,000; and in 1986 more than 12,000 applications were received, representing over 50 per cent of all Norwegian secondary school leavers in that year with the equivalent of A-levels (Amdam and Mordt 1992).[10] In the public sector, the regional polytechnics, which were set up during the 1970s, accomplished much with their two-year under-graduate programme in business administration (Amdam and Mordt 1992).[11]

This expansion in the number of students at Norwegian business schools was followed by an increase in the numbers of Norwegian students who went to foreign business schools – from 950 in 1980 to 2,400 in 1990 (Rasmussen and Wold 1992). Most of the latter studied at foreign business schools for at least four years, which gave them an opportunity to apply for the right to use the title *siviløkonom*, on equal terms with graduates from Norwegian business schools. Overseas graduates made up 34 per cent of all new members of the Norwegian professional association of *siviløkonom* in 1988 (Rasmussen and Wold 1992: 53).

The growth in business education reflected a new attitude towards business and management education among young people. It also reflected a change in the demand for this kind of education within business. Of course, not all business school graduates became managers. Statistics on salary and unemployment (Larsen 1985), however, suggest that business school graduates were doing quite well. In 1985, an examination of the average salaries of different groups of graduates ten years after graduation showed that no other professional group could compete with the *siviløkonom* (Edvardsen 1986: 51). In the 1980s, the *siviløkonom* also became the best-paid profession with regard to the level of salaries a year after graduation (Amdam and Mordt 1992: 32).

Corresponding with this change in the general condition of graduates from business schools, Norwegian industry began to recruit business school graduates instead of engineers as senior executives. A survey of the top managers in Norway's 150 largest companies in 1991 shows that 27 per cent had degrees from the business schools in Bergen or Oslo, 18 per cent had degrees from NTH in Trondheim, 9 per cent were lawyers, 4 per cent had degrees in economics, and 30 per cent had higher degrees from abroad.[12]

This trend is supported by various case studies. A closer look at some of the Norwegian multinational companies in the late 1980s reveals that a radical shift had taken place in the educational background of their managers. At Elkem, engineers were predominant at board level up until 1980; then business school graduates took over (Gammelsæter 1991). The board of directors at Hafslund Nycomed, after the merger in 1986 between the energy company Hafslund and the pharmaceutical company Nyegaard & Co, which were previously both dominated by engineers, was controlled by business school graduates (Amdam and Sogner 1994). In the insurance industry, lawyers were prominent among the top directors of casualty insurance companies until 1980, when business school graduates took over. Actuaries lost position gradually to business school graduates among the top managers of life insurance companies throughout the 1980s. Business school influence was especially strong in the largest of the insurance companies. In 1991, UNI and Storebrand merged to become the biggest insurance company in Norway – UNI Storebrand. Of the six members of the new board of directors, five had graduated from Norwegian business schools. The sixth had an MBA degree from Harvard (Amdam 1993b).

The move from managers with a specialist education to those with general skills in management – from engineers to business school graduates – may seem to be a radical shift towards the American pattern of educating and training managers. This impression that the American model was widely introduced into Norway during the 1980s is supported by the popularity of American consultancy firms, such as McKinsey, as well as by American management literature. However, a closer examination shows that Norway did not copy the American model completely. In particular, the Norwegian business schools did not transform themselves according to the American pattern.

Nevertheless, Norwegian business schools were significantly influenced by American scholars. American textbooks were used to a greater extent, and large numbers of their teachers had degrees or experience from the United States. At the Norwegian School of Management in Oslo in 1992, twenty out of the forty four who had their doctorates had American degrees (Amdam 1993a).

What did not change, however, was the traditional *Hochschule* structure: in other words, the business schools did not switch to a pattern which had a marked distinction between its under- and postgraduate programmes. In 1972, some large Norwegian companies established a post-experience business school based on the Harvard Business School model. But the North European Management Institute closed after only five years as a result of lack of support from both industry and students. In 1978–9, NSM in Oslo, which at that time was not recognized by government as an academic business school able to confer the degree of *siviløkonom*, seriously debated whether or not it should adopt the American MBA degree programme. In the end, it decided to embrace the German model used by NSEBA in Bergen. Inspired by the possibility of being given the right to award the degree of *siviløkonom*, the school worked hard to achieve this goal instead, which it did in 1985. It could thus be argued that the system of control and accreditation, which was established by the Norwegian government in collaboration with NSEBA in Bergen, encouraged NSM to evolve towards the traditional *Hochschule* model (Amdam 1993a).

The interest in developing an educational system that was unique to Norway is also demonstrated by the successful one-year programme in business administration at NSM in Oslo, and the two-year programmes at the regional polytechnics. By developing short programmes aimed at qualifying their students for employment without any additional education, these institutions chose a course that was different from the American MBA as well as from the traditional undergraduate structure at Norwegian universities. Their reason for doing this was the need to develop a system of business education that matched Norway's economic structure, with its many small firms (Amdam 1993a).

Finally, the American MBA degree was not introduced in Norway until 1988 when the Oslo Business School, a small private business school which in 1991 merged with NSM, established an MBA programme. NSM, itself, established its MBA programme in 1989. However, NSEBA decided not to offer an MBA programme at all, but rather to develop a Master of International Business degree. This has been actively marketed as a master's degree which is different from the American MBA. At NSM, the one-year MBA has been promoted as a European degree, different from the American model, and the MBA programme has been supplemented by a new Master of Science degree, with specializations in subjects such as European Management and Energy Management, which is closely related to Norway's oil and energy industry.

MANAGEMENT EDUCATION AND BUSINESS PERFORMANCE

It has been argued that the radical change which took place in Norway during the 1980s did not represent a shift from the German to the American model of management education. Instead, the change expressed a strong tendency within Norwegian education to develop its own style by adopting foreign influences that could be useful.

This interpretation of the recent evolution of Norwegian management education may be described as a positive view, and there are those who will disagree with it. During the last year or so, managers with a business school educational background have been criticized for some of the failures in Norwegian business, especially within the banking and insurance sector around 1990. After a period of expansion, the banking and insurance industry underwent some years of crisis, with huge losses. The state had to intervene and give financial support so that the largest private banks did not go into liquidation. In 1992, UNI Storebrand, the biggest Norwegian insurance company, went technically bankrupt, and the state had to take it over. This company, as well as some of the larger banks in trouble, was managed by directors with a Norwegian business school background.

These events have naturally focused on the responsibility educational institutions have for preparing their students for management (Lai 1994). Investigations so far point to the fact that some of the problems in the banking and insurance sector were caused by mismanagement. However, more research is needed before it can be concluded that this mismanagement resulted from the educational background of the managers. A more significant hypothesis than the one expressed here is that Norway went too far in transforming its general system of management education. Replacing managers who had specialist technical skills and experience with those who had general knowledge of management and experience from different industries meant that Norway was no longer able to adopt foreign influences in management education critically, and combine these with national traditions. Thus it may be claimed that, instead of developing her own style, Norway adopted the American pattern.

The essential point in any consideration of the Norwegian case is the change from engineers to business school graduates as managers. Debate on differing interpretations of the character of the contemporary system of management education in Norway may be linked to the question of why this change happened in the first place.

It has been suggested that the shift was caused by structural alterations between the 1960s and the 1980s (Gammelsæter 1990). The introduction of divisionalized firms combined with a change of focus within these firms from production to marketing, caused by a more open economy, favoured managers with a business school education.

An alternative interpretation has been put forward by Byrkjeflot, who emphasizes the radical shift towards an American model, and who suggests that this change may be explained by a combination of some deeper structural weaknesses in the Norwegian economy and various ideological factors (Byrkjeflot 1994). As far as the former are concerned, Byrkjeflot concentrates not so much on the structural changes after the 1960s as the fact that, traditionally, Norway has had an underdeveloped system of large independent companies. Big companies were set up either by the state or by foreign investors, which resulted in a weak national bourgeoisie. Norway did not therefore have the strength to resist strong foreign influences and, in the 1980s, became an easy victim to American ideology in management.

This hypothesis may be supported by the fact that management by its very nature has, as Locke has shown (Locke 1989), a weak scientific basis.

There may be disputes about the historical character of the Norwegian bourgeoisie and, as shown here, whether or not management style has shifted towards the American model. However, the ideological and cultural dimension is interesting in the way that it focuses on how the shift actually took place at company level. Based on case studies of two companies – the pharmaceutical company Nycomed and the insurance company UNI Storebrand – which both witnessed a radical change in management style during the 1980s, it can be said that the most remarkable thing about this change was not that several young men with a business school education were able to rise to the top, but that the old managers allowed them to do so (Amdam 1993b; Amdam and Sogner 1994). This may, of course, be interpreted as a demonstration of weakness in the face of a new, strongly ideological, movement in management.

However, there are also arguments against such an interpretation. Both companies were old companies which had been among the biggest within their industries, and neither of them had been set up by the state or foreign investors, nor had at any time been owned by the state or foreigners. Moreover, from the early years of the twentieth century up to the 1980s, both companies had continuously had top managers with a higher education in appropriate subjects. Thus each had developed its own criteria regarding the formal qualifications needed for its management, and neither company was known for radical changes. So, why did change take place in these companies in the 1980s?

Even though the companies were conservative as far as organizational change was concerned, UNI Storebrand, along with many other insurance companies, and Nycomed had routinely been open towards both new ideas in management and foreign influences.

In the case of the insurance industry, its training institute was, during the 1960s, among the most active supporters of American ideas in management, as these were taught by ARF at the business school in Bergen. And during the 1970s, many directors were sent to the United States to supplement their specialist knowledge and skills in insurance with a formal degree or a course in management (Amdam 1993b). In the case of Nycomed, the company had since the 1930s, when it was among the first Norwegian companies to set up an R&D department, relied heavily on expertise outside the firm, partly from abroad and partly from the universities. In the 1930s, Nyegaard, as the company was then named, developed close ties with the British pharmaceutical company Glaxo, in order to exchange ideas on new technology. This tradition was reflected in Nyegaard's attitude towards both German and American companies after the war. When it came to collaboration with universities, contacts were not limited to those in Norway. British, Swedish, and Belgian university researchers were also seen

32

as suppliers of knowledge to the company (Amdam and Sogner 1994). Moreover, even though the firm's exchange of information with foreign organizations has primarily been aimed at improving its technological knowledge, and not its skills in management, this tendency ought to be mentioned.

It will therefore be suggested that when UNI Storebrand and Nycomed altered their management style in the 1980s, it was not because of any weakness. The change should rather be explained as a natural continuation of their strong interest in importing new ideas. When this took the form of a shift in management, it was because both companies felt that, since they faced radical organizational changes, they needed some form of new expertise. For UNI Storebrand, the 1980s was a period of merger, concentration, and divisionalization. Nycomed, for its part, decided to develop into a multinational company, based on an innovation in X-ray contrast media.

CONCLUSION

This chapter has suggested the hypothesis that what matters for national competence in management's contribution to competitiveness is a country's ability to use foreign ideas critically, adopting those needed and moulding them with national traditions. This hypothesis has then been discussed in relation to Norway. In developing a specifically Norwegian style of training and educating managers, the country should not be described as moving from a German to an American model. Rather, Norway has developed a pattern of management education, with parallels to the Japanese model, which is characterized by a strong interest and ability in importing foreign ideas and combining these with national traditions. While German ideas mattered most before the Second World War, American ideas were the main influence after it. The latter influence was especially strong in the 1980s.

Norway has typically always had an open attitude towards foreign ideas and a system for transferring these ideas to herself. In this respect, the large numbers of foreign students abroad – and the numerous managers with a foreign educational background – have historically been very important. However, it is more difficult to analyse whether Norway has developed the skills to examine foreign ideas critically, and the strong national traditions necessary to enable it to resist pressure from outside.

In the first decades after the Second World War Norway demonstrated the skill both to examine imported ideas discerningly and to resist pressure from outside by combining some new influences with the traditional system of education and style of management. This conclusion is based on two facts. First, several case studies of Norwegian manufacturing companies show that engineers were still to the fore among managers (Gammelsæter 1991). Furthermore, most top managers in Norwegian insurance companies were actuaries or lawyers who had worked in the insurance industry since their graduation (Amdam 1993b). In other words, a manager should still qualify for managerial positions by becoming a specialist, through relevant education combined with practical experience from the industry itself. Training or education in general management was not a sufficient qualification for managerial work, but was in some cases regarded as a good additional requirement. In the second place, Norway has stuck to the traditional German-inspired *Hochschule* system in technical and business education.

If the changes that took place in the 1980s are considered, it is not so easy to defend the suggested hypothesis. Norway's traditionally strong and open attitude towards foreign ideas, and her way of transferring those ideas, still existed, and were expressed through the growing number of business students abroad and through an increasing interest in American management literature and the use of American management consultancy firms. But the question is whether Norway has lost its ability to examine imported ideas critically and to combine new influences with her own style and traditions in management education. The interest of the business schools in recruiting new scholars with an American PhD points to a tendency to copy the American pattern of management education. The same may be said about the radical shift that seems to have taken place among board members of Norwegian companies: namely, the change from engineers and other professional specialist groups to people with an educational background in general management from American business schools or business administration from their Norwegian counterparts.

Detailed studies will no doubt come up with examples of blind copying, as well as the resistance of isolationists towards new ideas. However, if the more successful cases are focused upon, the internal transformation of external ideas on a company level appears to be important. The case study of Nycomed suggests that the level of competence and experience gained by using highly educated managers, and developing a culture which is open to foreign influences, may be significant in this process. The appointment of a physician, Tore Talset, as the new CEO of Nycomed in 1993 following a CEO with an MBA, may have been an expression at company level of a readjustment towards a new balance between foreign patterns and national traditions after several years of domination of the board by business school graduates.

At the national level, the system of control exerted by the government also seems to be important. The Norwegian system of higher education has traditionally been strongly regulated as to the number of its students and its formal accreditation criteria. In particular, it has not been possible, as a rule, to set up new educational programmes without the approval of some of the existing universities. Critics of this system say that the result has been that educational institutions have not been able to change fast enough. On the other hand, a kind of stability has been secured and changes which are too hasty prevented. It may be argued that the system got somewhat out of control at the beginning of the 1980s, when the expansion of the one-year programme in business administration at private business schools took place without any government approval. This expansion led to increased numbers of business graduates, which strengthened the impression of radical change. However, recent developments suggest that government has changed its methods, which means that these programmes now have to be approved. The scheme of approval, to which state loans for students have also been linked, has served to hamper the growth of new master's programmes in management. As a result, business schools have been encouraged to develop a Norwegian or European style in order to be accredited.

Finally, there is the question of management education and business performance. It has been argued that the Norwegian system of management education matched the economy in the interwar period and in the 1950s and 1960s. However, as the problems of companies like UNI Storebrand illustrate, more research is needed for the 1980s before any conclusion can be reached. It should be stressed, however, that the Norwegian economy in the late 1980s was not only characterized by mismanagement and crises in the banking and insurance industry. Other large companies, such as those in the pharmaceutical industry, for example, contrived to change small firms into profitable multinational companies during these years. For them, the radical changes in management may have been a necessity.

NOTES

1 The secondary commercial school (*Handelsgymnas*) played a much more important role among the top directors of banking and commercial companies.
2 The degree of *siviløkonom*, which was received after a three-year programme (four years from 1975) in business administration, has been translated as Master of Management or Master of Business.
3 In 1947, seventeen of the textbooks used in the two-year programme were printed in the United States, and only two in Germany. Twenty six were from Norway, fifteen from Sweden, four from Denmark and two from other countries (Amdam 1993a).
4 BI Archive, F. Øien's report of his visit to the United States in 1958, and a letter from Øien to J.C. Dockerlay, George Washington University, 11 April 1958.
5 National Archives (NA), NPI, 1, Annual reports.
6 NA/NPI, 1, Minutes from Rådsmøte 28 June 1954, agreement between FOA and NPI.
7 NA/NPI, 1, Minutes from Rådsmøte 1953–63.
8 NA/NPI, 1, Minutes from Rådsmøte 23 February 1960.
9 NA/NPI, 1, Rådsmøte 20 February, 1958. Plan for 1958.
10 An unknown number of the 12,000 applicants had graduated from secondary schools earlier than 1986.
11 The number of students increased from 201 in 1970 to 488 in 1980, 884 in 1985, and 1,137 in 1990.

12 The remaining 12 per cent had a different kind of educational background. Unfortunately, the sort of higher education received by the 30 per cent who were trained abroad is unknown (*Inside* 1992).

REFERENCES

Aldcroft, D.H. (1992) *Education, Training and Economic Performance 1944 to 1990*, Manchester: Manchester University Press.

Amdam, R.P. (1993a) *For egen regning: BI og den økonomisk-administrative utdanningen 1943–1993*, Oslo: Universitetsforlaget.

—— (1993b) 'Utdanning og kompetanse i forsikring', (Unpublished paper).

—— (1994) 'Foreign Influence on the Education of Norwegian Business Managers before World War II', *Business History* 36(4): 79–94.

—— and Mordt, G. (1992) *Utdanningskonjunkturer*, Handelshøyskolen BI, Research Report No. 4.

—— and Norstrøm, C.J. (1994) 'Business Administration in Norway 1936–1990', in L. Engwall and E. Gunnarsson (eds) *Management Education in an Academic Context*, Uppsala: Acta Universitatis Upsaliensis, Studia Oeconomiae Negotiorum 35.

—— and Sogner, K. (1994) *Wealth of Contrast: Nyegaard & Co – A Norwegian Pharmaceutical Company 1874–1985*, Oslo: Ad Notam Gyldendal.

—— Hanisch, T.J., and Pharo, I.E. (1989) *Vel blåst! Christiania Glasmagasin og norsk glassindustri 1739–1989*, Oslo: Gyldendal Norsk Forlag.

Askvik, S. (1983) 'Et kurs for nåværende og fremtidige bedriftsledere? Rekrutteringen til AFF's Program for lederutvikling i perioden 1953–82', *Working Paper*, Bergen: ARF.

Bakke, E.W. (1959) *A Norwegian Contribution to Executive Development*, Bergen: NHH.

Barnes, W. (1989) *Managerial Catalyst: The Story of London Business School 1964 to 1989*, London: Paul Chapman.

Barry, B. (1989) 'Management Education in Britain', in W. Byrt (ed.) *Management Education: An International Survey*, London: Routledge, 56–77.

Byrkjeflot, H. (1993) 'Hvorfor har ikke det amerikanske ledelsesidealet fått gjennomslag i Tyskland?', *Working Paper*, No. 9353, Bergen: LOS.

—— (1994) 'Norsk bedriftsledelse – mellom amerikanske og tyske idealer', *LOS Kontakt* No. 2.

Byrt, W. (ed.) (1989) *Management Education: An International Survey*, London: Routledge.

Cheit, E. (1985) 'Business Schools and Their Critics', *California Management Review* XXVII(3): 43–62.

Collins, K. (1989) 'Management Education in Japan', in W. Byrt (ed.) *Management Education: An International Survey*, London: Routledge, 172–209.

Edvardsen, R. (1986) *Ti år etter eksamen*, Oslo: NAVFs utredningsinstitutt, Melding No. 5.

Gammelsæter, H. (1990) 'Toppledere i norsk industri: fra sivilingeniører til siviløkonomer', *Norsk Harvard 1: 90–2*.

—— (1991) *Organisasjonsendring gjennom generasjoner av ledere: En studie av endringer i Hafslund Nycomed, Elkem og Norsk Hydro*, Molde: Møreforsking.

Geiger, R.L. (1986) *Private Sectors in Higher Education: Structure, Function, and Change in Eight Countries*, Ann Arbor, MI: University of Michigan Press.

Gundhus, P. (1960) 'Langtidsplanlegging for organisasjon og medarbeiderstab', *Bedriftsøkonomen* 5.

Handy, C. *et al.* (1987) *The Making of Managers: A Report on Management Education, Training and Development in the USA, West Germany, France, Japan and the UK*, London: National Economic Development Council.

Hanisch, T.J. and Lange, E. (1985) *Vitenskap for industrien: NTH – en skole i utvikling gjennom 75 år*, Oslo: Universitetsforlaget.

—— (1986) *Veien til velstand*, Oslo: Universitetsforlaget.

Inside (1992), 1.

Jensen, O.H. and Strømme Svendsen, A. (1986) *Norges Handelshøyskole femti år*, Bergen: NHH.

Kalleberg, R. (1991) 'Kenning-tradisjonen i norsk ledelse', *Nytt Norsk Tidsskrift* 3: 216–44.

Keeble, S.P. (1992) *The Ability to Manage: A Study of British Management, 1890–1990*, Manchester: Manchester University Press.

Lai, L. (1994) 'The Norwegian Banking Crisis: Managerial Escalation of Decline and Crisis', *Scandinavian Journal of Management* 10(4): 397–408.

Lane, C. (1989) *Management and Labour in Europe: The Industrial Enterprise in Germany, Britain and France*, Aldershot: Edward Elgar.

Lange, E. (1989) 'Norske ingeniører i Amerika 1900–1950: En moderne svennevandring', in T. Bergh and H. Pharo (eds) *Historiker og veileder: Festskrift til Jacob Sverdrup*, Oslo: Tiden Forlag.

Larsen, K.A. (ed.) (1985) *Utdanning og arbeidsmarked*, Oslo: NAVFs utredningsinstitutt, Melding No. 2.

Lawrence, P. (1989) 'Management Education in West Germany', in W. Byrt (ed.) *Management Education: An International Survey*, London: Routledge, 151–71.

Locke, R.R. (1988) 'Educational Traditions and the Development of Business Studies after 1945 (An Anglo-French-German Comparison)', *Business History* XXX(1): 84–115.

—— (1989) *Management and Higher Education since 1940: The Influence of America and Japan on West Germany, Great Britain, and France*, Cambridge: Cambridge University Press.

Lorriman, J. and Kenjo, T. (1994) *Japan's Winning Margins: Management, Training, and Education*, Oxford: Oxford University Press.

Nerheim, G. and Nordvik, H.W. (1986) *Ikke bare maskiner: Historien om IBM i Norge 1935–1985*, Stavanger: Universitetsforlaget.

Nioche, J.P. (1992) 'The War of Degrees in European Management Education', *EFMD Forum* 1, 21–4.

Nordby, P.A. (1956) 'Utdannelse av bedriftsledere: Rapport fra de norske deltakerne i en studietur til USA', *Bedriftsøkonomen* 6.

NOS Utdanningsstatistikk (Educational statistics, several years).

NPI (1963) *Norsk Produktivitetsinstitutt gjennom de første ti år*, Oslo: Norsk Produktivitetsinstitutt.

Porter, M.E. (1990) *The Competitive Advantage of Nations*, London: Macmillan.

Rasmussen, L. and Wold, A. (1992) 'Utenlandsstudenter, hvorfor finnes de? En undersøkelse av årsakene til at norske studenter reiser til utlandet for å studere økonomi/administrasjon', Master's Thesis, Norwegian School of Management.

Steiro, J.R. (1974) 'Om opprettelsen av Norsk produktivitetsinstitutt', MA Thesis (History), University of Oslo.

Wilson, J.F. (1992) *The Manchester Experiment: A History of Manchester Business School, 1965–1990*, London: Paul Chapman.

Yasumuro, K. (1993) 'Engineers as Functional Alternatives to Entrepreneurs in Japanese Industrialisation', in J. Brown and M.B. Rose (eds) *Entrepreneurship, Networks and Modern Business*, Manchester: Manchester University Press, 76–101.

3

AMERICAN INFLUENCE ON EUROPEAN MANAGEMENT EDUCATION

The role of the Ford Foundation

Giuliana Gemelli

INTRODUCTION – IMITATION AND RESISTANCE

Until a few years ago there was general agreement that the United States had always led in the field of management education and that for this reason her models had been easily exported to Europe. Since the end of the 1980s, however, this statement has been open to question. American experts have begun to examine the deficiencies of business education in the United States and to compare these with the weakening of American management's organizational capabilities (Aaronson 1992). At the same time, they have begun to say that some European business schools, especially those that have developed a transnational focus and teach international business as a subject which is integrated throughout the curriculum, have reached a competitive position in the worldwide campus of management education (Greenhouse 1991). This revisionist attitude has stimulated scholars into analysing the historical heterogeneity and different patterns of business schools, in both their organizational design and training strategies. In the last few years, they have produced studies in which the historical approach has a crucial role in analysing the different solutions that each institution has given to similar organizational problems. As Herbert Simon (1967) has stated, these problems are principally related to the functional complexity of the business school and, in particular, to the necessity of integrating two different social systems and their cultural patterns: the social system of practitioners and the social system of scientists in relevant disciplines (such as mathematical sciences, behavioural sciences, and accounting) whose heterogeneity is also evident.

This heterogeneity is underlined if the development of commercial and entrepreneurial training, in the long period from the second half of the nineteenth century, is considered. It is important to stress that the level of coordination and integration between the university and the industrial economic systems was always the product of a long process of trial and error, which in some cases lasted for almost half a century. Even though the result of this experimental process presents qualitative and quantitative differences from one country to another, the process in itself was not a distinguishing element of such peripheral countries as Italy or Spain; this experiment was also relevant to Germany, as well as, to some extent, the United States. To date, only Robert Locke (1984, 1989) has tried a systematic comparison of the relationship between higher education and entrepreneurial performance, comparing the three main European countries – Britain, France, and Germany – with the United States. His analysis, however, does not succeed in avoiding completely the limits of the functionalist approach. This is especially true when he considers the German case study as opposed to the other European countries. In the early twentieth century, the latter were hardly interested in developing their own strategies of, and institutions for, management education, and later on – after the Second World War – they became in consequence more receptive to the impact of American management patterns. In fact, the dynamic of cultural resistance versus the imitation of foreign patterns is more complex than this, and less 'linear'! The process of integration and denial is not entirely the product of rational choices, but also the effect of a system of micro decisions taken over a long period, which are related not only to management education but to the complex articulation between the social system of scientific knowledge and the social system of professional practice and, selectively, to its results.

Locke argues that since the beginning of this century Germany has produced the right educational environment for the right economic and entrepreneurial development. Locke does not consider, however, that the outcome of this synthesis was the result of a long empirical process. Moreover, he does not think that the distinctive pattern of business education in Germany was shaped by the appropriate adaptation of German technical institutes to the demand of the industrial environment, but rather by other considerations. The factors which mattered were those that were internally related to the process of institutionalization in the higher education system. At the beginning of the twentieth century, the theoretical debates on such crucial and authoritative disciplines as political economy and sociology had a role in shaping the institutional and theoretical patterns of new disciplines. Recent studies demonstrate that, not only in Germany but also in Italy, the influence of positivism and, more specifically, the results of the *Methodenstreit*, which was prevalent at the beginning of this century, stimulated the emergence of a unified theory of the firm (Canziani and Brovetto 1995). This approach – mainly deductive – was very different from the 'case method' – basically inductive – which progressively became the dominant pattern of American business education.

European differences

The theory of the firm was a basic ingredient in the genealogy of both *economia aziendale* in Italy, at Bocconi University, and *Betriebswirtschafts-lehre* in Germany. In France, on the other hand, *les sciences de gestion* were characterized by a more empirical approach, avoiding any attempt to integrate *gestion* (both as a teaching subject and as a training scheme) into a general theory of the firm. With Fayol, *le gestion* was intellectually rather than theoretically founded. More specifically, it was a doctrine that was intellectually rooted rather than a theory with an applied aim, as in Germany (Fayol 1925/1979). Its disciplinary identity remained very fluid and was based on juridical disciplines in addition to engineering, with the added support of *l'art du commandement* which was a subject in military schools as well as in the *École Polytechnique*. Despite similar denotative characteristics, then, European institutions showed many connotative differences. In most European countries the education of managers only took place in the universities, broadly defined to include polytechnic schools and high schools of commerce. But the connotation of these institutions was very different from one country to another, relating to the different structural factors mentioned above.

Moreover, if the effect of historical change over the long period is considered – namely, the differing role from one period to another of such interacting factors as professional interests, institutional rivalries, national and international competition, financial constraints or opportunities, economic or organizational asymmetries – the changing patterns of business education become evident. For example, in the United States, business administration essentially consisted of engineering together with economics; later on, it was also centred on organizational behaviour. In Germany, it was accounting above all, and only included *Betriebswirtschaftslehre* in the second period of development of the study of economics of the firm. In the Italian *Scuole di Commercio*, it was mainly *ragioneria* and later, with the creation of Bocconi University, it was *economia aziendale*.

We are, then, confronting an evident asymmetry, both in space and in time, which was rapidly (and to some extent only apparently) reduced during a specific historical period – from 1950 to 1970 – by a process of homologation produced by the impact of the American management education system in Europe. This process, however, was part of a larger scenario of cooperative strategies relating to other sectors thought to be of crucial importance in reinforcing American political leadership of the West, such as for example technological cooperation in space. In particular, this occurred during the 1960s, when the relationship between technology and economic growth became a strategic element in the American–European relationship. This growing interest was mainly channelled into and institutionalized by the Organization for Economic Cooperation and

Development (OECD) (Sebesta 1984). OECD also had an important role in stimulating the development of European management education as a critical strategic factor in reducing the asymmetry – 'technological gap' – between the two continents.

Contrast of contexts

In analysing the dynamics between national patterns and the processes of homologation to a dominant system, a significant step is to define the conceptual tools required. It is also important to find strategic topics which can improve the comparative approach both in time (over the long period) and space (national and international). Important pointers can be found in the recent methodological literature on comparative analysis. The method based on the analysis of the 'contrast of contexts' (Ragin 1991), for example, seems to be particularly useful in developing a suitable generalization from empirical case studies. This approach aims to maintain the distinctive originality of case studies, especially when considering their historical framework, rather than to produce a simple inventory of institutional similarities and differences. On the contrary, the basic ground for comparison is the selection of some of the general and crucial questions which oriented the comparative analysis. The focus in this case is not the study of the distribution and diffusion of training patterns in managerial education but the interactive and cultural dimension which orients the historical development of these training patterns. The main goal is to develop an analysis which emphasizes a variety of answers to a rather homogeneous set of problems, such as how to integrate professional standards and practices into the curricula of business schools and how to adapt these professional standards and practices to scientific changes and methodological innovation in the relevant disciplines or systems of disciplines. This variety of answers is the product not only of institutional strategies but also of the inner factors which characterize cultural contexts. Anthropologist Yahuda Elkana (1981) defined these factors as 'images of knowledge': that is, socially based conceptions about knowledge, such as sources, legitimization patterns, rules, values, behaviours, and rituals.

In most European countries, management as a cultural pattern (that was developed by business schools and diffused in cooperation with such differing institutions as universities, firms, trade associations, private foundations, and so forth) has progressively imposed itself as the dominant motif, which has overlapped previous images of knowledge and their institutionalization as disciplines. Examples include *economia aziendale* in Italy, *gestion* in France, and *Betriebswirtschaftslehre* in Germany and some northern countries. Despite a certain familiarity with American management, these social practices of knowledge maintained, even after the powerful impact of American patterns in Europe, a basic heterogeneity not only from the connotative but also from the denotative point of view. It is a matter of fact that, until the present time, this heterogeneity has been frequently underestimated. Only recently have scholars, institution builders, and the designers of institutional reform seemed to consider the role of the inner factors of cultural resistance as important elements in shaping new educational strategies or institutional reform projects. In this case, reference to the comparative approach based on a 'contrast of contexts' could also be said to have an applied aim.

It is important to stress that this method becomes particularly useful when the field of enquiry requires the 'translation' and 'transmission' of cultural and organizational patterns in contexts which are heterogeneous not only in their historical development but also in their asymmetrical position within the systemic framework produced by this dynamic of transmission and transfer of 'dominant' cultural and organizational patterns. Indeed, the domination of American patterns in managerial education after the Second World War has evoked in the European countries a range of reactions, from hybridization to imitation and resistance to refusal. The historical analysis of these has become crucial, especially in the last few years when the asymmetrical map of managerial education in the international context has entered into a phase of transition. This is characterized by an inversion in the direction of the relationship between European and American patterns and by the emergence of pluralism as a strategic target.

The involvement of the Ford Foundation in developing European management education

The goal of this chapter is to develop some of these methodological issues and to investigate the historical background in which this inversion was set up through the exploration of a transversal subject: the Ford Foundation's financial and organizational involvement in developing European management education. In this context, the Ford Foundation acted as a cultural entrepreneur, trying to standardize management educational patterns and professional requirements through the dissemination of intensive training and research programmes. It was experimented on initially by the most important American business schools in the early 1950s (Schlossman *et al.* 1987). Then, from the mid 1960s, the Ford Foundation also acted as a translator of American methods into different European institutional and cultural frameworks. This aspect of the Ford Foundation's work will be analysed in more detail in two case studies.

A STRATEGIC TOPIC: CROSS-FERTILIZATION POLICIES

The Ford Foundation's work – initially directed towards American business schools, and then towards European institutions – was not automatic or the result of a carbon copy strategy of transfer. This is not an issue that can easily be included in the old idea of 'Americanization'. Instead, the concept used to analyse the transfer is that of cross-fertilization, which implies a process of translation from one context to another, rather than a mechanical transfer. From this point of view, the concept of cross-fertilization is also used as a detector to identify some crucial 'contrasts of contexts' in the development of management education, especially from 1954 to 1974. This is precisely the period of greatest development in the Ford Foundation's involvement with European cultural and institutional policies.

Early attempts at cross-fertilization

The Ford Foundation was not the only contender in the business of bringing cross-fertilization policies to management education. The role of other institutional or even individual actors should also be considered. The origins of the translation of American educational patterns are related to the role that Harvard Business School (HBS) had during the 1930s in diffusing the case method throughout Europe, and especially in France. Indeed, this process was mainly due to the individual initiative of one man: a man with a vision, General Georges Frederic Doriot.

Doriot was a Frenchman, educated in the United States, who became vice-dean of HBS when he was 28 years old. In 1930, in cooperation with a small group of French entrepreneurs, he took the initiative of creating, in Paris, the *Centre de Préparation aux Affaires* (CPA). This was the first European outpost to develop the case method approach, both in teaching and research training (Gemelli 1993). Doriot had a long career, both in the educational field and in capital venture enterprises (he was the founder of American Research and Development (ARD) and of its European agency, ERD). In the mid 1950s, he was also the ideas man and pioneer of INSEAD, which was founded by Doriot's former French students in the HBS class of manufacturing: Olivier Giscard d'Estaing, Roger Godino, and Claude Janssen. Doriot was also active in stimulating financial support for INSEAD, both from the Ford Foundation (where he was, in fact, an influential member of the board of trustees) and from many important American companies (see Table 3.1).

Cross-fertilization after the Second World War

The process of cross-fertilization through which the 'new look' in management education designed by the Ford Foundation was translated into Europe was also anticipated and stimulated by the clear and detailed studies of the educational and institutional situation of the various European countries produced, from the early 1950s, by the European Productivity Agency (EPA).

Table 3.1 The American contribution to INSEAD 1971–2 ($)

Firm	1971	1972
ACF Foundation	250	
ALCOA Foundation	5,000	5,000
American Express	500	
ARMCO Steel Corp.	500	
Arthur D. Little	2,000	
Avon Products Foundation	2,000	
Bois Cascade	1,000	
Chase Manhattan Bank	2,000	3,000
Chemical Bank of England	1,000	
Corning Glass Foundation	2,500	
Cresap McCormick & Paget & Co.	1,000	1,000
A. De Vitry	700	1,800
EG & G Inc.		400
Ford Motor Co.	2,000	
General Electric	5,000	
Goldman Sachs		100
Hancock Mutual Life Insurance Co.		1,000
IBM World Trade Corp.	5,000	5,000
International Paper Co. Foundation	1,000	
ITT	10,000	
Kimberly Clark Foundation		2,000
Kraft Food	1,000	
Merck, Sharp & Dohme	1,000	
Monsanto Co.	1,000	1,000
Morgan Guaranty Trust		2,500
Pfizer Int'l	2,000	
Schieffelin & Co.	1,000	
The Singer Co. Foundation		500
Standard Oil of NJ	7,000	
The Virgil & Judith Stark Foundation	9,000	
Texas Instruments	5,000	
Uniroyal Foundation	1,000	
Warner Lambert	1,200	
HE The Hon. Arthur K. Watson*	50,000	
Xerox Foundation	2,000	

Note: *American Ambassador in Paris

Source: GFD Personal Papers, French Library in Boston

44

EPA's detailed reports allowed the Ford Foundation to adapt its strategies to the highly differentiated European environment. Before analysing certain elements of the explicit strategies of this cross-fertilization process, the general context in which the Ford Foundation's involvement in European management education took place will be described, and then the reasons behind the selection of the two case studies presented here will be explained.

With regard to the first point, it should be stressed that the Ford Foundation's role in Europe was not merely the result of a strategy to export a successful national experiment. It was part of a grander vision of the role of the 'diplomacy of ideas' in strengthening the cultural and ideological unity of Western civilization through the development of programmes of higher education in research and training, which concerned management education as well as the social sciences (Gemelli 1994). Indeed, the basic elements of the 'new look' in management education projected by the Ford Foundation came to be a feature of the introduction of behavioural and social sciences to the curricula of business schools, and also to their structural goal, which was the stimulation of research as a relevant factor in the process of management professionalization.

In any event, the development of programmes, whose aim was the improvement and standardization of European research, has been associated since 1954, both in the social sciences and management fields, with the setting up of an autonomous European programme within the 'International Affairs' part of the Ford Foundation. Thanks to the initiative of one of its brightest officers, Shepard Stone, the Ford Foundation elaborated a grander vision of Europe which foresaw three goals: the strengthening of the Atlantic Community; the reinforcing of democratic institutions; and the widening of European perspectives, towards not only the Mediterranean countries but also those in the East. The origins of this project should be regarded as part of the very complex scenario in which the Cold War, at the end of its aggressive phase, moulded higher learning into a strategic factor in political warfare. As recent studies have pointed out, this was also the period in which, thanks to better coordination between scientists, entrepreneurs, and politicians, and the creation of a set of relationships between private experts and public agencies in the United States, an important transfer of know-how from military research to 'major science' was realized. In the field explored in this chapter there are crucial examples of this kind of transfer as well. Georges F. Doriot, who became a general in the American Army during the Second World War and was made head of the Army's Department of Research and Development which was created in 1946, transferred his experience of that Department to his work during the 1950s of organizing the first experimental venture capital enterprises. It should also be stressed that many of the directors and deans of the first European business schools came from an army background. One of these was Alexander King, who was an organizer of scientific strategies within

EPA. According to him, the idea of implementing productivity came directly from the previous experience of operational research applied to the technical problems of the war effort.[1]

In some respects the Second World War and the Cold War were a godsend for the development of social science and management education. The growth of plans for a unified Europe, strongly supported by such eminent American personalities as General William Donovan and Georges Ball, and the development in the Kennedy era of a more equal partnership between the United States and Europe, facilitated and accelerated the growth of American interests in Europe. In the mid 1960s, the momentous debate on the 'managerial gap', emphasized by the publication of Servan-Schreiber's widely acclaimed book, *The American Challenge*, gave another strong impetus to this dialogue, and increased the visibility of management problems as a strategic element in the relationship between the United States and Europe. The large private foundations were at the right stage to play a decisive role in this process. Their importance was accentuated by two factors: the increasing political supremacy of the United States in the international context, and particularly in Europe, and the expanding role of private foundations in dealing with specific problems of American public policy and cultural diplomacy.

International strategies in education and research were part of this scenario, the dynamics of which in the area of management education and training can best be described by specific case studies. In fact, the two case studies presented here – of INSEAD in France and IPSOA in Italy – have been selected in the first place because they are particularly relevant to an illustration of the dynamic context of the relationship between the United States and Europe, and in the second, because they allow for experimentation of the 'contrast of contexts' approach. Not only do they both relate to the same historical period, but also they both pertain to the first experimental phase which anticipated the extensive involvement of the Ford Foundation in European management education programmes. Moreover, these two case studies concern different countries which present, within very different institutional, social, and entrepreneurial contexts, a similar resistance to American educational and training patterns. Finally, the case studies are part of a very asymmetrical story. IPSOA had a very short institutional life, despite the intensity of its experience and the positive and innovative effects it produced within the social and cultural framework of Italian management. INSEAD, on the other hand, is not only still going but one of the best and most successful international business schools.

THE FORD FOUNDATION'S NEW LOOK IN MANAGEMENT

In 1953, Milton Katz of the Ford Foundation invited Thomas Carroll, then dean of the School of Business at the University of North Carolina and formerly an assistant dean at HBS, 'to spearhead Ford's developing interest in business education and, more specifically, to outline a proposal for strengthening the case method of instruction in business' (Schlossman *et al.* 1987: 9). An advisory committee was set up to study a specific programme for the Ford Foundation's intervention in the reform of business education. The committee concluded that:

> for business education to improve, rather than simply to follow established practice, the Foundation had to subsidize and encourage substantial imaginative research in a field where few conducted any research at all and where much of what was undertaken was descriptive, industry-specific, if not company-specific.
>
> (Schlossman *et al.* 1987: 14)[2]

This advice implied that research should have a central role in the professionalization of management.

The Ford Foundation's strategy was to invest in a few 'excellent' institutions (Carnegie, Harvard, Columbia, Chicago, and Stanford) and start a curricula reform based on the incorporation of behavioural and social sciences into such traditional disciplines as accounting, mathematics, and econometrics.

At the end of the 1950s, despite some criticisms and tensions between different sets of priorities, such as development of centres of excellence or improvement in the diffusion of the 'new look' to a larger range of institutions, the 'new look' was definitely on the offensive. The decision to transform this strategy into an international programme was not the automatic effect of its success in the national context. Indeed, it must be stressed that the Foundation had been experimenting in the development of European management education since the early 1950s: that is, before launching the 'new look' in American institutions. As will be seen later, however, when IPSOA's development is analysed, it was not an auspicious precedent. The reasons behind the Ford Foundation's substantial involvement in European educational policies later should be related rather to the simultaneous occurrence of several different factors. First of all, it was connected with some of the Foundation's structural changes during the second half of the 1950s. In this period, two new programmes were created – the International Affairs Program (IAP), established to carry out the Foundation's programmes in Europe, and the Economic Development and Administration Program (EDA), set up to support educational institutions concerned with the economy. These programmes found a productive field of interaction in management education. When the IAP was terminated in the second half of the 1960s, the development of European management education found a home for itself, and the right structure, mainly within the Higher Education and Research Program. Marshall Robinson, who, significantly, directed the EDA from 1964 to 1967, was the officer in charge of this new programme. It is also important to add that in 1957 the Foundation ended the Behavioral Sciences Program, which began in 1951 but was considered to have become too 'intellectual', abstract in content, and overformalized in its methods.[3] At that time, implementation of the role of behavioural sciences in management education was perceived as a way to give a more functional direction to these disciplines, whose effect on European social sciences was getting greater.

The Foundation's European programme was stimulated by other external factors, related to the dynamics of the international context at the beginning of the 1960s. As already mentioned, there was in this period a growing interest in the relationship between technology and economic growth and, at the same time, an increasing European anxiety about the 'technological gap' that existed between the United States and Europe. Management education was perceived as a crucial factor in reducing this gap, especially by some of the brighter members of OECD, like Alexander King and Jean-Jacques Solomon.[4] In the early 1950s, King had been the promoter of European productivity strategies; from the mid 1950s he became a key figure in the promotion of the scientific policies of EPA. Directed in Paris by Roger Grégoire, this organization had its own national agencies in many European countries. The men who directed these national agencies were often also promoters of institutional and organizational initiatives in the field of studies of human relations and management. Padre Agostino Gemelli, who was a member of the *Comitato Nazionale per la Produttività*, the Italian agency of EPA, was one of the few Italian experts in applied industrial psychology and played a part in the introduction of the study of human relations in Italy. The *Comitato Nazionale per la Produttività* (CNP) had an important role in establishing in 1956, with EPA's support, ISIDA, Italy's second school of management located in Palermo. Under the direction of Gabriele Morello, a bright young economist who had previously been an assistant professor at IPSOA, ISIDA, during the 1960s, successfully continued along the path that IPSOA, with financial and organizational support from the Ford Foundation, had previously delineated in Turin.

What is important to stress is the role of EPA in implementing the basically technical set of formulae for productivity, with a cultural background that was firmly rooted in European tradition. EPA's role is attested to by the following quotation in a 1956 report by Alexander King:

> There is a reluctance on the part of Universities in some parts of Europe to accept management as a subject of sufficient intellectual content for inclusion alongside the accepted disciplines. This has been supported by the tendency since the war . . . to introduce the subject in the form of particular techniques, sometimes trivial, apparently unconnected

with each other and often without consideration of underlying principles. At the same time there is recognition of the need for well trained, progressive managers in European industry. . . . It appears to us that accepted American methods of training for management, while developed more extensively and successfully than elsewhere, have tended to become somewhat traditional. On the other hand, the growing needs and complexities of industry are clearly making it necessary to develop managers of a new type, while the elaboration of scientific methods and the unfolding of the social sciences are offering new and dramatic possibilities.[5]

This statement contains a clear acceptance of the strategic and methodological orientation which inspired the 'new look' of the Ford Foundation as a positive opportunity to develop European management education. Moreover, it must be stressed that European experts for the most part agreed that their management education ought to be built on a cultural and cross-disciplinary foundation which integrated American patterns with European transnational culture. As Alexander King pointed out, this interdisciplinary orientation should be based on an increasing use of quantitative methods and mathematical analysis (e.g. the theory of games), scientific methods, and operational research techniques, as well as on the implementation of the research tradition of the social and behavioural sciences.

It seems paradoxical that the first experiment in European management education took place in a country like Italy where the university system was not only completely unaware of cross-disciplinary educational strategies but also totally opposed to innovative experiments. Why, then, did the Ford Foundation decide to support an HBS programme there and launch itself into the creation of IPSOA?

THE PIONEER STAGE OF THE FORD FOUNDATION'S EUROPEAN PROGRAMME

The Italian experiment anticipated the Ford Foundation's involvement in American business education reform, which, as mentioned above, started in 1953. The IPSOA project should be associated with Shepard Stone's commitment to work in Europe rather than viewed as an explicit experiment in management education. This commitment rested on his judgement that there were promising opportunities for the foundation in the modernization and reform of education as an impetus not only to the strengthening of the Euro-Atlantic alliance but also to the planning of a unified Europe. The main goal was to extend to Europe the 'organizational synthesis' patterns, carried out in the United States through the integration of social sciences and practical policies, of academic research and public policies, and of experts and state administration. The basis of support in

Italy for Stone's strategy was limited. In the universities and academic institutions, there was no idea of what a cultural policy could mean.

However, at the beginning of the project, Stone's strategy found particular support in a social and intellectual reform movement, *Comunità*, whose energetic and inventive pioneer was the Italian industrialist Adriano Olivetti. It is not surprising that the Foundation decided to support Olivetti's idea of creating a postgraduate school for management studies, to be located in Turin. In fact, IPSOA was the first European business school (after the creation of CPA in the 1930s) to imitate the methods and teaching strategies of HBS.

The case study of IPSOA is a good empirical example of the difficulties and obstacles which can characterize the automatic transfer of a set of organizational patterns from one context to another, especially when the industrial and higher education systems of the countries involved are strongly differentiated, as was the case with those of Italy and the United States.

The history of IPSOA

IPSOA was established in 1952 by FIAT's director Vittorio Valletta and by Adriano Olivetti himself. After participating in an international conference in New York, organized by the National Management Council, Valletta and Olivetti decided to start a new educational experiment in Italy, based on the pragmatic action-oriented type of education that existed in the United States. IPSOA was established with the financial means provided by their companies and with the weight of their personal support. It was run by a former Olivetti man, Giovanni Enriques, the son of the mathematician Federigo, who was the director of the institute. Thanks to an agreement between the Foundation and HBS, IPSOA could count, for nearly all of its first year, on the strong capabilities – particularly with regard to the case method – of Professor Melvin T. Copeland, former Director of Research at HBS, Pearson Hunt, and Professor Charles M. Williams, also from HBS. Moreover, in 1953, the first instalment of the Ford Foundation grant ($13,000) was entirely devoted to training in case method techniques and to the development of research in this field.

Under Enrique's management, the success of the school was very rapid. The first academic year started with ninety students, and a lot of enthusiasm. Furthermore, there was also a good deal of democratic cooperation (unusual in an Italian university) between the faculty; the younger assistants, often chosen by Adriano Olivetti himself (as were Pietro Gennaro, Gabriele Morello, and Piero Bontadini); and the students, who came from different educational backgrounds. IPSOA was an island of innovation in a feudal empire dominated by the usually rigid and bureaucratic style of the Italian university. The school rapidly became well known in Europe thanks to the energy of a young organizer, Richard Miller, who had an intimate knowledge of the Italian mechanical engineering industry. In France, CPA made regular contact with IPSOA's staff in order to organize the first European networks in management training and education and, in the second half of the 1950s, the pioneers of INSEAD consulted the founders of the Italian school when they started planning the new institute at Fontainebleau.

Presenting the new institute in *Fortune* magazine, Miller did not hesitate to speak of a 'second Italian Renaissance'. However, he did not conceal several critical problems. The *Turin Unione Industriale*, which decided to support the school, was an unreliable partner. It did not represent any large corporations, only those smaller companies which had neither the interest nor the means to send someone to IPSOA. Furthermore, a kind of undeclared war was developing within the university network over the new institute, whose innovatory and dynamic curriculum contrasted strongly with the static educational systems of most Italian universities.

In fact, IPSOA's attempts to make an alliance with the traditional university power structures were short lived and superficial. According to Gabriele Morello, an eyewitness of this era, a real alliance was never wanted. IPSOA was perceived as 'an esoteric transplant' by university professors. Moreover, IPSOA's training strategies were considered by the industrial networks to be too far from the needs of Italian companies. On the other hand, IPSOA was very proud of its atypical independence.[6]

Gradually, IPSOA developed – as a sort of *in vitro* experiment, a beautiful but almost useless greenhouse flower. Yet it was a crucial experiment in cultural innovation. The organizational, educational, and even cerebral and behavioural patterns of its management, and the cooperative and democratic climate distinguishing it, contrasted with the authoritarian and bureaucratic climate which characterized both the universities and most of the larger Italian firms, particularly FIAT. This climate stimulated the resistance of businesspeople to giving the information about the affairs of their companies which was necessary for the collection of Italian case studies, in addition to those imported from HBS, as teaching material. 'Another obstacle', Professor Copeland noted in his memorandum to the Ford Foundation,

> is the practice of many Italian firms of keeping two sets of books, one for the tax purposes and one for business administration. In as much as such a large proportion of Italian firms are family owned or closely held, furthermore, published financial statements are available in only a few instances.[7]

This was also the reason why many of the American instances of business finance had a limited applicability to Italy where publicly-held companies were rare.

51

Copeland agreed with Miller that the most serious obstacle to IPSOA's development was the antagonism from academic quarters. This hostile attitude was not only based on personal envy and criticism but also had deep roots in Italian intellectual tradition. Italians were accustomed to the deductive method of analysis, whereas the case method approach supposed an inductive approach. All these factors limited the prospect of integration between mere productivity policies and the development of a broader concept of training in business administration.

In order to develop a more expansive strategy, it was necessary not only to bypass the obstacles mentioned above, but also to develop cultural patterns which could fertilize the management sciences. EPA started to study these problems, at precisely the same time as the IPSOA experiment was taking place. Alexander King observed that any hope of developing a science such as management as an integrated and interdisciplinary field was strictly connected with the growth and institutionalization of the social sciences (industrial psychology, industrial sociology, organizational theory, and theory of the firm). In Italy, more than in any other European country, the questions were not so much how to introduce new techniques and disciplines as, first, the lack of a suitable institutional and intellectual context, and second, as stressed by Herbert Simon, the avoiding of the critical gap between a social system that produces scientific knowledge and one in which professional practice takes place.

The effect of the IPSOA experiment

Paradoxically, the most positive effect of the IPSOA educational experiment was not found at the level of entrepreneurial strategies, but at the level of the social and intellectual diaspora that IPSOA generated. IPSOA's underlying concepts and methods were the inspiration for two other management centres which started in the 1950s, CUOA (*Centro Universitario per l'Organizzazione Aziendale*) founded in Padua in 1957, and ISIDA founded in Palermo in 1956. On the other hand, the organic life of IPSOA – which closed its doors in 1964 – could be said to have continued by way of the large amount of organizational know-how that it offered to others who experimented in the setting up of European business schools – INSEAD's founders for a start. With regard to the dissemination of IPSOA's concepts and methods, it should be noted that many of its former assistants went on to spread the word in other Italian institutions, such as FORMEZ. A positive and imaginative result of this dissemination was the creation also of some important consulting companies. In particular, there was the case of former Olivetti employee and assistant at IPSOA, Pietro Gennaro, who became the leader of an important group of consulting experts in Milan. Later, at the end of the 1960s, Gennaro was one of the founders of a successful Italian business school, ISTUD, at Stresa. Other former assistants at IPSOA acted as catalysts and promoters of the managerial culture within the traditional system. Mostly, they were freelance professors (Flavia Derossi, Bontadini, Malinverni); less frequently they became full professors in the Italian faculties of *Economia e Commercio* (Sergio Ricossa, Giovanni Micheletti).[8]

What really happenned to IPSOA? In 1957, the institute was already in crisis. 'The causes', observed Waldemar Nielsen, a Ford Foundation officer, 'seem to be the usual Italian ones of sharp personality clashes and erratic management.' Another Ford Foundation officer, Stanley Gordon, in some notes taken during a trip to Europe in 1957, observed that Adriano Olivetti's attitude towards IPSOA was now less optimistic than in the past. Moreover, FIAT's willingness to continue giving the school financial support had become weaker and weaker.

> According to Olivetti . . . FIAT is apparently trying to merge the Turin school with the Turin Polytechnic Institute. The latter school is stuffy and traditional . . . and a merger would be the 'coup de grace' for the Turin school. Olivetti thinks that the new Nestlé school in Lausanne is apparently recruiting staff from the Faculty at Turin.[9]

Unfortunately IPSOA's crisis began just when the European engine was starting to run and when American–European policies of technological and scientific cooperation were entering their organizational phase. On the American side, this phase was depicted by tentatively activating cross-fertilization strategies rather than by automatically transplanting methods and educational patterns, as occurred in the case of IPSOA. Furthermore, the *effet Europe* acted as a strong impetus to the creation of a new business school with a transnational structure and multilingual culture. This applied particularly to INSEAD in Fontainebleau and IMEDE in Lausanne. It was also the main aim of the first network of European business schools, such as the *Fondation Industrie-Université*, created by Gaston Deurink in Brussels, the European Association of Management Training Centres (EAMTC), and the International University Contact (IUC) which began to organize European research and graduate studies programmes in cooperation with the most important American business schools. The most relevant effect of this organizational dynamism was that, between the end of the 1950s and the beginning of the 1960s, the most traditional institutions, such as the *École des Hautes Études Commerciales* (HEC) in France, also started to modernize their curricula according to American patterns. At HEC a small group of former students of CPA, headed by Guy Lherault, tried to transform a traditional *grande école* into a dynamic new school, well connected with the American and European institutions (Nouschi 1988).

The effect of an almost invisible process of cross-fertilization, which lasted for almost thirty years and whose origins are related to the CPA experiment in the 1930s, began to have results. The Ford Foundation plan for European management education acted as the catalyst for this dynamic context, which unfortunately did not include IPSOA. Adriano Olivetti died prematurely in 1962 and IPSOA ceased its activities two years later, in 1964. This was the precise moment when the Ford Foundation started its more extensive design for management education, with the appointment of Marshall Robinson (a former vice-dean of the Pittsburgh School of Management) to the directorship of EDA's programme. It was also, as will become apparent, the period during which a small institute in Fontaine-bleau transformed itself into one of the most prestigious business schools in Europe. As some crucial aspects of INSEAD's development are related to the Ford Foundation's cross-fertilization policies, it is essential to spend some time analysing its general structure and goals.

THE FORD FOUNDATION'S PLAN FOR EUROPEAN MANAGEMENT EDUCATION

The Ford Foundation's first step was to finance an EPA programme called 'Pool of American Professors in Business Administration'. The project's draft, presented to the Ford Foundation by Roger Grégoire in 1957, is clearly directed to improving management education by the creation of a good, permanent, and research-trained teaching staff. As already implied, IPSOA's development was entirely dependent on a non-permanent teaching faculty: this was also a weakness of most of the European business schools. 'The present project aims at overcoming part of the shortage of teachers of Business Administration in Europe', Grégoire wrote, and he continued:

> The EPA and other programs in this field have, in fact, resulted in the creation of numerous schools of business management, for which qualified professors are urgently needed. The EPA . . . is endeavouring to increase both the numbers and the quality of management teachers by means of its teacher training projects in the USA and in Europe; however, it must be recognised that demand has outstripped the availability, primarily because of the length of time required to train qualified personnel and steps must be taken if European management teaching is to develop as rapidly as desired.[10]

The Ford Foundation's reply was rapid and positive. It was clear that the need for this kind of investment was deeply rooted in Europe during the late 1950s, and it was certainly strengthened by European integration after the Treaty of Rome. The economic expansion, which took place as a result of the European recovery, had a direct impact on private firms and, in particular, on small and medium-sized enterprises. One result of this growth in the size of the firms was to create a demand for a greater variety of specialized skills at the middle management level. The universities and other training institutions in Europe were not geared up to provide individuals with these new skills. The programme proposed by EPA consisted of a two-phase scheme. First, there was a short-term design, based essentially on a series of executive development seminars opened both to managers who were holding posts of responsibility in medium-sized enterprises and to young graduates of traditional schools of economics. Second, there was a long-term plan, aimed at creating permanent institutions in Europe. The main goal of this second phase was not only to supply managers for the expanding and integrated economies of the European member countries, but also to create centres of study and research in management. It was this long-term scheme which captured the Ford Foundation's attention.

The first step towards the goal was the supply of American professors to the schools. Initially, there were twenty five of them. They came from different American institutions and also from different areas of the United States. However, a large percentage came from Michigan. This was an important factor with respect to the insertion of marketing and organizational behaviour as teaching subjects into the curricula of the new European schools, since both these disciplines were significantly developed at Ann Arbor and at the Chicago School of Business Administration.

American professors in Europe

The American professors had two main tasks: conducting courses, and giving policy advice to the new institutions to point them in the right direction. This direction was, naturally, related to the implementation of American standards, which were meant also to create a basic similarity among the institutions dispersed through the different countries. In addition, an important part of the work of these professors was to select young assistant professors who could receive scholarships to spend a year in the United States, during which time they could specialize in a particular aspect of business administration.

In 1957, the Foundation approved a grant of $98,400 for this purpose, which was renewed at the same rate in 1959. The main goal of the Foundation was clearly to translate into Europe the basic patterns of American 'organizational synthesis' rather than simply to export the educational content of curricula, and teaching programmes.[11] Clearly, however, the ability to develop this strategy largely depended on contexts: in countries where management (and not just management education) was still an unknown quantity, the transfer had, in the main, to centre on content and programmes. Considering the problem of the 'contrast of contexts', within a rather homogeneous strategy of dissemination, like that of the Foundation in the late 1950s and early 1960s, it is interesting to note that the requests of American guest professors for help came mostly from those

55

countries in which management education had met serious obstacles in its process of institutionalization: namely, from Italy (61 per cent) and from Britain (17.5 per cent). Other requests came from the Netherlands (15.5 per cent), Sweden (5.0 per cent) and Belgium (0.5 per cent). In Italy, especially at ISIDA in Palermo, there was, without doubt, the highest concentration of American professors.

It is evident that in its first three years of life (1957–9) ISIDA was able to profit from IPSOA's crisis, obtaining the best American professors available.[12] The reports of the American professors reveal that the ISIDA experiment, and Morello's interest in research and in organizing a general management curriculum (very different from the curricula of the Italian trade schools), were considered to be extremely positive. In this period, ISIDA was a very promising institution in the European context, as was IPSOA at the beginning of the 1950s. Indeed, it can be said that at the end of the 1950s Italy was at the heart of the American experiment of exporting management education to Europe. The backwardness of Italy in this field was probably an element which facilitated this somewhat mechanical transfer.

Changes in the early 1960s

The situation, on both sides of the Atlantic, changed rapidly in the first half of the 1960s when the dissemination of management education in Europe created an increasingly relevant asymmetry among institutions and national cultural strategies. Unfortunately the process of involution which character-ized the static 1960s generally came to typify Italy in particular. According to Gabriel Morello, the need for investment in human resources was not felt in Italy, and the number of executives who went through regular learning exercises could be counted in terms of a few hundred per year (Morello 1974: 60–2). With regard to the question of why new initiatives did not originate from the universities, Morello claimed:

Historically, Italy was probably the first country to conceive of the engineer as a man of vast and complex knowledge. . . . But the technician of general education [was] soon replaced, under the spurs of technological process, by specialists. And thus it happened that [Italian] faculties were divided into small bits and pieces of specialised sciences [and] the Italian educational model was frozen into a monolithic system which kept adding new departments and disciplines while leaving unchanged the structure of the system. . . . Since each small piece of science turned into a chair, meant status and personal gratification for somebody, the impetus for the citadels of knowledge to become citadels of power, was real and concrete.

(Morello 1974: 60–2)

One element should be added to this lucid analysis. Whereas in most

European countries a strategy and structure for postgraduate studies rapidly evolved in the majority of disciplines, in Italy, despite the energy devoted to this by a small group of enlightened intellectuals and administrators, strongly supported by the Ford Foundation, nothing happened. A structure for postgraduate studies was only created in the early 1980s, in order to avoid complete exclusion from Europe's educational framework.

This helps to explain two sequences of events. First, it indicates why Italy participated so intensively in the first phase of the Ford Foundation's international policies, but played an almost insignificant role in the second phase which was devoted to the strengthening of research and postgraduate programmes rather than just to the export of American patterns of training and education. Second, it reveals why the change between the end of the 1950s and the mid 1960s was so emphatic, especially in the relationship between the two sides of the Atlantic. The development of new attitudes of American cultural behaviour, basically oriented to a cross-fertilization policy which considered differences as well as similarities among countries and cultures, undoubtedly facilitated the already existing process of differentiation in size and strategies that described the evolution of European business schools during the 1960s. In fact, the most visible 'contrast of contexts' during this period depended on the asymmetry between the dynamic situation which characterized some European countries – like France, Belgium, and, to some extent, Britain – and the Italian involution. Despite the many shifts produced by the historical period, the basic ground for the new trend, which typified the Ford Foundation's policies towards European educational programmes during the 1960s, was to be found in the previous experimental phase. As described above, the aims and strategy of this phase were mainly inspired by the idea of simply exporting some dominant cultural patterns.

The reports that were written on the schools visited by the professors engaged in EPA's programme were of great value to the Ford Foundation. They both defined the Foundation's policy of investments in each country, with respect to the level of acceptance of management education at university, and assisted it to select those projects which were to have priority within its general policy.

In fact, at the end of the 1950s, when EPA's era had ended and the Foundation went into Europe alone, its agenda had changed. In the mid 1960s, the problem was how to reduce organizational asymmetry between Europe and the United States, and bypass the technological gap between the two continents, rather than how to educate European managers. On both sides of the Atlantic, prominent observers like Robert McNamara and Jean-Jacques Servan-Schreiber saw a strict relationship between the technological and managerial gaps at the same moment as, in Europe, the state of management education was attracting increasing attention, even in countries like Britain where the problem had been underestimated for a very long time. The Foundation had its own ideas about this: it considered that the managerial gap could only be filled by stimulating research and integrating it as a factor of development at the level of both industrial and educational strategies.

The Ford Foundation's 1967 programme

The formal launch of the Ford Foundation's own programme was in 1967. By that time, it had already acquired fifteen years' experience, thanks principally to the EPA programme, but also to a series of small grants, often devoted to improving teacher training through such international programmes as the International Teachers Program.

An overall view of the European Management Education programme reveals that it involved forty-seven major grant actions and eighty-one doctoral fellowship grants. Excluding individual fellowships, grant sizes ranged from $3,000 to $1,000,000. The average duration of a grant which included some schematic elements was two years. The European programme was ordered under different headings, corresponding to discrete needs and organizational strategies. Thus it was not a rigid and linear programme. On the contrary, it implied many experimental and articulated byways.

Many grants were devoted to institutional development: namely, to the strengthening of institutions which were mostly but not exclusively non-university training centres. This was done in two ways. Professional deanships were established and the creation of a permanent faculty supported. For example, INSEAD received a grant of $1,000,000 on a partial matching basis, and the *Centre d'Études Industriels* (CEI) in Geneva received $250,000. Then, research staff were improved and training in support of doctoral programmes was provided, as was the case for the London Business School and the Manchester Business School in Britain and for the *Centre de Recherche en Sciences de l'Organisation* (CEROG) in France (which received $300,000). CEROG was conceived as an implementation at postgraduate level of the activities of the already existing *Instituts d'Administration des Entreprises* (IAE). Other grants were devoted to 'visits and exchanges' from both sides of the Atlantic, the aim of which was the enhancing of European institutions. This was the case of the grant to the Stockholm School of Economics which aspired to bring specialists from different countries to Stockholm in order to enrich the school's curriculum and research standards.

A third type of support was related to network building.[13] Essentially, each institution supported by this kind of grant had its own distinct history, which it was important to recall in detail. Most of the grants were devoted to starting and strengthening research centres. The University of Warwick, in Britain, was given a $250,000 grant for the establishment of a Centre for

Industrial and Business Studies within the School of Social Sciences, for example. Another grant ($100,000) went to the International Institute for Management of Technology, sponsored by OECD and established in Milan in 1971. This last was a total failure: however, its short history is very interesting, because it was planned, on the basis of the INSEAD model, as a kind of European MIT. At the beginning, anyway, INSEAD was seen as the European equivalent of HBS.

The largest amount of money ($1,000,000) was devoted to doctoral fellowships, which allowed young European teachers to go to the United States to study at one of twelve participating American graduate schools of management. At the end of their time, the participants were required to return to an academic career in Europe. As was to be expected, they did not all return. Many of them preferred to find jobs in American multinational firms, or to teach in American schools. This was one reason why the Ford Foundation decided to develop simultaneously (with $1,500,000) some European networks, according to the more general trend symbolizing the American–European relationship during the mid 1960s, which was inspired by the philosophy of 'equal partnership'. The creation of EIASM was a kind of compromise, resulting from a very complicated experimental phase during which many options were confronted. All these options were discussed in 1968 at a key meeting in Rotterdam. The Foundation's officers, and many American consultants, recommended the establishment of an excellent doctoral-granting international institution to be located in Western Europe. The European experts and educators resisted the idea, however, and EIASM originated out of this disagreement:

> It was designed as an institution for graduate studies operated by US-European faculty, to supplement training at the student's home institution, not to compete with it.[14]

Actually, at the end of the 1960s, the network of European business schools was not only highly differentiated but had already developed its own lines of cooperation and competition, which were related both to the different institutional scales and to the articulated scope of each institution. The map of participants to EIASM doctoral programmes, both by country and by school, is a very interesting field for the analysis of the dynamic of cooperation and competition among the different business schools. As an example of this dynamic, it can be recalled that while the London Business School hardly valued EIASM at all, its most direct rival, the Manchester Business School, was one of EIASM's stronger supporters!

As a general statement, it can be said that some of the Foundation's grants were the basis of the rapid and gradually autonomous growth of European management, which really became an *apprentis sorcier* in this period. This was particularly the case with some institutions, which acted as 'poles of excellence' in the development of European management and management education strategies. A crucial case study in this context is that of INSEAD which succeeded in capitalizing on two sets of opportunities: those which were created by the dynamic French environment, both in the political and economic context (so very dissimilar to the Italian situation at the same time); and those created by strategies of American cooperation between the end of the 1960s and the first half of the 1970s.

COMPETITIVE COOPERATION: INSEAD'S CHALLENGES

From the time of its experimental phase, INSEAD's history was an important chapter in the Ford Foundation's programme for management education in Europe. Moreover, it was also possible to compare INSEAD's development with IPSOA's history. In the next phase, when the Ford Foundation's programme involved a large number of European business schools as well as their networks, INSEAD, which was considered the most 'American' of the European business schools, got the greatest support and was considered as a yardstick for excellence. Paradoxically, it was also one of the few European schools which succeeded in producing an articulate strategy of competitive cooperation not only *vis-à-vis* the other European schools but also towards the most important American institutions (including HBS), while transforming itself into an increasingly international educational structure (Gemelli 1993).

As mentioned above, INSEAD was proposed and established in 1957, which was also the year of IPSOA's greatest expansion as a result of the initiatives of General Doriot and a group of enlightened industrialists connected with CPA. From the mid 1950s, CPA started to internationalize its activities, and cooperated enthusiastically with IPSOA in pursuit of this goal.[15] In any event, the founders of INSEAD were able to profit from the know-how of their Italian colleagues. When the Fontainebleau school opened its doors in 1958, some former IPSOA students attended its classes. Among the small group of professors of the new school, there was a bright young Italian professor of marketing, Salvatore Teresi. In fact, he was not a product of IPSOA at all, but he did have good relations with its network. More importantly, he played a significant part in getting the *Comitato Nazionale per la Produttività* to involve itself in supporting and organizing management education in Italy.

Networks for industry

When INSEAD started up, the French industrial and institutional environment was as inhospitable as its Italian equivalent had been. The university system and the *grandes écoles* had had a monopoly of higher education, even in commercial studies. The *École des Hautes Études Commerciales* had existed in France since 1881, and had developed strong roots within the social milieu of the entrepreneurial elite. Until the Second World War, and even later, the French entrepreneurial environment was dominated by medium-sized and small enterprises which were only marginally interested in MBA programmes. Nevertheless, unlike their Italian colleagues, INSEAD's founders could count on certain possibilities which they were able to exploit to positive advantage.

An important opportunity, for instance, was created by the process of cross-fertilization achieved by CPA, whose methods and training patterns were assimilated by a large range of students who came from very different institutions and who subsequently had a variety of careers, not only in industry but also in bureaucracy, finance, and diplomacy. An excellent example of this process of 'horizontal fertilization' of different social and institutional segments is the career of Pierre Uri, a former CPA student who became head of the Commissariat au Plan.

As has been seen, in order to resist the opposition of the university system, IPSOA increasingly transformed itself into a kind of innovation bastion, which had less and less contact with the entrepreneurial and academic environments. On the other hand, INSEAD's founders, developing General Doriot's strategic orientation, tried to consolidate a large network of supporters and donors, not only in France but also in Europe and the United States. Instead of becoming exasperated by the opposition of the university system, INSEAD tried to avoid it and to find a financial base for its existence directly in the entrepreneurial environment. This factor also fundamentally set it apart from the organizational patterns of American business schools, which in most cases depended on attachment to a large university.

Another important opportunity was created, in the very short term, by a rapidly changing political situation, characterized at the international level by the implementation of European unification. This implied, at its most basic level, the strengthening of an intellectual (and, essentially, a political) identity. Nationally, INSEAD could profit from the effects of Mendés-France's policy, the main thrust of which was to create a solid and dynamic interface between the public and private sectors and between the bureaucratic system and the entrepreneurial milieu. Unfortunately, this sort of ambience was, despite the efforts of an enlightened group of reformers, totally lacking in Italy.

Links to American business schools

INSEAD was able to benefit from the intellectual and the social capital of its founders. These were former scholars who had been trained in the United States and had a good knowledge of American educational patterns (including the case method). As one-time students of Maurice Allais at the *École Polytechnique*, they also had an excellent training in operational mathematics. All these basic factors undoubtedly facilitated relationships with the most important American business schools (Harvard, Stanford, and Chicago), and also the placement of young graduates in American firms and multinationals, just at the time when European expansion was at its peak.

It is not surprising then that, when the Ford Foundation decided to support European management education, INSEAD was considered a strategic investment. Pressure in this direction came not only from General Doriot, who was one of the Ford Foundation's trustees, but also from HBS which, during the 1960s, became increasingly interested in developing European case studies as teaching material. In the first phase of institutional development, INSEAD participated vigorously in the programmes organized by Harvard, especially the programme for teachers, the aim of which was to produce a future European professor of management. However, INSEAD very quickly developed its own strategy as regards case study material, mostly directed at filling the demand coming from the European (and later also the international) entrepreneurial environment. From the mid 1970s, too, INSEAD evolved, on the organizational level, an increasingly autonomous strategy, to the point of launching a European programme for teachers which challenged Harvard's monopoly. Moreover, in the early 1970s, the school turned its face strongly against the idea of creating a European Harvard in France. In a short space of time, cooperation had begun to show its competitive side.

Paradoxically, the growth of this contrasting orientation was one of the effects of the Ford Foundation's sizeable grant. It allowed for the stabilization of INSEAD's faculty by creating a professional dean. Because of its financial constraints (which were based on a system of matching funding: for every dollar of American finance, INSEAD itself had to find one and a half dollars), the school was also stimulated into developing greater and more permanent contacts with the entrepreneurial environment. Indeed, INSEAD was impelled into organizing a structure of fund raising that was gradually integrated with research and development strategies. This led to the creation of CEDEP, a form of continuous education conceived of as a group of associated companies. Each enterprise which participates in CEDEP's programmes has to do so for almost five years. At the same time, the firm has to develop a system of continuing reintegration into its different sectors for managers who participate in these educational programmes. Moreover, in order to become partners, new CEDEP subscribers must have the agreement of the other members.

The development of the faculty

CEDEP was only one element of the institutional differentiation of the Fontainebleau school, which gradually implied a change in its size. The initial stabilization of INSEAD's faculty also allowed a more differentiated and articulated offer of its programmes. MBA programmes (whose duration was shorter than in American business schools) were complemented by continuous education and by a rapidly expanding executive schedule, which was crucial to the development of a productive relationship with the entrepreneurial environment.

As already seen, IPSOA lacked opportunities to take advantage of the stabilization of the faculty to begin with, and then the process of differentiation. The most negative consequence of this was the fact that the Turin school depended entirely on American teaching materials, and was unable to produce any case studies which could be of real practical use to Italian business. IPSOA's isolation could be measured by the lack of demand for its products by Italian firms. In contrast, INSEAD rapidly increased and disseminated its products from the beginning of the 1970s. In fact, just when IPSOA closed its doors in the mid 1960s, the institutional and historical situation began to change very quickly.

Another stimulus to INSEAD's development was the resistance that it presented to American donors when they pressed it to accelerate its process of academicization. The idea of strengthening an equal partnership between the United States and a Europe supported by the Ford Foundation implied that the most important European institutions could adapt themselves very rapidly to American standards. During the 1970s, the order of the day was professionalization of management through academic research. INSEAD accepted this challenge but with its own timing: that is, within the limits fixed by its own institutional development, which needed the making of strenuous efforts to improve relationships with the French and European entrepreneurial environments. In the long term, these links became a challenge in reverse, as well as a good opportunity.

The Ford Foundation's retreat from Europe

INSEAD's critical transformation from a mere training institute into a proper educational structure occurred in the mid 1970s, when not only the international, economic, and financial context changed dramatically, but the whole system of American–European relationships also came to a decisive turning point. Ironically, 1973, which was declared by Henry Kissinger as the 'year of Europe', marked the entry to a significant period as well. A key actor here, the American Ambassador to the European Community, Robert Schaetzel, affirmed:

Dans la periode antérieure, l'accent dans les rélations américano-européennes était sur la co-opération, la tension était présente mais manifestement au second plan. En 1970, cet accent était renversé désormais.

(Quoted by Melandri 1988: 53)

In fact, many elements converged to create a particularly troublesome period in American–European relations: elements such as the changing priorities in American foreign policy due to the loss of legitimacy of its global hegemony as a consequence of the Vietnam War, coupled with the international economic and financial crisis. It is not surprising, then, that in the mid 1970s the Ford Foundation programme for the development of European management education was also in retreat.

This retreat suited the general orientation of the Foundation's policy during the 1970s, with the new presidency of McGeorge Bundy, well. Waldemar A. Nielsen, a former Foundation officer who participated in many European ventures, wrote in his book *The Big Foundations*:

The Foundation's international programs, which some had thought might be Bundy's primary interest, were simultaneously given a lower priority than the domestic programs. The European segments, under a rapid succession of chiefs, almost disintegrated.

(Nielsen 1973: 96)

Nielsen's statement needs to be corrected on one point. Bundy actually contrived to create a new and well-supported programme – Higher Education and Research. Under its aegis the most important results in management education cross-fertilization strategies (both in Western and Eastern Europe) were gained. It should be added, however, that the Higher Education and Research Program does not have as comprehensive a concern with Europe as a geographic and political entity as the IAP once had. Just before the mid 1970s, the era of the Ford Foundation's European venture, as a strategic target, was coming to an end. During McGeorge Bundy's presidency, Europe was not yet the core but only a part of the Foundation's international strategy. Moreover, since the mid 1970s, management education has become of international rather than merely American–European significance.

INSEAD was, indeed, one of the few (and probably the first) European business schools to meet this challenge, with the increasing internationalization of its faculty, students, programmes, and research centres. It created, for example, a Euro-Asian Centre in 1975. Since the late 1970s, and especially during the 1980s, the institutional dynamics, cultural framework, and pattern of communication of business schools within their worldwide campus changed profoundly. American patterns ceased to be the unique reference and competition increasingly demanded shared patterns. The latter even became a necessary strategy within the battle to maintain or impose educational standards. This implies a critical challenge. Competition between educational systems is in fact coupled with the desire to internationalize education: that is to say, the wish 'for concepts and international norms which . . . allow for some compatibility between the different systems' (Nioche 1992: 21). Since the end of the 1970s, INSEAD has made strong efforts to anticipate and then to meet this challenge by following its own direction, whose basic element was and still is to develop in each of its institutional areas, and for each of its set of products, a 'transnational focus'. Should one consider in the 'war of degrees', along with the German, the American, and the Latin model, an INSEAD model also? What alternatives will stimulate a coordinated European educational strategy? These questions clearly extend beyond the confines of this chapter, but they are certainly implied in its conclusions.

CONCLUSION

Problems of transfer and cultural translation as well as of 'contrasts of contexts' are now, in fact, perhaps more than ever before, at the heart of the debate on management education.

The case study of INSEAD, in contrast with the almost contemporary experiment of IPSOA, provides an interesting historical background against which to analyse how a positive and innovative imitation of dominant patterns suggest a flexible institutional strategy and a creative mental map. American influence on INSEAD's development principally had the effect of stimulating this flexibility and this mental map. INSEAD's institutional choice was that of selective imitation: that is to say, it chose to translate American patterns into its own institutional culture, the first imperative of which was the development, at each level and stage of its structure, of an intimate contact and extensive communication with its national, European, and, later on, international environment. From this point of view, it may be affirmed that INSEAD was established and matured in the unstable equilibrium between a social system which produces scientific knowledge and a social and information system which depends on professional practice.

IPSOA's organizers perceived flexibility as a problem, and even a danger, when they were faced with academic power and university supremacy. They chose to isolate themselves in their ideal strongholds. In contrast, the INSEAD founders, transforming the impetus created by the *effet Europe* after the Treaty of Rome into a cultural strategy, considered flexibility as a challenge. Moreover, with the bonus of the historical change produced by the petroleum crisis and by the growth of European multinationals in the mid 1970s, they succeeded in changing the need to be flexible into an opportunity to compete on the worldwide campus of management education.

What seems to have differentiated INSEAD's development from that of the American business schools over the last few decades is rather the former's capacity for internalizing a complex environment, which is related to different social systems, than its growth as an academic institution with its own programme of PhD studies, which is, in any event, only recent. The rise of INSEAD's academic excellence seems to be the product rather than the cause of its institutional growth. It has implied a strategic commitment, by the school, to strengthen simultaneously, through a shared transnational focus, its different sectors (MBA, executive programmes, continuing education, academic research, and fund raising). The most relevant effect of this strategic orientation is the consolidation of an institutional dynamic, which could be described in Alfred Chandler's (1962) theoretical terms in this way: INSEAD developed its structure following the variations of a strategic design whose steps and stages were related to its progressive changes of size. The uncalculated effect of this rational choice was the growth of a synergetic interface between INSEAD's two aims – that of an academic institution, and that of an enterprise capable of stimulating and even creating its own market.

NOTES

1 Interview with Alexander King, 24 October 1993.
2 See also J.E. Howell, 'The Ford Foundation and the Revolution in Business Education', Ford Foundation Archive (FFA), Report 006353, pp. 1–2.
3 See B. Berelson, 'Oral History Transcript', FFA, pp. 20–8.
4 J.J. Solomon was head of the *Division des politiques de la science et de la technologie* at the OECD.
5 A. King, 'Studies on Management Organisation in Various European Countries', EPA Project 347, FFA, Reel 0068, Grant No. 56–51, Section III, pp. 3, 6.
6 See R. Miller, 'Summary for Fortune', FFA, Reel 0950, Grant No. 54149, pp. 4–5.
7 M.T. Copeland, 'Memorandum to Dean David', FFA, Reel 0950, Grant No. 54149, pp. 5–7.
8 For a first attempt to analyse IPSOA systematically, see Faliva and Pennarola (1992).
9 FFA, Reel 0850, Grant No. 54148, Section 3: Reports.
10 FFA, Reel No. 57265, Section I.
11 Discussion on 'European Productivity Agency Business Management Training (1957)', FFA, Reel 0527, Grant No. 57265.
12 Ezra Solomon from Stanford and Mervin Waterman from Ann Arbor School of Business Administration taught Finance and Controls; Joseph W. Towle from Washington University and Pearson Hunt from Harvard University taught General Management; Paul Converse from the University of Illinois and Edward Cundiff from the University of Texas taught Marketing; and Norman Maier from Ann Arbor taught Industrial Relations and Psychological Research.
13 This is a very rich and interesting chapter of the Ford Foundation saga in Europe and deserves more attention than can be given in this chapter.
14 E.F. Cheit, 'The European Management Education Program', FFA, Report 005777, p. 28.

15 The Ford Foundation's officers also underlined the strict relations between the two institutions: 'Professor Grégoire believes that the projected international business school inspired by Professor Doriot of the Harvard Business School will be a new IPSOA'. (Visit to M. Roger Grégoire, Director, European Productivity Agency – Inter-Office Memorandum, 7 November 1957.) FFA, Reel 0527, Grant No. 57265.

REFERENCES

Aaronson, S.A. (1992) 'Serving America's Business? Graduate Business Schools and American Business, 1945–60', *Business History* 43(1): 160–82.

Canziani, A. and Brovetto, P.R. (1995) 'The Economics of the Firm in Continental Europe during the 1920s: Betriebswirtschaftslehre and Economia Aziendale as Methodological Revolution', in S. Todd-Lowry (ed.) *Perspectives on the History of Economic Thought*, Vol. VIII, Aldershot: Elgar.

Chandler, A.D., Jr (1962) *Strategy and Structure: Chapters in the History of the American Industrial Enterprise*, Cambridge, MA: MIT Press.

Elkana, Y. (1981) 'A Programmatic Attempt to an Anthropology of Knowledge', in E. Mendelsond and Y. Elkana (eds) *Science and Culture*, Dordrecht: Reidel, 1–76.

Faliva, G. and Pennarola, F. (1992) *Storia della consulenza di direzione in Italia: Protagonisti, idee, tendenze evolutive*, Milan: Edizioni Olivaris.

Fayol, H. (1925/1979) *Administration industrielle et générale*, Paris: Dunod.

Gemelli, G. (1993) 'Per una storia delle business schools in Europa: Le origini dell'INSEAD', *Annali di storia dell'impresa* IX, 339–407.

—— (1994) 'The Ford Foundation and the Development of Social and Public Sciences in Italy (1954–1973)', in G. Gemelli (ed.) *Big Culture: Intellectual Cooperation in Large-Scale Cultural and Technical Systems. An Historical Approach*, Bologna: CLUEB, 61–116.

Greenhouse, S. (1991) 'Studying Business? Why stick to just one continent?', *The New York Times* 30 June.

Locke, R.R. (1984) *The End of the Practical Man: Entrepreneurship and Higher Education in Germany, France, and Great Britain, 1880–1940*, Greenwich, CT.: JAI Press.

—— (1989) *Management and Higher Education since 1940: The Influence of America and Japan on West Germany, Great Britain, and France*, Cambridge: Cambridge University Press.

Melandri, P. (1988) *Une incertaine alliance: Les États-Unis et l'Europe 1973–1983*, Paris: Publications de la Sorbonne.

Morello, G. (1974) 'Changing Organizations and the Role of Management Development', *EFMD IIIrd Annual Conference Proceedings, Turin, 19–22 May*.

Nielsen, W.A. (1973) *The Big Foundations*, New York: Columbia University Press.

Nioche, J.P. (1992) 'The War of Degrees in European Management Education', *EFMD Forum* 1: 21–4.

Nouschi, M. (1988) *Histoire et pouvoir d'une Grande Ecole HEC*, Paris: Robert Laffont.

Ragin, C. (1991) 'Comparative Sociology and Comparative Method', *International Journal of Comparative Sociology* XXII(1): 102–20.

Reild, D. (1986) 'Genèse du fayolism', *Sociologie du Travaile* IV: 234–79.

Schlossman, S., Sedlak, M., and Wechsler, H. (1987) 'The "New Look": The Ford Foundation and the Revolution in Business Education', *Occasional Paper*, Los Angeles: Graduate Management Admission Council.

Sebesta, L. (1984) 'The Politics of Technological Cooperation in Space: US-European Negotiations on the Post-Apollo Programme', *History and Technology* II: 317–41.

Simon, H.A. (1967) 'The Business Schools: a Problem in Organizational Design', *Journal of Management Studies* 4(2): 2–12.

4

CONTINUITIES IN DUTCH BUSINESS EDUCATION

Engineering, economics, and the business school

Huibert de Man

INTRODUCTION

Academic business education in European countries should be understood as a product of its own history. Our view of the present system of academic business education in the Netherlands, in the form of the new discipline of *bedrijfskunde* (business studies), rests on this assumption. The American idea of a business school and the related ideas of a science of management and a profession of management were received after the Second World War in an existing context of business education, which had been developed in the interwar period.

In this system of business education, which like that in Germany had found its academic recognition in the form of business economics, there were tensions between two diverging views of the (economic) science of business. The view developed in the Faculty of Economics of Amsterdam stressed the purely economic aspects, and was based on a restrictive and deductive conception of science; that developed by the Rotterdam Superior School of Commerce, based on an existing *bedrijfsleer* (the practical discipline of business) tradition in which engineers also had an important role, was closer to practice and rested on a non-restrictive and inductive conception of science.

When American ideas became influential in the Netherlands, and *bedrijfskunde* arose as a discipline in the Dutch universities, the tension between the two conceptions of business science was an important background. The American ideas fitted in better with the more loosely structured Rotterdam ideas than in the deductive system of Amsterdam. So, one of the conclusions of this chapter is that a high degree of continuity existed between the *bedrijfsleer* of Rotterdam and the new *bedrijfskunde*, which was developed as a result of the inspiration of the American business school.

Another continuity dealt with in the chapter is the persisting debate on the scientific character of the business sciences. The dialogue between the Amsterdam and Rotterdam schools of business economics was concerned with the legitimacy of a science of business within academia. Given the distance between the business world and the university, this was undeniably a difficult issue. And, in spite of all the changes since the 1920s, the basic question remains, and now manifests itself in discussions among *bedrijfskunde* professors on the subject of methodology. The need to justify practical science seems still to be of concern.

The role of the university in managerial careers also shows some continuity. The actual function of the schools is to be a broad preparation for business careers; the management aspect is not emphasized.

The future of academic business (not management) education is expected to be built upon the traditional strengths of the Dutch business sciences. The professional and academic elements are likely to receive increasing emphasis in the *bedrijfskunde* faculties. There is some doubt, therefore, whether business economics and *bedrijfskunde* will continue to exist as two separate disciplines.

ACADEMIC BUSINESS EDUCATION IN THE NETHERLANDS: CONTINUITY AND CHANGE

Academic business education in the Netherlands, as in other European countries, arose from a combination of a national heritage of commercial and technical education and the American idea of a business school and the integrated science of business administration (Locke 1989). The American innovations came after the Second World War in the context of the reconstruction of Dutch society and the economy. The Technical Assistance Programme, part of the European Recovery Programme (the Marshall Plan), played an important role. In the 1950s and early 1960s, the national productivity centre (COP) was active in the propagation of American management ideas through the organization of visits to business schools and companies in the United States (de Man and Karsten 1994).

The new ideas on management and management education, which were brought to the Netherlands by businesspeople and university professors, concerned a wide range of issues. On a general level, the American ideas introduced a kind of pragmatism and an optimistic belief in technical solutions to organizational and social problems, which were to some extent alien to the Dutch culture. A specific example of this pragmatism was the belief that management could be taught in business schools. This idea involved a view of the university which radically differed from the prevailing ideas on scientific education in the Netherlands, where the acquisition of knowledge was seen as good for its own sake, and applied sciences were considered second rate.

Substantive innovations could be found especially in the fields of marketing, finance, managerial accounting, production, and personnel management. Marketing and finance were relatively well developed in the United States, where multidivisional enterprises required knowledge on strategic issues which could not be dealt with on the operational level of single-product enterprises. The underdevelopment of finance and market-ing in the Netherlands may have been related to the industrial structure. On the one hand, there was the majority of small and medium-sized, often family-owned, enterprises. As in Germany (Locke 1985: 237), such enterprises had no need of financial or marketing specialists. On the other hand, there were the big multinational companies (Shell, Unilever, Philips), state-owned enterprises (PTT, Railways), and banks. In these large organizations, functional structures prevailed until the 1960s (for the multinational companies, see Jagersma 1994). Within such structures, there was little need for MBAs, and managers were primarily recruited internally.

Production management and production-related accounting techniques had, since the introduction of Taylor's work to the Netherlands, been influenced by American ideas. A renewed interest can be seen after the Second World War, however, in the pragmatic and efficiency-oriented style of the American managers. Among Dutch experts, there was some amazement at the simplicity, if not underdevelopment, of American tools, combined with the ingenuity with which they were used in practice (see, for example, *Organisatiemethoden en efficiëntie-controle in Amerikaanse bedrijven* 1952). In addition to this new injection of American pragmatism, there were the fresh contributions to the methods of production control and organization, which became known as 'operations research' and, on a more philosophical level, 'systems theory' and 'systems methodology' – the idea of the organization as a system. These innovations took longer to become part of management thought in the Netherlands – it was not until the 1960s and 1970s, when engineers and economists in particular became interested in the new philosophy and methods, that they were fully accepted by the academic world.

The 'human relations' ideas on personnel and organization formed the last ingredient of the American innovations. Here also the pragmatic American belief that the relations between individuals and the organization could be improved through managerial intervention was an important innovation in a culture where moralism was the prevailing reaction to social problems. The idea of 'human relations' had its greatest impact on the training of lower and middle management in the 1950s. And after this period, the interest in American psychology and its application to management remained a continuing feature of Dutch management thought (de Man and Karsten 1994).

Business education in the 1990s

What happened to this American pragmatism – the ideas of production, management accounting, operations research, systems theory, and human relations? And what happened to the idea of the business school? Dutch attitudes towards American management ideas were generally positive, but as Lawrence (1991: 136) writes 'the Dutch do not seem to share the British view that the Americans are exemplars of best management practice'. Nevertheless, the Americanization of business and business education cannot be denied. Current textbooks on management and organization in the Netherlands are to a great extent based on American sources. Management jargon, from 'overhead value analysis' to 'linking-pin organization' and 'learning organization', is inspired by American examples and most terms are used without translation. The management subjects mentioned above have all become part of academic curricula. The business school of the American type, however, has never become a reality in the Netherlands, as will become apparent.

The present situation with regard to academic business education in the Netherlands is complex. It is neither comparable with the situation in the United States – with 'business administration' taught in 'business schools' – nor to the German and Swedish situation where an integrated approach to management evolved from 'business economics'. Today, although the German and Swedish faculties involved represent themselves in English terminology as faculties of 'business administration', they continue to refer to themselves as *Betriebswirtschaftslehre*, that is centres of 'business economics'.

In the university system of the Netherlands, however, there are two different disciplines, both of which represent themselves in English terms as 'business administration', but refer to themselves as *bedrijfseconomie* and *bedrijfskunde* respectively. The former, which may be translated here as 'business economics', is the older discipline and is part of the faculty of economics which has a reputable history. The latter, translated here as 'business studies', came about in the 1960s as an attempt to introduce the American business school into the Netherlands. The term *bedrijfskunde* is older than the new academic business school, however, and originally referred to the specialization in management and organization which arose in departments of mechanical engineering at the superior schools of technology (now the technical universities).

The precise origin of *bedrijfskunde* is expressed in the *ingenieur* (engineer) degree of the business studies curriculum at the technical universities, in contrast to the *doctorandus* degree at the other universities. At the present time, the formal length of an *ingenieur* or *doctorandus* degree is four years, but most students need five years and some even six. The difference between the two varieties of *bedrijfskunde* is also expressed in their English translations. For example, the Eindhoven faculty represents itself as a faculty of 'industrial engineering and management science', and not as one of 'business administration'.

In addition to the academic business education dealt with above, there is an increasing supply of post-experience MBA programmes. These come from foreign universities operating in the Netherlands, and also from Dutch educational institutions (universities and schools of higher vocational education) which have licensing agreements with foreign (American and British) universities. A special case is Nijenrode, a business school in the American tradition, which after some years of offering education on a bachelor degree level acquired full academic status in 1982.

At this point, it may be useful to be more specific about the terminology used in this chapter. The term 'management education' has been reserved for a type of education in which the training of managers is the central purpose. The term 'business education' is used for a type of education which prepares for management-related functions in business, such as organization, accounting, logistics, and marketing. The word 'general' has often been added: 'general business education'. In this case, a type of education is meant which is supposed to give a general background for various positions in business. Business economics and business studies are both considered as 'business education' here, whereas the term 'management education' applies to the American MBA. Of course, the dividing line between management and business education is not always as sharp as the distinction suggests.

This chapter concentrates on the typical Dutch schools of academic business education which prepare students for the *doctorandus* and *ingenieur* degrees. The main schools providing academic business education for the *doctorandus* degrees are:

- business economics at Amsterdam
- business economics at Rotterdam
- business economics at Tilburg
- business studies at Rotterdam
- business economics at Groningen
- business studies at Groningen
- business studies at the Open University
- business economics at the Open University
- business economics at Nijmegen
- business studies at Nijmegen.

Two schools offer curricula for the *ingenieur* degree:

- business studies at Eindhoven
- business studies at Twente.

The curricula of both 'business economics' and 'business studies' have adopted American innovations. In 'business economics', marketing and finance have been introduced alongside the existing accountancy subjects.

73

Operations research techniques, such as linear programming, have become standard tools of the business economist, and Dutch business economists have been among the first to introduce general systems theory and methodology to the field of management.

The behavioural aspects of human relations and industrial psychology have become important ingredients of the business studies curricula, especially in the schools outside the technical universities. The techniques of operations research and systems methodology, on the other hand, have become essential ingredients of business studies, particularly in the technical universities. General conceptual systems theory has often been seen as a meta-theory, which justifies the existence of a new science of business studies in the academic community. In the 1960s and 1970s, especially, general systems concepts were used to point to the difference between integrative, interdisciplinary business studies and mono-disciplinary business economics. Marketing has become a regular part of business studies curricula, with the result that two marketing departments may be found in one university, as in Groningen, teaching the same subjects in the faculties of economics and business studies. The difference between business economics and business studies is still quite pronounced when financial subjects are considered. Although some attention is given to financial management and accounting in business studies courses, this cannot begin to compete with the depth and specialization accorded to such subjects in business economics disciplines.

Thus there are, in fact, three varieties of academic management education (apart from MBA courses) in the Netherlands: business economics, technical business studies, and general business studies, all of which in some way reflect the special ways in which the American business school and the American science of business administration have been received in an existing academic context.

Growth and stagnation

Academic business education became a quantitative success in the 1980s. Management developed into a favourite subject for many students, and both the old and respectable discipline of 'business economics' and the young and not yet established one of 'business studies' profited from the growing demand for this type of education. Currently, the schools of business economics and business studies enroll some 25,000 students, which is about 15 per cent of all university students. After a period of growth in the 1980s, student numbers have now stabilized or even decreased somewhat.

Growth was a mixed blessing for both types of school. Increased teaching loads, and the difficulty of finding qualified teachers, hindered the balanced development of the schools. In the same period, too, doing research – 'publish or perish' – was becoming more important in the academic world of the Netherlands, including the faculties involved in management education. Moreover, in the last few years, there has been a noticeable change in the way practical subjects in the universities are evaluated. After a period in which the trend was towards integration between academic and higher vocational education, more recently there has been a renewed tendency in the Dutch educational system to emphasize the fundamental differences between both types of education. Mass participation in academic education, however, makes it hard to maintain academic standards in universities, which in turn has led to proposals by the government to adopt the American distinction between graduate and undergraduate education. Eventually, this might lead to undergraduate status for existing business studies curricula in the Netherlands, which would be a threat to the academic status of this new discipline.

It is obvious that questions of identity, which did not seem acute in the period of growth, arise in this situation of decrease in student numbers. And it also seems logical that the new faculties of business studies should feel more vulnerable than the long-established faculties of economics. Typical of the present quest for identity in the faculties of business studies is the debate on methodology, which is taking place in various forms. In a recent issue of *Bedrijfskunde*, various authors discuss the methodological bases of their trade. The feeling of insecurity, even inferiority, is expressed in statements which imply that the field of business studies is not yet a science. Van Aken (1994a), for example, considers the development of business studies as a 'normal scientific discipline' with its own paradigm, research programme, and methodology, as a condition of getting rid of its 'subservience to the mono-disciplines'. He is quite negative about the alternative concept of business studies 'as a supermarket of techniques, ideas and methods' (de Man 1993). Much of the management literature, which is based on either practical experience or metaphysical reasoning, does not meet scientific standards. According to van Aken, it should be considered pre-scientific. The objective for *bedrijfskunde* must be to become a true science, while retaining its practical orientation. The *bedrijfskundige* (business scientist) is a professional who develops science-based heuristics, which can be used by practitioners (van Aken 1994b).

Business economists seem to care less whether their discipline is a science or not. Perhaps being part of the faculty of economics gives them all the acceptance they need in the academic community. However, some outstanding business economists have started a debate on the relationship between business economics and business studies. Although no one suggests publicly that both disciplines should be considered as one science, some go a long way towards doubting the relevance of the lines drawn between them. Douma (1991) suggests that business economics and business studies should be combined in one faculty of 'business sciences', thus avoiding the problem of who is going to dominate whom. Schreuder

(1985) advocates a non-restrictive view of business economics, which brings him close to a conception of business studies as an interdisciplinary science that finds its problems through practice. Such nods in the direction of *bedrijfskunde* reveal tensions inside economic faculties between the ideals of economics as a pure and deductive science and those of practice-oriented business economics.

PERSISTENT DICHOTOMIES IN DUTCH BUSINESS EDUCATION

What will be the result of the self-doubt and philosophical reflection of business studies, and the growing awareness of the unproductive lines drawn between business economics and business studies? Will a unified science of management arise in the spirit of American business administration? Will business economics return to its purely economic identity, or, conversely, broaden to become an integrative science of management? Will business studies acquire full academic acceptance by defining its own goals and methodology?

These questions are hard to answer. It is obvious, however, that the present debate is strongly shaped by attitudes and values rooted in the history of Dutch business education. There is a specific culture surrounding academic business education that has shaped the way American ideas were received after the Second World War, and which is expressed in its institutions. Insight into this cultural context is essential if the further development of academic management education in the Netherlands is to be understood. Some aspects of this cultural context that have played a significant part in Dutch academic management education since its beginning will now be sketched.

These will be presented in terms of the dichotomies that have been largely responsible for structuring the debate on academic management education, and have continued to be so to the present day. The underlying idea, inspired by the literature on organizational culture (e.g. Schein 1985), is that discussions are shaped by assumptions which in themselves are not the object of the debate and which act as generative principles. Fundamental assumptions are concerned with the dimensions of reality; such dimensions can be expressed in the form of dichotomies (compare Hall 1959).

An important dichotomy in business education is, by the very nature of the subject, the theory/practice dichotomy. It is not unique to development in the Netherlands, but the form it took right from the start of Dutch academic management education will be described.

With regard to the relation between theory and practice, two views arose at the beginning of the century which continue to have an impact. The first of these is associated with the idea of a practical doctrine; the translation of *kunstleer*, the Dutch equivalent of Schmalenbach's *Kunstlehre* (Locke 1984), considers theory as a summary of what can be observed in practice, an attempt to distil a systematic body of practical knowledge from practice. This idea, with the addition of the concept of an improvement of practice by means of hypothetical and constructive reasoning, is then, in a more refined version, known as 'applied science'. Typical of both practical doctrine and applied science is that the origin and inspiration of knowledge is practice. A close relationship between the educational institution and the business world is the logical consequence of this view.

The second view is the complete opposite, and turns the relationship around. Practice must be informed by pure knowledge, which does not follow from a systematization of practice. It is the task of science to uncover the essential nature of reality. The ensuing insights can then be used to inform and to judge practice. This view implies a high degree of independence for the scientist and a distance between practice and science.

In the Netherlands, the first – 'inductive' – view became a characteristic of engineers. The second – 'deductive' – view became dominant in business economics, although there was always a strong undercurrent of inductive business economics in the country.

A second dichotomy exists between the 'restrictive' and 'non-restrictive' definitions of the discipline dealing with business (van Rossum 1985). In the restrictive conception, the discipline has a well-defined formal objective, delineated by a special point of view. Reality can be neatly divided into a part which lies within the competence of the discipline and a part outside it. The non-restrictive view takes the empirical phenomenon as its starting point and deals with all aspects relevant to that phenomenon.

There is a logical connection between the deductive/inductive dichotomy and the restrictive/non-restrictive dichotomy. Inductive reasoning leads to a non-restrictive view and deductive reasoning to a restrictive one. Thus the dominant view in business economics became restrictive, with a non-restrictive undercurrent, whereas the engineers were non-restrictive in their approach.

The third dichotomy is between approaches which deal with discovering the structure of the world as it is, on the one hand, and those which deal with the construction of possible future worlds, on the other. This might be labelled the 'explanation/construction' dichotomy, which can also be seen as the conflict between orientations towards the past and the future. Most outspoken in their constructive emphasis are the engineering sciences; from the outset, engineers involved in management education took the constructive position. The dominant trend in business economics, however, was to refrain from all constructive work. The business economist studies the principles of economic action, develops techniques to get an adequate view of the economic reality of business, and judges decisions from an economic point of view. But the business economist is neither a manager

77

nor an engineer. He or she uses facts from the past and does not engage in speculative reasoning about the future. This view has become central in Dutch business economics, and has led to a clear distinction between the roles of business economists and engineers in the Netherlands.

These three closely related dichotomies were in turn related to status differences in Dutch society and to the educational system. Since the introduction of the civil high school (the translation here of *Hogere Burgerschool*) by the liberal government of Thorbecke in 1863, alongside the existing classical high school (the Dutch gymnasium), two channels for upward mobility have existed. The classical high school prepared students for university; the civil high school prepared them for practical careers in commerce and industry. Delft Superior School of Technology, which educated engineers, remained part of the practical, lower-status stream, although its academic level was recognized as early as 1905 (Lintsen 1980: 347). So did commercial education institutions which were outside the universities. The view of education prevailing in this 'lower stream' was that young men had to be prepared for their job: the emphasis was on practical knowledge, skills, and character development. In the 'higher stream', the emphasis was on general culture and intellectual breeding: the German *Bildung* ideal.

The two views of management education which developed in the Netherlands clearly had their place in the status system. The inductive, non-restrictive, and constructive approach, originating in engineering and commercial education, belonged to the lower-status stream of practical education. The deductive, restrictive, and explanatory view of business education, on the other hand, became part of the high-status stream of the universities. This conjunction of views on the nature of science with feelings of class superiority and inferiority give an extra dimension to the meaning of the dichotomies dealt with above. The main dichotomies can now be summarized in Table 4.1.

To give an idea of the specific content of these dichotomies in academic business education in the Netherlands before the Second World War, two

Table 4.1 Major dichotomies in management education

Object of debate	Option 1	Option 2
Relation between theory and reality	Inductive	Deductive
Domain of science	Non-restrictive	Restrictive
Relationship with practice	Construction	Explanation/judgement
Time orientation	Future	Past
Type of knowledge	Practical doctrine	Science
Typical discipline	Engineering	Business economics
Educational philosophy	Preparation for practice	*Bildung*
Class orientation	Middle class	Elite
Typical author	Goudriaan	Limperg

typical writers have been chosen to represent each column of Table 4.1. Limperg, founder of the influential school of business economics in Amsterdam, represents the second column. Goudriaan, an engineer teaching at the Rotterdam School of Commerce, represents the first column.

TWO EARLY VIEWS OF BUSINESS EDUCATION: J. GOUDRIAAN AND TH. LIMPERG JUNIOR

J. Goudriaan (1893–1974)

J. Goudriaan has been chosen here to represent the inductive, non-restrictive, and constructivist view of management which became typical both for the engineering approach to management and for a trend in business economics that developed at the Rotterdam Superior School of Commerce (later, Economics). He belonged to both. If he were alive now, his profession would certainly be classified as *bedrijfskunde*.

Goudriaan, the son of a school master in Amsterdam, did not attend the classical high school, but the civil high school. At the age of 17 he enrolled at Delft Superior School of Technology, where he graduated as an engineer within five years with very good results (*cum laude*). He finished his dissertation in 1922 and gained his doctorate, also *cum laude*. In 1926, at the age of 33, he was appointed professor at the Rotterdam Superior School of Commerce (van der Zwan 1991).

He was a student of J.G.Ch. Volmer, who had held the chair of management and book-keeping at the Delft Superior School of Technology since 1908. Volmer, an accountant, was the great advocate of Taylorism in the Netherlands. Retrospectively, he may be considered the first professor of *bedrijfskunde* in the Netherlands. His students, especially Goudriaan, Hijmans, and Van Gogh, formed the first generation of organizational consultants, and their ideas have influenced Dutch organizational thought up to the present day. As for his economic ideas, Volmer was strongly influenced by the historical school of Schmoller, which had a virtual monopoly in Germany between 1870 and 1914.

Like his fellow students mentioned above, Goudriaan combined a belief in scientific management with socialist views. He believed in the rational construction, not only of business, but also of society. When Goudriaan was appointed at Rotterdam, he continued to work as an engineer for Fijenoord, a shipbuilding enterprise. From 1928, he worked for Philips where he was a major architect of the survival strategy during the years of the Great Depression. He was also appointed professor at Delft Superior School of Technology in 1935.

In his 1926 inaugural lecture, Goudriaan gave a clear view of the subject of management (Goudriaan 1926). With the advantage of hindsight, this lecture can be seen as the first formulation of an applied science of management and organization. As a student of Volmer, he used the term *bedrijfsleer*, the Dutch equivalent of the German *Betriebslehre* or the practical doctrine of business. Philosophically, Goudriaan showed an absolute belief in the moral superiority of science over other forms of knowledge. Basing his views on the positivism of Auguste Comte (1798–1857), he saw a hierarchy of sciences in which the sciences further up the hierarchy made use of the truths provided by those lower down. *Bedrijfsleer* was part of economics, which was itself part of sociology, the highest science in Comte's system.

Bedrijfsleer is an applied science, according to Goudriaan. Whereas pure science has knowledge as its central value, applied science wants to know in order to control. Applied science is future oriented. The phenomena of the *bedrijfsleer* cannot be studied, like those of the natural sciences, under controlled conditions. According to Goudriaan, this gives special relevance to the development of pure theory. The theory is:

> a system of hypotheses and deductions which see a certain phenomenon as a logically necessary result of a number of conditions, but there is no necessity that these conditions have become reality in today's society. On the contrary, the theory should show a series of possibilities and should develop an elaborate system of possible cases, a network of abstract truths, which makes it possible to choose on the basis of critical comparison that case which comes nearest to the concrete observable reality.
>
> (Goudriaan, 1926: 12; our translation)

Applied science should not be confused with technical knowledge, nor should it be considered pure science in a different form. Applied science has an identity of its own. It is concerned with both existing and imaginable technical practice. Technology – Goudriaan used the Dutch word *techniek*, equivalent to the German *Technik* (Locke 1989: 77–9) – is the knowledge and practical management of resources to attain specific objectives. Applied science studies this technology in order to improve it. It does not judge objectives; these are considered to be outside the scope of science. This view of applied science is directly relevant to the objective of the *bedrijfsleer*, which is not just business reality as it is, but more specifically the technology of management that is studied in order to improve it.

As a practical science, *bedrijfsleer* has its place in a hierarchy of practical sciences. Each practical science draws on the results of the previous science. At the top of the pyramid Goudriaan placed *bedrijfsleer* and public administration (including law). The pedagogical and medical sciences were found one step lower down. Engineering and agricultural sciences were at the bottom. There was also a hierarchy of objectives, as presented in Table 4.2.

The essence of *bedrijfsleer* is thus organization, which presupposes the

Table 4.2 Hierarchy of applied sciences according to Goudriaan

Objectives	Applied science
Organization	Business and public administration
Breeding	Agriculture, pedagogics, and medicine
Construction	Engineering

construction of a technology and the health and education of people. Goudriaan sees this. His lectures in Rotterdam on *bedrijfsleer* were entitled 'the organization of the enterprise'.

This conception of *bedrijfsleer* has definite consequences for academic management education. The hierarchy of sciences implies that the curriculum must involve a number of subjects lower in the hierarchy such as mechanical engineering, hygiene, pedagogics, and psychology. As for the area of management itself, Goudriaan distinguished five functions: technical, commercial, socio-economic, accounting, and financial. He opposed an early specialization in one of the functional areas:

> If one wishes to achieve that persons of varying educational background join hands and work at making an enterprise flourish in friendship and mutual respect, then it is first of all necessary that each of these persons has obtained a harmonious view of the whole.
>
> (Goudriaan 1932; our translation)

The definition of *bedrijfsleer* as an 'applied science' requires that students study current practice and learn to discover possibilities for improvement. Goudriaan insisted that students should learn that variable situations require flexible rules. Theory should be seen as a reservoir of logical possibilities, not as a dogmatic system of transcendental truths.

The idea of business education that Goudriaan had in mind did not materialize in exactly this form in Rotterdam or Delft. Not until the 1960s would business studies curricula, which would come close to Goudriaan's ideas, be developed in the superior schools of technology (the present technical universities). However, the concept of a constructive, practice-oriented, and non-restrictive science of business did become a central ingredient of the growing profession of organization and management consultancy in the Netherlands, with its close ties to the superior schools of technology, and in this sense is still visible in the business studies curricula of the technical universities. It also continued to play a role at the Rotterdam Superior School of Commerce (Economics), from 1973 the Faculty of Economics of the Erasmus University. Rotterdam business economics continued to some extent the *bedrijfsleer* tradition of Volmer, and remained relatively open to problems as defined by practice.

The future-oriented and relatively open model of business education at

Rotterdam and Delft later formed a relatively fertile soil for the seeds planted by the American innovations. American pragmatism resounded more clearly in the *kunstleer* tradition of Delft and Rotterdam than in the closed system of transcendental economic truths that had been constructed in Amsterdam. To show why this was the case, the career of Th. Limperg Junior, the man who not only founded the Amsterdam school of business economics but in a sense *was* this school, will now be examined.

Th. Limperg Jr (1879–1961)

Th. Limperg Jr was both the most important pioneer in academic business economics and the founder of modern accountancy in the Netherlands.

Accountancy became professionalized around the turn of the century. In 1895 the Dutch Institute of Accountants was founded; among the founders was J.G.Ch. Volmer. Limperg, introduced to accountancy by Volmer, was among a group of coming men who led an open attack on the alleged conservatism and prejudices of the old guard. This led to his expulsion from the Institute. On leaving the Institute, together with several others, including Volmer, he founded the Dutch Accountants Association in 1907. Typical of Limperg's view was that the accountant should not rely on samples and superficial observations: instead the accountant should base a judgement upon systematic research, and verify all books. In the professional ethic which Limperg helped to develop, the independence of the accountant was the central element (de Vries 1985: 53–6).

As the accounting profession developed further, the contrast between advising engineers and accountants became more pronounced. Volmer could still belong to both groups, but increasingly this combination became less likely, and was indeed seen as undesirable. Debate on the division of work between accountants and engineers took place in the 1920s and 1930s. The accountant R.W. Starreveld formulated the difference in terms of the opposition between organizing and controlling. This also involves a difference in time perspective. The engineer who is involved in organizing – or management – has an active role; the accountant involved in control has a retrospective orientation. Although organization and control are related, the two functions are fundamentally different (de Vries 1985: 187).

This distinction of management and control (in the original French meaning of verification or inspection) remained crucial for the accountant's attitude to management. It explains the fact why Dutch business economics, with its close ties to accounting, has never developed a genuine management orientation. It also explains problems of developing management tools in the field of management accounting, where financial and engineering views of management and control meet.

Limperg was not only among those who defined the accountancy profession in the Netherlands, but also the first to give an identity to business economics, setting it apart from the practical doctrine of business: the *bedrijfsleer*. In 1922, he was appointed the first professor of business economics in the Netherlands at the new Faculty of Economics at the University of Amsterdam. This change from *bedrijfsleer* to *bedrijfs-huishoudkunde* (business economics) involved a new view of the subject. Limperg's problem with the practical *bedrijfsleer* was its low scientific level. It was still *kunstleer* – an artificial doctrine constructed on the basis of practical experience. He rejected the inductivist historical method, still typical of Volmer's work. His own philosophical approach was probably inspired by the Leyden philosopher G. Heymans, who saw the law of egoism as the principle on which the science of economics was based (Klant 1979).

According to Limperg, whose ideas are reminiscent of the neo-Kantian philosophy of Rickert, a true science is abstract and emphasizes the aetiology, or causal structure, of phenomena. A science is built up around abstract causes, which are the ultimate object of that science. Each science specializes in such abstract causes, which Limperg also sees as forces or laws. The force or law which gives rise to the science of economics is the economic principle. Economics as a science is thus concerned with the causal analysis of phenomena that obey this economic principle. The economic principle or economic motive – the formal object of economics – is defined by Limperg as follows:

> Economics is the science that has the economic motive as its formal object. By virtue of this motive economics looks for the smallest means, that is the sacrifice with the greatest useful effect on the welfare of the individual or the community.
>
> (Limperg 1954: 391; our translation)

Economics is both a causal and a normative science. The economic principle is the norm by which economists can judge decisions. This normative principle is not a moral value; decisions have always to be taken in situations where the economic principle is only one of the norms that should be taken into account. The weighing of norms in a specific situation is called politics, which cannot be the object of science. Economists should therefore refrain from giving integral advice (Limperg 1954: 389).

Economics, according to Limperg, is not founded on psychology. It is a rational science, based on objective criteria. He criticized the Rotterdam school for applying psychological reasoning to the subject of organization (Muysken and Schreuder 1985: 31). Business economics shares its formal objective with general economics. Only its empirical objective is different. This is, according to Limperg, the 'business economy' (a translation of *bedrijfshuishouding*). It is not the business organization (or *bedrijf*), the technical–organizational unit which was central in the *bedrijfsleer*. The term *bedrijf* lacks a theoretical basis and cannot be the object of a scientific discipline; it was 'a vague and indeterminate concept, like many concepts in daily life, which seemed very suitable to the doctrine (*bedrijfsleer*) which then used it to apply it in the same indeterminate way' (Limperg 1946: 26; our translation). The business economy is defined as 'the system of actions and resources which are directed at a specialized part of production' (Limperg, 1946: 24; our translation).

Limperg divided business economics into four main doctrines: the doctrine of value and profit, the doctrine of cost and cost prices, the doctrine of finance, and the doctrine of (internal and external) organization (Muysken and Schreuder 1985: 29). His definition of the formal and empirical object of business economics made him critical of American approaches to management, which still had the character of practical doctrine (*kunstleer*):

> The systematic division of work between economists, as we know it in this country, has been applied in an identical way in Belgium and Germany. In other countries, and especially in the Anglo-Saxon world, no such specialization has come about. . . . Business economics retains a predominantly technical orientation there and does not transcend the level of a practical doctrine (*kunstleer*).
>
> (Limperg 1946: 23; our translation)

This was written just after the Second World War, when engineers, in particular, were becoming quite enthusiastic about American achievements in management!

Limperg's view of business economics made the distinction with the *bedrijfsleer* very clear. Economists should limit their work to the purely economic aspects and not be involved in technical and social issues. His emphasis on logical consistency and closure created a distance between the self-contained system of business economics and the ambiguities of managerial practice. The difference between engineers and economists, still relatively unclear in Volmer's day, was now seen as fundamental.

Limperg's philosophy introduced an idealist tone to business economics, which even had a mystical quality to it. The identification of the formal objective with fundamental laws and abstract causes gave the Amsterdam school of business economics its own character, which remained visible well up to the 1960s. Limperg's followers emphasized systematic and logical thinking, consistency, responsibility, and intellectual distance. His economics was not only a science; it also had the qualities of a conviction.

The academization of business economics, which Limperg attained by breaking out of the *bedrijfsleer* tradition, was realized at the expense of practical involvement in management issues. The relationship between accountancy and business economics was strengthened, but management consultancy and management were not part of the environment of Amsterdam business economics. The refusal to play an active role in business decisions can be seen in the relative underdevelopment of finance and management accounting.

Limperg developed his ideas without much involvement in international discussions. There was a certain provincial quality in his work. Most of the examples in his lectures were taken from domestic industry, which was managerially still relatively underdeveloped. Although he emphasized the unity of economics, Limperg was not really involved in advanced economic debates. He was a typical system builder, who built up his system by isolating himself from both the ambiguities of practice and international economic discussion.

At the Rotterdam Superior School of Commerce (Economics), the academization of business economics was not carried so far. The term *bedrijfsleer* continued to be used, and the curriculum was broader than in Amsterdam. N.J. Polak (1887–1948), who was appointed professor at the Rotterdam Superior School of Commerce in 1922, shared Limperg's view that the *bedrijfsleer* should become part of economics, but he was less radical in this respect. In his view, the *bedrijfsleer* could be compared with the economics of Quesnay or the work of the Cameralists. Both had focused on the description of existing practice being in the service of commercial and administrative education. According to Polak, like economics which developed into a science, *bedrijfsleer* could evolve into a scientific discipline and become part of economics (Polak 1953). Polak thus took a middle position between the *kunstleer* inspired by Schmalenbach and the German historical school on the one hand, and the new business economics of Limperg on the other. The existing *bedrijfsleer* was valued as a stage in the evolution of a science. Indeed, it was remarkable that Polak should continue to use the term *bedrijfsleer*, which Limperg rejected so furiously. The focus of Polak's work, moreover, also testifies to his practical interest in current business issues.

With Limperg's work, two schools emerged in the Netherlands: the deductive and restrictive Amsterdam School of Business Economics and the more open and inductive Rotterdam school, which did not break away from the *bedrijfsleer* of Volmer and Schmalenbach. In the further development of business economics, the distinction between the two schools remained evident. When using the word 'school', however, the fact that the Amsterdam economists, with their coherent intellectual system, deserved this word more than their colleagues from Rotterdam, with their more loosely structured and varied approach, should be acknowledged.

Conclusion

The views of Goudriaan and Limperg give an idea of how the academic community of the Netherlands dealt with business themes before the Second World War. On the one hand, there was the idea of a practical doctrine, rooted in practice. This idea was typical of the *bedrijfsleer* which was taught in the superior schools of technology and commerce. Its theoretical background came from the German historical school of economics, American scientific management, and positivist conceptions of natural science. In the work of both Goudriaan and Polak, a wish for this doctrine to become a science is discernible, but the orientation towards practice was not abandoned. There was, however, a gradual differentiation between the economic *bedrijfsleer* and the more technical version. In the latter conception of *bedrijfsleer*, the core of the subject is seen as organization, and the profession of organizational consultancy in the Netherlands arose from it. The economic version of *bedrijfsleer* gradually developed into the Rotterdam conception of business economics.

Limperg's ideas led in quite a different direction. Academization involved a restrictive view of business economics, defined both by its formal objective, the economic principle, and its empirical objective, the business economy. Business economists were not involved in problems of organization. They constructed a normative economic science, which could provide valid principles for practice but was not actively involved in the daily management and organization of business.

The image of academic education and business between the world wars shows that management as such was not an important subject. The engineers did not develop a science of business administration, but a practical doctrine of organization, which became known in the Netherlands as *organisatiekunde*. Business economists became closely linked to the profession of accountancy. In Amsterdam, especially, the customary and formal view of the business economist was emphasized. Only in Rotterdam were there some signs of a shift towards a more management-oriented view, by Goudriaan in particular. His concept of a broad interdisciplinary education came close to the American ideal of the business school.

Put crudely, there were two possible ways for business subjects to become accepted in the Dutch academic world. The first was to concentrate on the relatively technical problems of organization. Students could be trained to become specialists in the field of *organisatiekunde*. The second was to become an academic business economist, a specialist in normative economic reasoning, with an accent on accounting. Both possibilities excluded a management-oriented approach to academic business education. As will be shown in the final section of this chapter, this emphasis on non-managerial, scientific, or technical, themes has remained a feature of Dutch business education until the present day.

NEW IDEAS AND THE OLD DEBATE: THE FURTHER DEVELOPMENT OF ACADEMIC BUSINESS EDUCATION

The reception of American management

After this excursion into the ideas of two early thinkers who represent two distinct currents in Dutch management thought, it is now time to see how American concepts of management were greeted in the Netherlands. The work of the founding fathers gives a hint as to the intellectual context in which the ideas were received.

It has become clear that the *kunstleer* tradition of both engineers and Rotterdam economists was more congenial to American pragmatism than the normative–idealist thought of Limperg and his school. Not only was the existing *kunstleer* already strongly influenced by American scientific management through Volmer's work, for example, but American business thought can itself be shown to have been influenced by the German *Kunstlehre* tradition and the ideas of the German historical school (see, for example, Jones 1992 on the subject of marketing). The innovations in American management thought in the 1950s and 1960s (Locke 1984, 1985, 1989), which went beyond this purely practical and empiricist tradition, and which became the basis of the business school ideal that also spread over Europe, were added on to the existing pragmatic legacy. While this approach tried to turn management into a science, it retained some of the central assumptions of the older current of management thought. First, there was a continuing positivist belief in the connection between knowledge and control. Second, was the idea that management required a variety of scientific inputs, often with an assumption of a hierarchy of sciences. The really new development in postwar American management thought was the assumption that there could be a science of sciences to integrate all the bits and pieces of knowledge into a meaningful whole. Such integration, by means of the new systems philosophy, could become the basis for the rational control of business organizations. All this became the essence of what Locke (1989) has named the 'new paradigm' in management – the basis of the new business school curricula in North America.

It is evident that this philosophy would fit better with the tradition of Goudriaan than that of Limperg. In terms of the dichotomies of Table 4.1, the new systems approach to management was non-restrictive, future oriented, and concerned with the construction of a new reality. It gave up the inductive and purely practical orientation of the old *bedrijfsleer* and promised the creation of a science of management, without degenerating into narrow academic specialism. The object of the new paradigm was the business enterprise as a system, which came close to the techno-organizational entity *bedrijf* (business organization), which according to Limperg could never become the object of a true science.

87

The definition of the business organization, *bedrijf*, as a system also implied the prospect of taking sociological and psychological aspects into account. In contrast to those economists of the Limperg tradition who rejected psychology, the engineers involved in business had long shown an interest in the psychological and social sides of business organization. The systems approach legitimized and formally recognized these non-technical factors.

Indeed, the initiatives for schools of *bedrijfskunde* (business studies) in the 1960s came from engineers and those business economists who favoured a broad, non-restrictive definition of their discipline. Sociologists and psychologists joined forces with these economists and engineers to form the new discipline of *bedrijfskunde*.

In the superior schools of technology (the present technical universities), *bedrijfskunde* evolved from the departments of mechanical engineering. In the universities, the new discipline could have remained part of business economics, but this did not happen. The dominance of the restrictive Limperg tradition certainly played a part. However, in the 1960s when the initiatives towards *bedrijfskunde* were taken, this was not the only current in business economics. At Groningen University, for example, the work of J.L. Bouma and A. Bosman, both working in the Faculty of Economics, showed a vivid interest in the new paradigm of management, especially operations research, R.L. Ackoff's systems methodology, and the behavioural theory of the firm of Herbert A. Simon and James G. March. Cooperation between business economists and behavioural scientists in the field of management and organization, which had existed since the 1960s, eventually led to the creation in 1976 of a new Faculty of Business Studies there (van Gils *et al.* 1987).

The continuity between the old *bedrijfsleer* of people like Goudriaan and the new interdisciplinary business studies can be seen in the objective of the new science, which was often defined as the organization. *Bedrijfskunde* was frequently equated to *organisatiekunde*, the practical science of organization, rooted in the Dutch organizational consultancy firms. J. Joele, one of the business economists involved in the founding of 'business studies' in Groningen, defined *bedrijfskunde* as the 'interdisciplinary action science, which has the behaviour of organizations as its object' (Joele 1973: 21; our translation). The influence of the Carnegie school of March and Simon, mentioned above, can be seen in the term 'behaviour of organizations'. Organizational diagnosis, organizational design, and the design and guidance of change processes in organizations were the central subjects of study according to Joele. The first course prospectus of the new faculty equated business studies (*bedrijfskunde*) with organization studies (*organisatiekunde*) (*Studiegids Interfaculteit Bedrijfskunde* 1977).

With the definition of *bedrijfskunde* as an applied science of organization, the Dutch version of the American business school acquired a character of its own, which showed a great deal of continuity between the old *bedrijfsleer* and *bedrijfskunde*. Organization, rather than management, became central to the discipline. Financial subjects were certainly not the core of the curriculum. The difference between the old *bedrijfsleer* and Limperg's business economics also continued to exist, first between *bedrijfskunde* and business economics and second between the two currents in business economics.

Continuities amidst change

Although this chapter emphasizes continuity, change has undoubtedly been the overall reality in the development of academic business education between the time of Goudriaan and Limperg and the present. A few examples follow below.

The growth of the universities since the 1960s, from the small elite institutions which existed before the Second World War into mass educational institutions, and their democratization, have radically changed the academic world. Moreover, the disproportionate growth of business economics and business studies, especially from the 1980s, has created large faculties quite unlike those in which the pioneers developed their ideas. The increasing importance of research – the idea of 'publish or perish' – is changing the work of the academic staff. Whereas Goudriaan and Limperg were first and foremost teaching professors, who wrote their books for educational purposes, the staff in present-day faculties of business economics and business studies are writing more and more for the forum of professional colleagues. This in turn is related to the internationalization of business studies and business economics: it is the international publications that count.

In the business world, many management and staff positions are now filled with academics, whereas internally recruited practitioners would have been favoured before the Second World War. This seems to be related to the change in company structures, with a consistent movement away from functional patterns (Jagersma 1994), and transformations in the working of the internal labour markets of large organizations in the Netherlands. The antagonism between university and business may not have disappeared, but it is undoubtedly less sharp than it used to be.

The philosophical roots of Limperg's and Goudriaan's work, eighteenth-century rationalism, and nineteenth-century positivism, have long been surpassed by more adequate views of the nature of scientific knowledge. The debate between the inductive style of the *bedrijfsleer* and the deductive style of business economics appears to be outdated; more recent philosophical ideas, like constructivist thought or ideas on the role of paradigms in science, give a more adequate account of scientific work. The absolute demarcation between science and non-science, typical of the older philosophy of science, is no longer accepted and science is increasingly understood as a human and social construction.

The growing influence of sociology and psychology on management thought and the further development of such conceptual tools as systems theory have opened fields of enquiry and problems which fall outside the old debates between engineers and economists.

In the light of such changes – in the education system, the business context, and the content of the business sciences – it is remarkable to see significant continuities. The most important continuity is the preoccupation with science; with *wetenschap*, a term which, like the German *Wissenschaft*, includes the humanities. The methodological and theoretical debates in business studies have already been mentioned. Van der Zwaan and van Engelen (1994), for example, note that the scientific status of *bedrijfskunde* (business studies) is still under criticism. Is it a science? They, like several others in the debate, give the implicit answer 'not yet'; only the further development of theory and methodology can eventually transform *bedrijfskunde* into a science. The applied nature of *bedrijfskunde* needs a methodology of application. Theories in this field, according to van der Zwaan and van Engelen, are only complete if they also specify their application in practice by means of diagnostic, design, and change technology. This is a new formulation of Goudriaan's view that applied science has an identity of its own. Van Aken (1991) compares the young discipline of organization studies (*organisatie-kunde*) with the long-established sciences. It has not yet reached the stage of being a science, but it can become a science by developing a consistent research programme. This programme must not be based on the empirical sciences, with their 'physicalist' theories; *organisatiekunde* is a design science, providing professionals with the knowledge of how to design and change organizations. Jansen (1994) observes that most knowledge in business studies is still a combination of a priori theorizing and eclectic case studies. Jansen favours a broad empirical approach for the business enterprise, in which all relevant aspects are covered. Researchers should acknowledge that very little is known still. Jorna (1994), who criticizes the ideas of van Engelen (1992), presents a number of arguments against the idea that *bedrijfskunde* is a field of engineering. It lacks the scientific theory upon which design technologies can be based. He is not very clear on what the core of *bedrijfskunde* should be; but this new science should learn from sociology and psychology. All these are just some recent examples of the growing consensus that *bedrijfskunde* is not (yet) a science, and of the idea that concentration on theory and methodology may help to bring about such a science.

A second continuity is the engineering approach to management, and its underlying positivist assumptions. The idea of the (business) organization as the central object of business studies, combined with the notion that the cooperation between human beings and technology can be rationally designed on the basis of objective knowledge, is a continuing feature of Dutch business studies. The combination of the engineering approach with the wish for *bedrijfskunde* to become a real science is interesting: it leads to attempts to develop a scientific methodology which extends into the domain of application. This could lend academic respectability to the traditional field of engineering which was often considered inferior by the established sciences.

A third continuity is the divorce of financial management and accounting from organizational issues. The separate development of business economics and business studies has reinforced this tendency.

A final point of continuity is the general philosophy of business education. As in Germany, the prevailing idea in the Netherlands has always been that managers cannot be trained in a university. The *Bildung* ideal in the universities, with its basis in the ideas of the Enlightenment, implies that it is the primary task of the university to develop an individual's intellectual faculties. In the engineering schools, the orientation has always been more towards a professional ideal: training technical specialists. Typically, a young university graduate starts a career in industry in a relatively specialized position. Managerial abilities are developed along the way. An academic education may help to prepare the student for business by developing his or her required background and intellectual levels, but does not provide him or her with the necessary management skills. To use German words: the student can become *betriebsfähig* (having the potential to become a manager), but is not *betriebsfertig* (ready to manage), at the end of his or her studies. This continuity of educational philosophy is consistent with the fact that the faculties of business economics and business studies concentrate on first-level degrees and offer curricular subjects to young people without practical business experience.

The future of academic business education

The central assumption of this chapter is that the future of academic business education will be shaped by its history. The persistent patterns of the culture surrounding business economics and business studies will shape the future role of universities in preparing young men and women for managerial careers. The actual future will of course depend on the interactions between changes in the educational system and outside pressures on this system. Some issues which are likely to play a major role in the near future will now be dealt with.

The first issue is the tension between management education on the one hand and general business education on the other. Both the academic culture and the labour market have favoured functionally oriented professional or scientific education at the expense of managerial orientation. The emphasis on undergraduate education at the universities in the last few years has reinforced this tendency. But there are also two major problems becoming manifest. In the first place, the labour market may not be able to absorb the large number of business studies and business economics graduates, in the sense that jobs are provided on the professional level assumed by the faculties. This may lead to a devaluation of the *doctorandus* and *ingenieur* degrees involved. The other problem is developing inside the academic schools. It concerns the growing wish for business education to become a science and be recognized as a science-based profession, which is likely to conflict with the actual educational functions of the schools as a general preparation for business.

The second issue is the *raison d'être* of two faculties in business education: business studies and business economics. The historical background of this divide is clear and the wish of business studies to be recognized as a science fits perfectly in the Dutch tradition. The tension comes primarily from abroad. The more Dutch management or business scientists become part of the international scientific community, the less real any lines drawn between the faculties will seem. Furthermore, financial considerations may stimulate university administrators to integrate business studies and business economics on an organizational level.

The third issue is the scientific status of the business sciences. In the Dutch academic culture the word *wetenschap* symbolizes the values of the university and marks the boundaries between the university and other educational institutions. Attempts to define a science of organization or business and the debate on methodology among professors in business studies demonstrate a wish to become fully accepted in the academic world of the Netherlands. As Whitley (1988) has shown, the field of management and organization does not readily combine with a scientific conception of knowledge: the scientific community is not likely to obtain control over the production of knowledge in this field to a degree which can be found in other sciences and professions. This makes it especially difficult for business subjects to be taught in an academic environment, such as the universities of the Netherlands with their *wetenschap* tradition. If this tradition is to survive the changes now taking place in the universities, the present tendency of faculties of business studies to defend their scientific status by emphasizing methodology will continue; and a professional, non-managerial definition of *bedrijfskunde* will be the result. If, on the other hand, the Dutch *wetenschap* tradition becomes less strong, there could be room for more managerially oriented curricula.

In countries with a strong national tradition of management or business education, innovations build upon existing strengths. This also applies to the Netherlands. The tensions and issues dealt with above are not likely to be resolved, for example, by copying the American system of management education. However, useful elements from foreign educational systems will be incorporated into the existing national tradition.

It seems likely, therefore, that in the faculties of business economics and business studies the professional elements will be strengthened in the years to come. In business economics, the link with general economics will continue to legitimize those business subjects which are taught in the university. In the faculties of business studies, the functionally defined subjects will be strengthened at the expense of general management; specialization of students in relatively technical subjects will be stimulated. The impending devaluation of the *doctorandus* and *ingenieur* degrees on the labour market will lead to an upgrading of the level of courses in terms of scientific and professional criteria, even if this leads to a decrease in student numbers.

The existence of two faculties of academic business education is likely to remain an issue. The specialization of business studies in the direction of engineering and organization seems probable and absolutely in line with past definitions of the tasks of engineers and economists. However, integration of business economics and business studies, perhaps within the faculties of economics, is another possibility. Management education in the American MBA tradition is likely to remain somewhat outside the universities, although faculties of business administration and business economics will continue to be actively involved in this type of education.

CONCLUSION

This chapter has tried to show the continuity of certain patterns of academic management education in the Netherlands. The work of two early pioneers in the field, Goudriaan and Limperg, who developed their major ideas between the two world wars, was used to demonstrate some of the major dichotomies in Dutch management education. Two images of academic management education resulted from a combined analysis of these dichotomies. The first image continues to play a role in business economics, especially in the Amsterdam tradition. The second image, having materialized in business studies, is also still relevant. Both, however, exclude a third image: the idea of academic management education.

Given the prevalence of the two Dutch images of academic business education, it seems obvious why the American ideal of management education has never found much resonance in the Dutch universities. The courses did adopt American subject matter, but the faculties did not adopt the corresponding educational philosophy. The faculties of business studies and business economics have witnessed phenomenal growth in the 1980s, and are now in a stage of reorientation. Their future will depend on their ability to combine the persistent characteristics of the Dutch heritage with innovative ideas and inspiration from abroad.

REFERENCES

Aken, J.E. van (1991) *Organisatiekunde, uil of jonge zwaan*, Intreerede, Eindhoven: Technische Universiteit.

—— (1994a) 'De bedrijfskunde als ontwerpwetenschap: de regulatieve en de reflectieve cyclus', *Bedrijfskunde* 66: 1.

—— (1994b) 'Het ontwikkelen van wetenschappelijke kennis voor organisatieprofessionals vanuit spelersperspectief: de rol van ontwerpmodellen en heuristieken', *M & O Tijdschrift voor organisatiekunde en sociaal beleid* 48(4): 388–404.

Douma, S.W. (1991) 'Bedrijfseconomie + bedrijfskunde = bedrijfswetenschappen', *Maandblad voor accountancy en bedrijfseconomie* November: 522–3.

Engelen, J.M.L. van (1992) *In het bijzonder bedrijfskunde: de integrende rol van de technologie en de ontwerphenadering*, Alphen aan den Rijn: Samson.

Gils, M.R. van, Karsten, L., and Man, H. de (1987) 'Bedrijfskunde: verleden, heden en toekomst', in S.K.T. Boersma and O.A.M. Fisher (eds) *Strucureren van het ongestructureerde*, Groningen: OFIR, 13–46.

Goudriaan, J. (1926) *Bedrijfsleer als theoretische en als toegepaste wetenschap*, Rede uitgesproken bij de aanvaarding van het ambt van buitengewoon hoogleeraar an de Nederlandsche Handels-Hoogeschool te Rotterdam op 23 April 1926, Rotterdam: Nijgh en Van Ditmar.

—— (1932) 'De ontwikkeling van de bedrijfsleer als toegepaste wetenschap' in E.G. de Jong *et al.* (eds) *Bedrijfseconomische studiën, verzameling herdrukken*, Haarlem: Erven F. Bohn, 534–54.

Hall, E.T. (1959) *The Silent Language*, New York: Doubleday.

Jagersma, P.K. (1994) 'Concernstructuren: theorie, praktijk en verklaring', *MAB* April: 179–89.

Jansen, P.G.W. (1994) 'Op weg naar een empirische bedrijfskunde', *Bedrijfskunde* 66(1): 45–56.

Joele, J. (1973) 'Bedrijfskunde in Groningen: nieuwe loot aan een snel groeiende stam', *Intermediair* 9(34): 21–3.

Jones, B. (1992) 'Die deutsche Historische Schule: Begründerin des nordamerikanischen Marketingdenkens', *Marketing Zeitschrift für Forschung und Praxis*, 1(1 Quartal): 5–11.

Jorna, R.J. (1994) 'Een nieuwe inhoud voor de bedrijfskunde', *Bedrijfskunde* 66(1): 36–44.

Klant, J.J. (1979) 'Grandeur en zwakte van een systeem', in *Reflecties op Limperg: opstellen over ontwikkelingen in onderneming, bedrijfseconomie en accountancy sinds de jaren dertig*, uitgegeven ter gelegenheid van de honderdste geboortedag van prof. dr. Theodore Limperg jr. onder auspiciën van het Limperg instituut interuniversitair instituut voor accountancy, Deventer: Kluwer, 33–42.

Lawrence, P. (1991) *Management in the Netherlands*, Oxford: Clarendon Press.

Limperg, Th. (1946) *Het object der bedrijfshuishoudkunde*, Purmerend: Muusses.

—— (1954) 'De normatieve taak van de economie', *Maandblad voor accountancy en bedrijfshuishouding* 28(9): 383–94.

Lintsen, H. (1980) *Ingenieurs in de negentiende eeuw: eenstreven naar erkenning en macht*, s-Gravenhage: Martinus Nijhoff.

Locke, R.R. (1984) *The End of the Practical Man*, Greenwich, CT.: JAI Press.

—— (1985) 'Business Education in Germany: Past Systems and Current Practice', *Business History Review* 59(2): 232–53.

—— (1989) *Management and Higher Education Since 1940: The Influence of America and Japan on West Germany, Great Britain and Japan*, Cambridge: Cambridge University Press.

Man, H. de (1993) 'Managers wetenschappelijk opleiden: de geschiedenis van een moderne idee', in A. Wattel (ed.) *Management Development*, Deventer: Kluwer, 29–49.

—— and Karsten, L. (1994) 'Academic Management Education in the Netherlands', in L. Engwall and E. Gunnarsson (eds) *Management Studies in an Academic Context*, Uppsala: Acta Universitatis Upsaliensis, Studia Oeconomiae Negotorium 35: 155–66.

Muysken, J. and Schreuder, H. (eds) (1985) *Economische wetenschappen: eenheid in verscheidenheid?*, Assen: Van Gorcum.

Organisatiemethoden en efficiëntie-controle in Amerikaanse bedrijven (1952), Den Haag: Contactgroep Opvoering Productiviteit.

Polak, N.J. (1953) 'Het huidig stadium en de naaste taak der bedrijfsleer', in H.T. Go and J.P. Kikkert (eds) *Verspreide geschriften van prof. dr. N.J. Polak*, Purmerend: Muusses.

Rossum, W. van (1985) 'De economie als niet-restrictieve discipline', in J. Muysken and H. Schreuder (eds) *Economische wetenschappen: eenheid in verscheidenheid*, Assen: Van Gorcum.

Schein, E.H. (1985) *Organizational Culture and Leadership: A Dynamic View*, San Francisco: Jossey Bass.

Schreuder, H. (1985) 'Economie (en) bedrijven: over de bedrijfseconomie als discutabel, spannend en eigenaardig onderdeel van de economische wetenschappen', in J. Muysken *et al.* (eds) *Economische wetenschappen: eenheid in verscheidenheid*, Assen: Van Gorcum, 199–223.

Studiegids Interfaculteit Bedrijfskunde 1977–1978 (1977) Groningen: Rijksuniversiteit Groningen.

Vries, J. de (1985) *Geschiedenis der accountancy: aanvang en ontplooiing*, Assen: Van Gorcum.

Whitley, R. (1988), 'The management sciences and managerial skills', *Organization Studies* 9(1): 47–68.

Zwaan, A.H. van der, and van Engelen, J.M.H. (1994) 'Bedrijfskundige methodologie 1: wetenschapstheoretische context', *Bedrijfskunde* 66(1): 27–35.

Zwan, A. van der (1991) *Goudriaan in botsing met NS: Koopman in dienst van de gemeenschap*, Schiedam: Scriptum.

5

BUSINESS STUDIES AND MANAGEMENT EDUCATION IN JAPAN'S ECONOMIC DEVELOPMENT

An institutional perspective

Tamotsu Nishizawa

INTRODUCTION

The broad expansion of higher education by the University Order after the First World War and the educational reform under strong American influence after the Second World War were probably the two greatest turning points in the development of Japan's higher education system. The formal and general education that resulted seems to have provided a good sound basis for the later training and continual upgrading of the human resources which served to promote flexibility and all-important diagnostic skills. In each company, this further training and upgrading was, for the most part, suggested and encouraged by various business organizations and training centres.

Although Japan has a very high proportion of business leaders with a university or college education, its business community seems not to have recognized specialist and professional training at graduate schools as an important qualification. Characteristically, the *gakureki* (academic credential) of Japan's business leaders was somewhat limited to university first degrees, especially when compared with the United States, where 44 per cent of the business elite had postgraduate degrees, and Germany, where 50 per cent had doctorates. Instead, training after graduation in Japan was largely 'in-firm training', both on the job and off the job (Aso 1991: 21–3). Since the 1960s, moreover, in-firm management education and training were widely diffused against a background of very rapid economic growth. This chapter will point out some of the attributes of the prewar development of formal business studies and explain the evolution of postwar management training, with particular reference to their institutional aspects.

BACKGROUND

Prewar development of business studies

The prewar development of Japanese formal higher education has been primarily discussed in relation to the imperial universities and their affiliates.[1] Tokyo Imperial University headed this hierarchy. The imperial universities grew under powerful government protection, in line with industrialization 'from above'. Their graduates were, as privileged elites in Japan's modernization process, largely absorbed into government service.

However, this chapter will also be concerned with the commercial universities and their associates and the private universities, whose hierarchies were headed by Hitotsubashi and Keio Gijuku respectively. These institutions were called 'Colleges' (*Senmon Gakko*) before the University Order of 1918. They had evolved and thrived through their own efforts in response to social changes and demands 'from below', and had played a central part in educating the human forces needed for Japan's industrialization. Indeed, until the 1920s, Keio Gijuku and the Tokyo Higher Commercial School at Hitotsubashi were the two most prominent providers of business leaders and commerce teachers (Amano 1978: 4–5).

First, the making of Tokyo University of Commerce (now Hitotsubashi University), which was at the top of the hierarchy of institutions offering business studies and education in prewar Japan, and the model for other higher business education schools, will be briefly outlined. To some extent, it seems to have achieved what might be called a unique 'balanced excellence' of the vocational and academic models. Tokyo Imperial, Hitotsubashi, and Keio Gijuku were the three largest suppliers of executives and managers in prewar Japan, but the proportion of graduates who later became executives and managers in relation to all graduates was by far the highest at Hitotsubashi (Aonuma 1965: 116–33).

Foreign observers admired the new Japanese institutions for commercial education that emerged in the late nineteenth century. One of them was Rudolph Beigel, who in his booklet *Der Kampf um die Handelshochschule* (1898), highly praised the Tokyo Higher Commercial School, which had originated in 1875 and later evolved into Tokyo University of Commerce. He wrote that the school was 'most nearly allied to what the German people tried to establish as [the] Handelshochschule'. Because the *Handelshochschule* at Leipzig had not yet been formed, Beigel thought Japan was more advanced than Germany (Beigel 1898: 31–4).[2]

On the other hand, Japan also received know-how from abroad in this formative period of the Japanese system of higher education. Students went overseas, some to England where a faculty of commerce was created at Birmingham in 1902. The number of students in its early years was astonishingly low and, worse still, many of them were foreigners. One of the five graduates in its second intake was Shinji Tazaki from the Tokyo Higher Commercial School (later, the first president of Kobe University of Commerce) (Nishizawa 1994: 205–6).

However, it was first intended that the Tokyo Higher Commercial School should follow the Belgian model, and a number of students and staff went to Antwerp. In 1885, Julian van Stappen, a graduate of the highly successful *Institut Supérieur de Commerce d'Anvers*, was invited to teach at the Tokyo Higher Commercial School. After him two other Belgian scholars were appointed. No other foreign teachers of specialized subjects came to the school until 1897, when Ernest Foxwell, a Cambridge graduate, was appointed as a lecturer in commercial economics. Apparently it was commercial science, not political economy, which characterized the curriculum of the school in its early days. This was in striking contrast to both Keio Gijuku and Tokyo Imperial University, where the subjects taught, under the influence of the German historical school, centred on political economy.

The curriculum of Tokyo Higher Commercial School was also strongly influenced by the requirements of the local business community. Yonekawa argues that Japanese companies employed a conspicuously larger number of university graduates than their Western counterparts. The most outstanding firm was Mitsui Bussan, which, in 1914, employed 731 university graduates out of a total workforce of 1,676. Nearly two-thirds of the graduates were from the Tokyo Higher Commercial School (Yonekawa 1984: 199, 1987: 206–10).

In its early days, two streams of thought prevailed among the students of the Tokyo Higher Commercial School, exemplified on the one hand by the enlightened reformist group and on the other by the conservative group, who tended to be the young scions of old merchant families. The latter were inclined only to learn business techniques for their immediate employment as common clerks, whereas the former were eager to pursue the new arts and science of commerce and thought that the school should be a place for training business leaders. The conflict between these two streams of thought about commercial education – namely, vocational education for the acquisition of useful techniques as against a more advanced academic education – underlay the evolution of the school up until its inauguration as Tokyo University of Commerce in 1920 (*Hitotsubashi 50 Nenshi* 1925: 22–3).

The German impact and generalist education

Around the turn of the century, a number of promising young scholars were sent abroad, this time to Germany; indeed, some actually moved from Antwerp to Berlin and Göttingen, where they were drawn into the maelstrom of the *Handelshochschulen* movement.

The avowed object of the *Handelshochschulen* was the training of future 'business elites'. In their early years, the *Handelshochschule* appeared to aim at both raising the social status of current businesspeople and broadening the outlook of future businesspeople. However, in the event they provided neither a thorough training in business administration and techniques nor business strategies. This was the essence of the movement around the turn of the century, when political economists were in key positions and economic subjects tended to dominate curricula. Fukuda and Seki, and their studies overseas, came long before Schmalenback's inauguration as professor of *Privatwirthschaftslehre* at Cologne (Sugiyama and Nishizawa 1987: 167–9; Shiryo 1982).

The years after the Russo-Japanese War of 1904–5 are said to have been the 'age of business', and higher commercial schools and commerce faculties were created one after another. In 1906, Japan's first academic journal for economics, *Keizaigaku, Shogyogaku, Kokumin Keizai Zasshi* (*Economics, Commercial Science, the Journal of National Economy*), was founded and edited by the professors of the Higher Commercial Schools in Kobe and Tokyo, who now appeared to overwhelm those from Tokyo Imperial University and Keio Gijuku. It was the mouthpiece of the Society for Social Policy, which was inaugurated in 1896 by the young economists who had recently returned from Germany. The economic ideas of this journal were born out of commercial science or economic studies, being focused on the private economy at Hitotsubashi (Ouchi 1970 chs 1–2; Shiryo 1983a). In 1909, Teijiro Ueda published *What is Business Economics?* following W.J. Ashley's *The Enlargement of Economics* (1908), after returning from studies at Birmingham and Berlin. He was founder of business economics in Japan, a discipline which was advanced by him and his adherents at the growing number of higher commercial schools. Subsequently, the Japanese Society of Business Economics was formed in 1926 (Sakamoto 1964: 113; Ueda 1975a: 45–54, 1975b: 385–97).

In 1920, the official organization of Tokyo University of Commerce was sanctioned. In the same year, Keio, Waseda, Meiji, Hosei, Chuo, Nihon, Kokugakuin, and Doshisha were authorized as private universities; and, one by one, the faculties of commerce or economics were institutionalized. The number of universities which had commerce or economics faculties rose from eleven in 1920 to twenty in 1930, and the number of students from 5,434 to 11,378. With the inauguration of Tokyo University of Commerce, the existing Higher Commercial School was abolished. A professional school, which was attached to the university (*Fuzoku Shogaku Senmon-bu*), was immediately substituted for it so that vocational education could be completed. This showed that the requirement for vocational training remained strong among the business community. A teachers' training school, which supplied large numbers of teachers to the numerous higher and ordinary commercial schools, was also attached to the University. Thus the ideals and practice of business studies and education of Tokyo

University of Commerce were widely diffused, and permeated commercial schools throughout Japan.

The curriculum of the new Tokyo University of Commerce still had five courses – foreign trade; economics; business administration and accounting; banking, transport, and insurance; and consular service – which apparently intended to meet the requirements of end-users as well as those of the graduate labour market. Fukuda remarked critically that the curriculum still retained a large element of vocational education: moreover, the new university looked like an 'import and export School'. He did not want education of the Antwerp type any longer. He argued that the university should be a place for academic study and research – not for mere vocational training. The curriculum of the new university of commerce should, therefore, be organized so that *gründlich* studies could be promoted. Instead of five courses, he proposed a two-faculty system of commerce and economics. Law and literary culture could also be added. The four-faculty system of the postwar Hitotsubashi University dates back to this period (*Hitotsubashi Senmon-bu* 1951; Shiryo 1983b).

Hitotsubashi seems never to have separated part of itself into a specialist business education and training institution, as did the Harvard Business School, or to have looked exclusively towards such specialist training, even after the Second World War. Keio University, on the other hand, established an independent institution for management education, and, from 1956, started various seminars with the cooperation of the Harvard Business School. This developed into the current Keio Business School.

AMERICANIZATION AND POSTWAR MANAGEMENT TRAINING

Introduction of American methods

Tokyo Imperial University changed its name to University of Tokyo under the postwar New Education Law. The Department of Commerce in the Faculty of Economics became the Department of Management in 1962, so as to match the current trend which was strongly influenced by the United States. The name change symbolized the end of German influence on business studies. The study of commerce and economics at Hitotsubashi University was, at this time, divided into the Faculties of Commerce and Economics. Courses directly relevant to business needs and practices in the prewar period remained, however, particularly in the Faculty of Commerce.

After the Second World War, Japan's university business education showed a greater tendency to stress arts and general studies subjects rather than practical and specialist ones. Notwithstanding the strong American influence, practical education had been increasingly neglected, and there was a widening gap between what the universities provided for the students and what 'end-users' expected from the universities. Unlike the United States, business schools did not develop in Japan. However, intensive efforts to train graduates were undertaken – primarily by the companies themselves – but also by various intermediate organizations and external training centres. This seems to have been highly efficient and effective, particularly at its initial stages, and reveals a prominent characteristic of the Japanese economic system (Yonekawa *et al.* 1990: 59).

The postwar history of in-house management training first started at the end of the 1940s with the introduction of various American management methods, and spread widely in the early 1950s. These methods included CCS (Civil Communications Section) seminars for top management, MTPs (Management Training Programmes) for middle management, and TWI (Training Within Industry) for supervisors or inspectors. In 1949, the Civil Communications Section of the American Occupation General Head-quarters (GHQ) convened its CCS management seminars, which marked the start of an epoch in postwar Japanese management education. From 1953, CCS seminars for top management were conducted by the Japanese Federation of Management Associations (Nihon Keieisha Dantai Renmei or Nikkeiren, founded in 1948), and from 1955 they became the ordinary business of the Japanese Society for Industrial Training (Nihon Sangyo Kunren Kyokai) which was founded in 1955 under the auspices of Nikkeiren (*Nihon Kindai Kyoiku 100 Nenshi* 1973: 579–86; Nihon Sangyo Kunren Kyokai 1971: 333–5).

Then there were TWI and QC (Quality Control), both of which characteristics were very extensively dispersed in the postwar industrial world and were largely responsible for the recovery of the Japanese economy. First of all, in 1950, the late Dr Deming gave a series of lectures which transmitted the rudiments of statistical quality control. Then, and also of great importance, there was the formation of various organizations dedicated to the promotion and diffusion of quality control – such as the Japanese Union of Scientists and Engineers (Nikka Giren) founded in 1946, the Japanese Standards Association (Nihon Kikaku Kyokai) founded in 1945, and the Japanese Management Association (Nihon Noritsu Kyokai) – to which almost all the companies seeking to introduce quality control sent their employees for training. These organizations also did a great deal in the promotion of management education and training in general.

TWI developed in the United States during the Second World War. Then it was introduced into Britain. It was a guidebook issued by the British Ministry of Labour that was offered by the American Occupation GHQ and translated into Japanese by Japan's Ministry of Labour which introduced the concept to Japan. TWI spread throughout Japan in a surprisingly short period of time, and was used for the training of supervisors. In the process of its spread, however, the ambiguous character of Japanese supervisors and consultants presented some problems. They began to appreciate the gap between American theory and Japanese reality, and tried to establish a more realistic training method which combined the new methods with the traditional Japanese management style. Because of these problems, other methods of company education were also re-examined, making the late 1950s a period of reflection on the wholesale introduction of the apparently easy-going American methods (Institute for International Cooperation n.d.; Nonaka 1994).

Yoichi Ueno and the Japanese Management Association

Even in the prewar period, business studies at Japan's universities was in general rather theoretical, oriented towards bibliographic study, and had little in common with a task-oriented business education. The notion of scientific management was never considered seriously by Japanese academics, who were critical of its pragmatism and of its apparently inhuman approach to workers. Yojiro Masuji of Tokyo University of Commerce, whose study was based on the German *Betriebswirtschaftslehre*, was highly sceptical of Taylor's system. Practitioners of it, such as Yoichi Ueno, who pioneered the introduction of the Taylor system in Japan and founded the Institute for Industrial Efficiency (*Sangyo Noritsu Kenkyusho*) in 1922, had to work as management consultants outside academia. This tradition was to be continued throughout the postwar period.[3]

Ueno worked towards spreading the ideas of industrial efficiency among practising managers, helping forward the regional associations which had been born spontaneously and were to be organized into the Japanese Federation of Management Associations (*Nihon Noritsu Rengokai*) in 1927. In 1925, he also founded the Japanese branch of the Taylor Society. As its chairman, and through writing, lecturing, consultancy, and committee work, he continued to spread the idea of scientific management, transforming it so as to adapt it to the Japanese business climate. Indeed, it was widely diffused as *Noritsu* (efficiency). Ueno's management philosophy, based on both scientific management and oriental Buddhism, was well on the way to creation. The efficiency movement was even seen as a kind of traditional spiritual movement. This is the reason why it was called *Noritsu-do*; as in *Ju-do* or *Ken-do*, the term *do* means not only physical practice but also spiritual training. Ueno opened the Noritsu-do School in 1941. It developed into the Nihon Noritsu Gakko; then, from 1942, Ueno issued a new version of the monthly journal, *Noritsu-do*.

In the same year, the Japanese Federation of Management Associations and the Japanese Industrial Association (*Nihon Kogyo Kyokai*, created by the government in 1931) were brought together by the Ministry of Commerce and Industry to form the Japanese Management Association (*Nihon Noritsu Kyokai*), for training production management engineers and increasing wartime production. After the war, the Japanese Management

Association was freed from government control and grew into a powerful management education organization. In 1949, Ueno presided over the newly formed All-Japan Federation of Management Associations (*Zen Nihon Noritsu Renmei*), a body which was developed as an umbrella association for the various management education organizations, giving accreditation to the business qualifications conferred by its members. Ueno also continued to work on developing his school as a vehicle for the promotion of industrial efficiency. It was upgraded to a junior college – the Industrial Efficiency (*Sangyo Noritsu*) College – in 1950, and after his death, in 1978, became a four-year management science university, *Sangyo Noritsu Daigaku*. Ueno was also a pioneering spirit in the evolution of management consultancy as a profession. In 1951, he established the Institute of Management Consultants, which is very highly regarded today (Saito 1984: chs 4–6; Ueno 1967: II).

Later, in 1979, the Sanno Management School was established as a subsidiary of Sanno College to develop the abilities of managers and executives. The school aimed to provide a high-level curriculum with a mixture of Japanese traditional business know-how and modern American production management. In 1981, the JMA Management School was formed to bring together all its educational activities and to function as a comprehensive specialist organization for management education. JMA runs annually more than 1,400 seminars and course meetings, in which around 60,000 people participate, and about a hundred conferences and symposia for executives and specialists on a broad range of subjects. Moreover, each year, approximately 2,500 training programmes are conducted by JMA's instructors on the premises of client companies. These programmes cover management development, sales-force development, worker training, motivation, and so on. Together, in the late 1980s, they had 1,250 full-time employees, with educational activities accounting for 40 per cent of total business (Okazaki-Ward 1993: 462–71, 487; Yonekawa *et al.* 1990: 62–3).

DEVELOPMENT OF THE MANAGERIAL FUNCTION

'New managers' and Keizai Doyukai

It has been argued that the silent characteristic of management in postwar Japan was the separation of ownership and management and the development of control of leading enterprises by professional managers. As a result of radical economic democratization, such as the *Zaibatsu* Dissolution, large-scale owners disappeared and control was increasingly exercised by management. This has also been described as employees' sovereignty (*Jugyoin Shuken*), instead of stockholders' sovereignty, which means that companies belong to managers and workers rather than to stockholders, and that the providers of human resources, not the capitalists or financiers, have the sovereignty (Itami 1993: 50–2; Okamoto 1973: 163).

In the course of postwar economic reform, the top managements of leading companies were totally reshuffled. More than 2,000 of Japan's foremost business leaders were purged, and were largely replaced by 'new managers'. This extensive purge of the leading executives of large firms left a sudden void, which was filled by promoting senior middle managers within their own companies. Kazuo Noda, a founding member of Keizai Doyukai, argues that 'the purge brought new and fresh opportunities for [the] young generation of corporate managers', and shows that 'the average ages of those who were presidents at the time of surrender and of those who had become new presidents by early 1952 were 60.2 and 51.8 years old, respectively' (Noda 1963: 260–1). Freed from the control of the holding company and from stringent government regulations, the long pent-up energies of younger men found fresh outlets.

The managerial elite in postwar Japan had a very high level of educational background. Around 90 per cent of the business executives of the 1960s were graduates of universities and colleges, which were, as mentioned above, largely inaugurated as a result of the epoch-making decision to expand higher education after the First World War. Professor Wakimura suggests that, in the 1920s, these young executives were the first generation to have studied seriously economics and management. Japanese universities started to take business education seriously around 1919–20. In 1919, independent faculties of economics were set up at the Imperial Universities of Tokyo and Kyoto (Wakimura 1983: 96). In 1920, Tokyo University of Commerce came into being, as well as a number of private universities. It was the graduates of these institutions who became the 'new' management executives in postwar Japan.

The new system of 'control by management' was to accompany certain institutionally patterned motivational orientations, which may provide some clues to understanding the behaviour of postwar managers. The younger managers formed the organization of business leaders, advancing new ideas and aiming to promote the development of the capability of incumbent managers. While *Nikkeiren* played the most significant role in the making of postwar industrial relations, and energetically drove vocational and technical education, *Keizai Doyukai* was assiduous at seeking the development of the managerial function. It took as its model the United States Committee of Economic Development, but was stronger on ideas. In Japan, the organization was known as the 'representative spokesman of the philosophy of new business leaders' (Yamashita 1992: 1).

Keizai Doyukai was founded in 1946 as a fellow union of 'progressive businessmen', under the presidency of Kanichi Moroi, who also presided over *Nikkeiren* when it was inaugurated in 1948. Moroi was a graduate of the economics faculty at Tokyo in 1921 and an intimate friend of the Marxist economist Tatsuo Morito, who had been jailed. At its inception, the committee of *Keizai Doyukai* was composed of progressive young business leaders who were concerned with the problems of reconstruction and democratization of the Japanese economy. Of the twenty-nine committee members elected from its eighty promoters, twenty one were in their forties. They had spent their youth or student life in the late *Taisho* era, when the popular democratic movement known as the *Taisho* Democracy was booming. It was also the age of the great expansion in higher education, and the time when Marxism emerged and flowered among Japanese intellectuals. The influence of liberalism and Marxism was so great that these young intellectuals were to be very sympathetic to labour problems and disputes when they became managers. These factors seem to have had a very significant meaning during the turmoil of postwar reconstruction (Keizai Doyukai 1956: 11–24; Okamoto 1973: 165, 171–4; Toba 1970: 327–31, 338–41; Yamashita 1992: 7–25).

The members of *Doyukai* started declaring themselves as 'the men of the management function', and they tried to bring about the revolution of democratization from that viewpoint. As a committee member, Banjo Otsuka organized the study group on economic democratization in 1947. He insisted on radical economic democratization, and called it 'modified capitalism'. Otsuka was a classmate and good friend of Nobusuke Kishi, who graduated from Tokyo in 1920 and became an able Minister of Commerce and Industry. Since the late 1930s, Otsuka had energetically advocated the separation of ownership and management, which was also promoted by the 'Innovative Bureaucrats' (*Kakushin Kanryo*). Much earlier, Teijiro Ueda of Tokyo University of Commerce had stressed the social significance of the managerial function in his article on 'Socialism and the Function of Entrepreneur' (1921) (reprinted in his *Social Reform and Business Enterprise* 1926).

Otsuka's proposals for economic democratization were something like the following. First, he advocated the co-ownership of business enterprise by management, capital, and labour – managers and workers who provided management and labour should be equal to stockholders. Second, he proposed the democratization of joint stock companies by means of the *Keiei Kyogi-kai*, where workers, like managers, would have voting power – the General Assembly (*Kigyo Sokai*), consisting of the triple representatives of management, labour, and capital, should be the highest decision-making organization. Third, stockholders would only be constituent members of the company and provide capital, in the same way as managers provided management and workers provided labour – profits should be shared equally by the three parties. Although this proposal was quite progressive, it remained a tentative plan of the study group. However, its basic concepts seem to have materialized eventually during the course of the productivity movement (Keizai Doyukai 1956: 73–84; Otsuka 1947: 2–9; Ueda 1926; Yamashita 1992: 17–21).

The Japanese Productivity Centre and the diffusion of in-firm training

The year 1955 is said to have been the beginning of the age of the development of the managerial function. It marked an era of the institutionalization of management education as part of in-firm training. On the political front, the Liberal Democratic Party won the election in that year, and remained in power until very recently, providing a stable and pro-business environment. Two prominent external training organizations were also born in 1955, with powerful backing from both business organizations and government: *Nihon Sangyo Kunren Kyokai* and the Japanese Productivity Centre. They met the need for management development in industry, with which the graduate schools of the higher academic institutions were neither willing nor equipped to deal. Essentially, that need was concerned with the practical competence to manage specific and individual problems rather than the acquisition of theoretical and abstract notions (Okazaki-Ward 1993: 34–5; Sakamoto 1964: 172).

The Japanese Productivity Centre (JPC – *Nihon Seisansei Honbu*) was founded in 1955 as a result of a nationwide campaign for the improvement of productivity, against the background of a flowering European productivity movement under the United States' Marshall Plan. The idea of JPC dates back to *Doyukai*'s annual meeting in 1953. In that year, *Doyukai*'s intellectual leader and secretary, Kohei Goshi, communicated his recent experiences in Europe, where he had been very impressed by the industrial relations and cooperation of managers and workers in West Germany and the productivity movement in Britain. Graham Hutton's *We Too Can Prosper* (1953) greatly stimulated Goshi, and he was especially and profoundly interested in the following remarks: 'The secret of the high productivity of the U.S. is not in the machine . . . it lies in the unreserved collaboration of the worker and the boss.'

The United States' government representative suggested to Goshi that United States technical aid for higher productivity in European countries might also be extended to Japan. As a result of Doyukai's efforts, four leading business organizations in Japan – the Federation of Economic Organizations, the Japanese Chamber of Commerce and Industry, *Nikkeiren*, and *Doyukai* – met and reached an agreement that the productivity movement should be launched in Japan. As a result, the Japanese Productivity Council was set up in 1954. At the time, Japan's Labour Ministry was concerned with improving labour productivity and translating International Labour Organization (ILO) reports; and the Japanese Ministry of International Trade and Industry (MITI) itself intended to establish a non-governmental productivity centre. The Japanese Productivity Council then dissolved itself into the Japanese Productivity Centre, composed of representatives of workers, managers, and neutrals, under the vice-presidency of Ichiro Nakayama, president of Hitotsubashi University and also of the Central Labour Committee. Professor Nakayama was a serious and conceptual advocate of the Management Council (*Keiei Kyogi-kai*) and the Workers–Managers Joint Consultancy (*Roshi Kyogi-sei*), the in-firm organization designed to promote the collaboration of managers and workers. The Workers–Managers Joint Consultancy was the pivotal notion of Japan's productivity movement, and has been disseminated into almost all leading companies (Carew 1987: ch. 9; Goshi 1990: 28–44, 242–54; Nihon Seisansei Honbu 1985: chs 1–2).

The members of *Keizai Doyukai* determined on 'the recognition and practice of social responsibility by the managerial persons' in 1956. They stressed the importance of fostering and training their successor managers – not merely for business itself but also for society. Then *Doyukai* stated that 'business corporations are now [the] public instruments of [the] national economy' and that 'the constant development of the business firms is the great responsibility of the managers'. It asserted that the 'long term development of business firms could not be expected without [the] quantitative enlargement and qualitative advancement of the managerial persons', and emphasized the significance of the self-development of managers and the fostering of successor managers who had both intelligence and management technique. In 'the opinion on the development of managers' resolved in 1958, *Doyukai* stressed the necessity of institutionalizing management education and set up a long term education programme in business firms (Keizai Doyukai 1961: 391–7, 414–19, 422–4).

Doyukai, who had already opened the Management Academy (Keiei Daigaku), presented a statement about 'the development of the managers' in 1958 and stressed the importance of self-development of managers and the fostering of their successors. By means of an 'Income Doubling' Policy (*Shotoku Baizo Seisaku*), attention to the training of human resources was rapidly strengthened and management education was diffused. Against this background, education and training by JPC was accelerated. In 1960, JPC asserted that it would 'carry out . . . systematic and organized management education with the idea of industry-university cooperation'. The Labour Productivity Academy was opened in 1964 for the training of specialists in labour problems and to inform on the concept of industrial cooperation. In 1965, the Academy of Management Development was established as a part-time graduate business school: the prospectus states that 'it is not too much to say that the most important thing for today's business is the problem of "manpower", not the power of money' (*Nihon Kindai Kyoiku 100 Nenshi* 1973: 673–5; Okazaki-Ward 1993: 455–62).

Around the year 1960, Japan's management education was in transition – from the assimilation of American management techniques to systematization and Japanization. Japanese experts had begun taking over from American ones in management seminars and consultancy activities. In 1958,

JPC started a full-time one-year management course for training consultants. The first *Karuisawa* seminar for top management was also held in the same year. A boom in management studies was created, and the publication of books on management flourished – that year, too, Fujiyoshi Sakamoto wrote a textbook in layman's language. Two years earlier, in 1956, Peter Drucker's *Automation and New Society* had been translated, and Keio held its first top management seminar, with the cooperation of the Harvard Business School. Systematization also meant, at the same time, Japanization. The Fifth Anniversary Declaration of JPC said, in 1960, that it should be aimed at the application of new overseas management techniques to the Japanese social and economic climate. Japanization had to be practised and carried out through firm-specific education and training.

JPC conducted a wide range of programmes of management development – from new recruits through to board directors, overseas study teams, management guidance teams, workers–managers cooperative committees, the Labour Productivity Academy, and the Academy of Management Development. With the philosophy of 'business depends on people', the section on management education provided a variety of seminars and courses. In 1961, thirty-eight kinds of seminar were conducted; and, in the following year, fifty-four varieties of seminar and six sorts of course. The numbers of people who attended the seminars were 1,147 in 1960 and 1,285 in 1961; in 1962, 1,871 people attended seminars and 367 went to courses (Nihon Seisansei Honbu 1985: ch. 3; Okazaki-Ward 1993: 35–6, 455–62; Sakamoto 1964: 143–4, 172–3, 180).

As shown by a questionnaire survey conducted by the Japanese Society of Industrial Training in 1970, about 42 per cent of the 855 companies which replied were undertaking education for 'executives' (*Keieisha*), 85 per cent for 'management' (*Kanrisha*), and 75 per cent for 'middle management'. With regard to the onset of this, 75 per cent was concentrated in the period after 1961. The content of education for 'executives' consisted of various seminars – such as top management seminars, overseas study teams, study meetings within the company, and so forth. However, with the progress of management education, executives were getting through the programmes organized by their own companies quite rapidly: in 1965, for example, training within companies reached 36 per cent (Nihon Sangyo Kunren Kyokai 1970; *Nihon Kindai Kyoiku 100 Nenshi* 1973: 658–62).

During the 1960s, in-firm management education and training were diffused very extensively, against the background of high-speed economic growth. Many pioneering companies had their own educational policy or educational programme to meet their firm-specific needs on the condition of 'lifetime employment'. The diffusion of in-firm education and the formation of firm-specific training presaged the progress of Japanization. Business organizations such as *Kaizai Doyukai* and *Nikkeiren*, and external bodies like the Japanese Management Association and the Productivity

Centre, appear to have played a vital role in the diffusion of firm-specific training – especially at the initial stages.

NOTES

1 Where no other reference is given, this part of the chapter is based on Nishizawa (1994).
2 The book was translated in an abridged form by Fukuda in 1930; see *Koyama Kenzo Den*, Osaka: Sanjushi Ginko.
3 For Yoichi Ueno and his work, see Saito (1984) and Ueno (1967). For scientific management in Japan, see, for example, Daito (1989: 1–28), Hara (1990) and Sasaki (1992).

REFERENCES

Amano, I. (1978) *Kyusei Senmon Gakko*, Tokyo: Nihon Keizai Shinbunsha.

Aonuma, Y. (1965) *Nihon no Keieiso*, Tokyo: Nihon Keizai Shinbunsha.

Aso, M. (1991) *Nihon no Gakureki Elite*, Tokyo: Tamagawa Daigaku Shuppanbu.

Beigel, R. (1898) *Der Kampf um die Handelshochschule*, Leipzig: Verlag der Handels-Academie Leipzig.

Carew, A. (1987) *Labour under the Marshall Plan*, Manchester: Manchester University Press.

Daito, E. (1989), 'Railway and Scientific Management in Japan 1907–30', *Business History* 31: 1–28.

Goshi, K. (1990) *Goshi Kohei: Seisansei to Tomoni*, Tokyo: Nihon Seisansei Honbu.

Hara, T. (ed.) (1990) *Kagakuteki-kanriho no Donyu to Tenkai*, Kyoto: Showado.

Hitotsubashi 50 Nenshi (1925) Tokyo: Tokyo Shoka Daigaku.

Hitotsubashi Senmon-bu, Kyoin Yoseijo-shi (1951) Tokyo: Hitotsubashi Senmon-bu, Kyoin Yoseijo.

Institute for International Cooperation (ed.) (n.d.) *Japan's Industrialization and Human Resources Development*, Tokyo: Japanese International Cooperation Agency.

Itami, H. (1993) *Jinpon-shugi Kigyo*, Tokyo: Chikuma Bunko.

Keizai Doyukai (1956) *Keizai Doyukai 10 Nenshi*, Tokyo: Keizai Doyukai.

—— (1961) *Keizai Doyukai 15 Nenshi*, Tokyo: Keizai Doyukai.

Komiya, R. (1963) *Sengo Nihon no Keizaiseicho*, Tokyo: Iwanami Shoten.

Nihon Kindai Kyoiku 100 Nenshi (1973) Tokyo: Kokuritsu, Kyoiku Kenkyujo, 10.

Nihon Sangyo Kunren Kyokai (1970) *Wagakuni no Kigyonai-kyoiku no Genjo*, Tokyo: Nihon Sangyo Kunren Kyokai.

—— (1971) *Nihon Sangyo Kunren 100 Nenshi*, Tokyo: Nihon Sangyo Kunren Kyokai.

Nihon Seisansei Honbu (1985) *Seisansei Undo 30 Nenshi*, Tokyo: Nihon.Seisansei Honbu.

Nishizawa, T. (1994) 'The making of Japan's business elites: Tokyo University of Commerce in its historical perspective', in T. Yuzawa (ed.) *Japanese Business Success: The Evolution of a Strategy*, London: Routledge.

Noda, K. (1963) 'Sengo Nihon no Keieisha', in R. Komiya (ed.) *Sengo Nihon no Keizaiseicho*, Tokyo: Iwanami Shoten.

Nonaka, I. (1994) 'The Process of Company-wide Quality Control and Quality Circles at Toyota and Nissan', Paper presented at the 21st Fuji Conference, 6 January 1994.

Okamoto, H. (1973) 'Management and their Organizations', in K. Okochi *et al.* (eds) *Workers and Employers in Japan*, Tokyo: University of Tokyo Press.

Okazaki-Ward, L. (1993) *Management Education and Training in Japan*, London: Graham & Trotman.

Okochi, K. *et al.* (eds) (1973) *Workers and Employers in Japan*, Tokyo: University of Tokyo Press.

Otsuka, B. (1947) 'Keizai Minshuka to Sono Gutaisaku', *Keieisha*, 1: 2–9.

Ouchi, H. (1970) *Keizaigaku 50 Nen I*, Tokyo: Tokyo Daigaku Shuppankai.

Saito, T. (1984) *Ueno Yoichi: Hito to Gyoseki*, Tokyo: Sangyo Noritsu Daigaku.

Sakamoto, F. (1964) *Nihon Keiei Kyoiku-shi Josetsu*, Tokyo: Daiyamondosha.

Sasaki, S. (1992) 'The Introduction of Scientific Management by Mitsubishi Electric Engineering Co. and the Formation of an Organized Scientific Management Movement in Japan in the 1920s and 1930s', *Business History* 34: 12–27.

Shiryo (1982) *Hitotsubashi Daigaku Gakuseishi Shiryo*, 2 (1886–1901).

—— (1983a) *Hitotsubashi Daigaku Gakuseishi Shiryo*, 3 (1902–9).

—— (1983b) *Hitotsubashi Daigaku Gakuseishi Shiryo*, 8 (1924–45).

Sugiyama, C. and Nishizawa, T. (1987) '"Captain of Industry": Tokyo Commercial School at Hitotsubashi', in C. Sugiyama and H. Mizuta (eds) *Enlightenment and Beyond*, Tokyo: Tokyo University Press.

Toba, K. (ed.) (1970) *Zaikai-jin no Kyoiku-kan, Gakumon-kan*, Tokyo: Daiyamondosha.

Ueda, T. (1926) 'Shakaishugi to Kigyosha no Shokubun' (1921) in *Shakai-kaizo to Kigyo*, Tokyo: Dobunkan.

—— (1975a) *Ueda Teijiro Nikki (1905–18)*, Tokyo: Keio Tsushinsha.

—— (1975b) *Ueda Teijiro Zenshu*, 1, Tokyo: Daisan Shuppan.

Ueno, I. (ed.) (1967) *Ueno Yoichi Den*, Tokyo: Sangyo Noritsu Tanki Daigaku.

Wakimura, Y. (1983) 'Sengo Keieishi no Shuppatsuten: Zaibatsu Kaitai', *Hitotsubashi Business Review* 31(2): 88–98.

Yamashita, S. (1992) *Sengo Keieisha no Gunzo*, Tokyo: Nihon Keizai Shinbunsha.

Yonekawa, S. (1984) 'University Graduates in Japanese Enterprises before the Second World War', *Business History* 26: 193–218.

—— (1987) *Hitotsubashi 100 Nen: Captain of Industry no Ayumi*, Tokyo: Josui-kai.

—— Yuzawa, T., and Nishizawa, T. (1990) 'The Development of Economics and Business Education in Japan', *Shiryo Supplement* 58–9.

6

MANAGEMENT EDUCATION IN A COUNTRY IN TRANSITION

The case of Slovenia[1]

Marjan Svetličič and Andreja Čibron

INTRODUCTION

Among a variety of problems, all countries in transition are also faced with the major bottleneck of a lack of adequate managers. No transition programmes, even those which might seem ideal, can be efficiently executed if there are no managers who can implement well-designed market-oriented reforms and make former state-owned enterprises efficient and internationally competitive. Many laws and regulations are therefore not being put into effect, and the results of the transition lag substantially behind expectations because of the lack of appropriate leadership and management. It is only now being recognized (at least in some countries) that implementation of the transformation process is just as important as the ideas behind it.

The managerial gap is without doubt one of the very pressing needs which face all countries in transition (Kraljič 1990). It is inconceivable that managers of previously state-owned companies can become efficient overnight at the transformation of newly privatized companies into internationally competitive ones. Nor can it be readily imagined that the newly emerging political or business elite can play this role without additional instruction: namely, without substantial on-the-job training in the new market-economy conditions, together with substantial exposure to international competition. Management education seems, therefore, to be a much more important part of the transformation process than is usually recognized. Nevertheless, it is not enough to be satisfied with just any kind of management education. Countries in transition often tend automatically to copy foreign, particularly American, experience; but there are other approaches.

In order to correct the past errors of not developing management education at all, or only on a very limited scale, most countries in transition have immediately started up a wide variety of management training

111

programmes. There is certainly an impression of 'inflation', of differing design and quality, in the number of such programmes. According to some commentators, after the almost total absence of this kind of education, many countries in transition are moving to the opposite extreme of establishing too many management education programmes, which are too thrown together, pushing the issue of quality into the background. Management education has become so popular that many students interested in economics want to study general management even at the undergraduate level.[2]

Some programmes of management training have emerged from the bottom, on the basis of companies' own initiative and financing; others have been initiated from the top by the government. Regarded objectively, countries in transition are in the position of latecomers – a situation that can be beneficial, provided that they are able to learn from the past experiences of their predecessors and not repeat their mistakes.

Although nearly all such programmes are of very recent origin, it seems important to start evaluating their performance – their role in the transition process and the impact of the newly educated MBA graduates on the improving performance of their companies – at once. It has been decided, therefore, that certain aspects of managerial education in Slovenia, and of the role of MBA graduates in the transition process, should be assessed through a survey of these graduates. Of course, such an approach has many bottlenecks, but fewer, it is thought, than a mere academic evaluation would have.

The objectives of this chapter are threefold. First, the different MBA programmes in Slovenia will be assessed by their graduates. Second, the major characteristics/problems of such programmes will be identified. Finally, the extent to which management training is instrumental in speeding up the transformation process, and improving the performance of companies, will be estimated.

The questionnaires used covered the major MBA programmes in Slovenia and each contained twenty-three questions.[3] With one exception, the questionnaires were distributed to those students who had already graduated from MBA courses.[4] The exception applied to students of the course at Radovljica, which had not then produced its first graduates. While taking the results of the survey as a basis for this chapter, separate observations will also be made.

SOME CHARACTERISTICS OF THE SLOVENE ECONOMY

The role of managers in the Slovene economy, particularly in the transition period, cannot properly be understood without stating some basic facts about that economy. Slovenia, an almost fully developed country with a

GDP of about $6,000 per capita, achieved legal independence on 8 October 1991, after the disintegration of Yugoslavia. Slovenia's 'transition' process is therefore fourfold: from a regional to a national economy, from a planned to a market economy (marketization), from a socialized to a private property-owning economy (privatization), and from a single-party to a democratic political system (democratization) (Senjur 1993: 121). It thus has additional problems – related to building up the national economy – which other countries in transition do not face.

The relatively well-developed industrial structure is reflected in a high rate of exports per capita (higher in 1993 than that of Japan). The share of agriculture in the GDP is under 5 per cent. Moreover, owing to an early political and economic opening, the activities of Slovene companies have achieved a rather high level of internationalization. In 1993, more than eighty-seven Slovene companies were established abroad, as well as some banks. Moreover, quite remarkable market shares were acquired in the export of some articles. High-technology goods constituted nearly 20 per cent of total Slovene exports in 1993, and the trade balance was positive. This serves to indicate that the structure and level of development of the Slovene economy is somewhat higher than that of most other former socialist economies. The 'natural' consequence is that there is also a higher level of managerial expertise, and the capabilities of Slovene managers have been considered as better than those of other former socialist countries. Interviews of eight foreign investors in Slovenia in 1991 demonstrated that, in 57 per cent of cases, they assessed the skills and abilities of Slovene managers as being the same as those of the foreign parent; in 63 per cent of cases, as being better than those of Central and Eastern Europe; and, in 67 per cent of cases, as being better even than those of other less-developed European countries (Rojec and Svetličič 1993: 149).

This merely proves that the transition process in Slovenia is somehow different from that of other former socialist countries, not less painful or problem free. From a managerial point of view, indeed, the major difficulty in building up the national economy is the loss of market in the former Yugoslav republics. Managers have to compensate for this by exporting to other markets. This task is the more formidable in view of the fact that, previously, the Yugoslav market accounted for more than 50 per cent of sales. A high export orientation, however, traditionally to the European Economic Community countries, makes the necessary transformation easier.[5]

THE GENESIS AND CHARACTERISTICS OF MANAGEMENT EDUCATION IN SLOVENIA: THE SUPPLY SIDE

Although the real boom in management education started in 1990 – that is, prior to independence – its origin dates well back into the structure of the earlier socialist system.[6] Perhaps one of the most important reasons for this is the fact that Slovene companies had achieved a relatively autonomous status – due to a more modest market-oriented economic reform in 1965.[7] The need for modern management techniques, and knowledge of world markets, started to emerge in parallel with the strengthening of the export orientation of companies. First, by 1977 the Chamber of Economy had already organized specialized short courses for sales managers and others dealing with foreign markets in general.[8] These were compulsory for all those involved in foreign trade operations. With the growing demand for more complex knowledge, the Chamber of Economy initiated the establishment of another training centre at Brdo, which later became the independent International Executive Development Centre, offering a wide range of different courses.

While these programmes were mostly initiated from the top down, the University of Ljubljana started management education from the bottom up in spite of the fact that the social sciences at the University were strongly influenced by Marxism. Indeed, many programmes have begun to include more micro-economic issues. Marketing started to be taught at the Faculty of Economics at Ljubljana as early as 1970.[9] In addition, more formal business education programmes started well before the fall of the Berlin Wall: for instance, at the Faculty of Economics and the Faculty of Social Sciences (both at Ljubljana) in 1969 and 1988 respectively. The new School for Economics and Commerce, with its two-year undergraduate programme which evolved into a four-year programme in 1968, was established in Maribor in 1959, in order to undertake a more business-oriented syllabus. Later, it developed into the Faculty of Business and Economics. Some companies – like Iskra[10] (the largest exporter in Yugoslavia at the time) and Slovenijales, which had two of the more ambitious and permanent approaches – initiated their own courses for managers. There are also some other institutions which undertake short courses for managers – such as GEA College, established in 1989 as a joint venture between some professors from the Faculty of Economics and some entrepreneurs.

MBA curricula now take different forms in Slovenia. They consist mostly of a combination of theoretical or classroom lectures with case studies – seminar discussions, group and individual presentations, and hands-on experience in companies. Different schools differ over the share that each of these constituents should have. All schools try to combine their own local experiences with those of 'foreign experts in order to get a new quality' (Purg 1993). There is, however, a great variety in the extent of foreign teaching in MBA programmes in Slovenia, ranging from 95 per cent in the most internationally oriented school (IEDC in Brdo) and 70 per cent at ICPE in Ljubljana to two programmes at the Faculty of Economics at Ljubljana and the Faculty of Business and Economics at Maribor where approximately 30 per cent of the curricula are carried out by foreign teachers. Part of the programmes is carried out abroad, or in firms, in order to combine theory with practice. Foreign partners are usually found among well-known MBA schools in the United States or Europe. For example, IEDC Brdo has developed a long-standing cooperative relationship with such institutions as IMD, Harvard University, and INSEAD. The Faculty of Economics at Ljubljana has developed a similar relationship with Indiana, Cornell, and Kellog Universities, and the Faculty of Business and Economics at Maribor with, mostly, neighbouring universities in Austria, but with some universities from the United States as well.

Schools also differ in terms of the duration of their courses and the number of candidates they accept. Moreover, some of the programmes are for local candidates only, while others include, in addition, foreign participants (IEDC Brdo and ICPE Ljubljana, for instance). And in some schools, teaching is only in English (IEDC and ICPE), while in others it is partly in English and partly in Slovene.

IEDC trains annually about thirty students. The duration of their study is one year: seventeen weeks of training, divided into four time periods. ICPE's MBA course is also of one year's duration. The Faculty of Business and Economics at Maribor has a two-year MBA course with 910 hours of teaching. Students participate in one week's training, after which they return to work; then they again have one week's training, and so on. The MBA course at Radovljica's Faculty of Economics takes 700 hours and students have to stay at the school and study for the whole time. The sample quoted here was evenly distributed between those who concluded IEDC's one-year programme and those from other programmes, who took an average of three years to graduate.

The survey shows that MBA graduates in Slovenia found almost all elements of the different MBA programmes there adequate. The selection of themes, the proportionate share of theory, the format of training, were all well accepted by the students. The style of the courses and the volume of the programmes were considered as adequate by a large majority of the sample (85 per cent). Training methods, the quality of foreign teachers, and the proportionate share of practical knowledge were considered less adequate, but still very satisfactory (71 per cent, 68 per cent, and 65 per cent of respondents respectively).

In spite of the fact that foreign teachers are considered better than local ones, the survey clearly demonstrated that foreign teachers, although highly qualified, are not sufficiently familiar with the local environment. Assessing the general performance of local as compared with foreign teachers, MBA students rated the former better than would have been expected. Only 18 per cent of the survey's respondents considered local teachers as inadequate. For 48 per cent they were partly adequate, and 33 per cent were of the opinion that they were completely satisfactory. If these results are combined with those in Table 6.1, which demonstrate a more detailed comparative evaluation of the quality of local and foreign teachers, an even more promising conclusion could be drawn: namely, that the large majority of students were of the opinion that some local teachers could compete with their foreign counterparts though others could not. Respondents seemed to believe that if local teachers specialized abroad it would make them competitive.

The results support the opinion of many experts that a productive combination of local and foreign expertise is probably the best. A good example of this is the style of Norwegian management education which tries to combine eclectically foreign, particularly American, experience with local comparative advantages, tradition, and mentality (see Chapter 2 above). A similar combination is also sought in Slovenia.[11]

DEMAND FOR AN MBA EDUCATION

Although the present expansion of management education in Slovenia can be taken as a sign of the belief that managers can be educated and are not necessarily born or trained on the job, the clear conclusion of the survey was that good managers have to have plenty of 'hands-on' experience as well as a proper formal training.[12] They have to have special personal characteristics, and adequate knowledge and skills. It is not surprising, therefore, that the first wave of management education has targeted existing managers – with short courses and, later, with the development of more regular postgraduate MBA courses.[13] Interest and demand have now increased so much that regular general management education programmes

Table 6.1 Evaluation of the quality of teachers (per cent)

Statement	Agree fully	Agree	Neither agree nor disagree	Disagree	Disagree fully
Some local teachers can compete with foreign ones others cannot	32	51	15	2	–
A combination of foreign and local teachers is best	49	32	17	2	–
If sent abroad for specialization, local teachers would be competitive	23	46	28	1	1
Foreign teachers are good but are not familiar with the local environment	9	5	28	11	1
Local teachers lag behind in quality but know the local environment better	11	38	25	21	5

have already started at the undergraduate level.[14] Indeed, there is an impression that universities are going from the extreme in the past of neglecting the need for such programmes, to the other extreme of overemphasizing them at the undergraduate level, as though management skills can only be taught in the classroom.

Individual or micro-economic demand is best illustrated by the factors which contributed to the decision of those MBA graduates who were interviewed for the survey to start their studies. It was unquestionably their own personal decision: for as many as 74 per cent of them, it was their own initiative.[15] It is important to note, however, that the general characteristic of this group of MBA students is above-average motivation and self-confidence which is sometimes referred to as 'cold-blooded arrogance'. Companies influenced MBA study in only 17 per cent of cases. Personal initiatives nevertheless mostly met with support from firms, since 75 per cent of students were financed by their companies and only 11 per cent had a scholarship. Clearly firms are stimulating management training, but this is not (yet) a systematic policy for strengthening their competitive advantage nor a means of promotion in a business career. In view of the dearth of scholarships or any other sort of methodical support of such programmes, it is not yet systematic government policy either. However, the climate improved in 1993–4 when the government of Slovenia launched a special support programme: 'Training of Managers for Restructuring', according to which companies and training institutions were able to get up to 50 per cent of co-financing for their management training programmes. The demand for co-financing was so high that the government had an almost insurmountable difficulty in selecting those who would get such support. The first such programme was launched in October 1993 and the second one in June 1994. Part of the 1993 programme was transferred to the 1994 one in view of the lack of funds.[16] In addition, the government is thinking of submitting to parliament a special law according to which large and medium-sized companies will have to invest 2 per cent of their income for the training of managers and employees in general.

Demand for MBA graduates by firms is evenly distributed among industrial and service companies (45 per cent and 47 per cent respectively). Demand by the civil service is apparently very low, although the quality of governance is one of the most important factors in the success of the transition. There are two explanations for lagging demand by the government and civil service. First, the inherited culture of the traditional civil service does not require modern business-like attitudes. Second, the 'push' factors of the transition are much stronger in industry: it is forced to become efficient in order to survive. This pressure is not so strong in the civil service. Government spending which is too high is often criticized by business, but this criticism is usually countered by the argument that it is a necessary stage in the building of a new state.

The large share of MBA graduates coming from service sector firms demonstrates their greater flexibility and responsiveness to the needs of the transition process. Such firms plainly need good managers and new ideas in order to prosper in the new market environment and on the international scene. Many of the new companies demanding MBA graduates are also embarking on innovative types of business like consultancy.[17] When deciding to study for their MBA, some young professionals now working for large firms are thinking of starting their own companies if and when the opportunity presents itself.

As shown in Table 6.2, large firms are the major customers of the MBA schools, especially some of them. They are usually among the most efficient companies, from sectors characterized by powerful international competition, and with a strong need to export or internationalize their activities. Other companies have not yet developed the need for a better educated younger generation of managers, partly because many still enjoy a monopoly or oligopoly position and partly because old managerial structures are not too keen to create competition for their own position within firms. This can be applied particularly to companies without clear personnel promotion criteria, where career advancement is more the result of kindness, friendship, and so forth, than of achievement or knowledge.

Table 6.2 MBA graduates according to the size and ownership of the company

Size	Number	Per cent
Large (over 250 employed)	32	49
Medium (50–250)	16	25
Small (up to 50)	15	23
No answer	2	3
Total	65	99
Ownership		
Social ownership	25	38
Private ownership and those in transition (the process of privatization)	24	37
State ownership	10	15
Mixed ownership	4	6
No answer	2	3
Total	65	99

The very high proportion of socially owned firms which remains is a reflection of the fact that the privatization process in Slovenia lags behind that of some of the other countries in transition.[18] Otherwise private companies would easily top the list of firms sending their young managers to MBA schools.

The relatively low proportion of economists and social scientists among MBA graduates (46 per cent of the sample) demonstrates that the demand for such new knowledge is higher among engineers. It also reveals the very high proportion of engineers among those holding middle management positions, who deal with commercial and not technical operations. This is partly a consequence of the salary structure, which is biased against those in direct production, even if they have a university education. Salaries of sales managers were, and still are, substantially higher than those of engineers in narrowly defined technical production positions ('blue-collar' engineers). The latter probably feel very forcefully the lack of commercial knowledge, and are therefore the more keen to enrol in an MBA programme.

MBA courses are rather expensive.[19] High prices effectively reduce the demand for them, along with sufficient adequate candidates able to take study leave from their regular jobs. Many of the best managers, or others in leading positions in firms, are so involved in the restructuring of their companies – in the privatization processes – that they simply cannot afford to take time off to study full time for a year or be away from their companies even for a week each month over a one- or two-year period. Moreover, many potential MBA candidates are not personally interested in doing an MBA course in view of the privatization process which is in progress. They feel that if they are away they might lose out on better chances arising as a result of management buy-out schemes. Families are also considered an important barrier, particularly for students abroad.

IS MBA EDUCATION IN SLOVENIA INSTRUMENTAL IN SPEEDING UP THE TRANSITION PROCESS?

Full-scale implementation of MBA education really started at the same time as the beginning of the fundamental transition process in Slovenia. One of the major criteria for the evaluation of the impact of the MBA, therefore, is whether it has contributed to the speeding up of this process. Have MBA graduates been instrumental in overcoming the various gaps, such as technology, productivity, marketing motivation, and, above all, management (Kraljič 1990)? Of course, it is too early for any complex evaluation. What is possible, is an indirect evaluation which assesses the motives of people who enrol in the MBA programme, their opinions, and whether their new knowledge has had a positive effect on their career advancement.

Although a small country, Slovenia has a number of MBA and other management training programmes. Public opinion quite commonly holds that Slovenia is too small to have so many MBA courses; it is a waste of resources. MBA graduates do not agree. The majority of them welcome such competition; they see competition in this field as productive – as an instrument for improving the quality of the programmes (46 per cent). Moreover, some regard the programmes as complementary (18 per cent). It seems that the market mentality has also penetrated this previously government-dominated field of education.

Managers and other potential MBA students tend to be selective when making a choice from among the different MBA programmes in the country. In the first place, they are convinced that quality programmes exist in Slovenia (69 per cent of the sample) and they therefore try to take advantage of the best curriculum available, in view of their needs. Studying for an MBA abroad has so far not been a real alternative. Slovene MBA students are not usually very familiar with the courses offered. Further reasons are the high cost of such programmes (29 per cent of the sample), and business responsibilities within their companies (13 per cent), which prevent the longer absence of would-be participants (19 per cent).

When answering the question 'Are MBA programmes instrumental in speeding up the transition process or in improving management practices in Slovenia?,' the initial step is to see what determined the decision to start such courses in the first place. An MBA title was not the major motive, nor was the pursuit of a further academic career, nor the reputation of the training institution. Students look for greater knowledge for their business activities rather than formal titles.[20] They seek quality, not prestige. The overwhelming majority claimed that the major driving force was to improve their knowledge (see Table 6.3). This is certainly a very good basis for their future impact on improving the performance of their firms.

Graduates do not consider the MBA title itself as very important, although,

Table 6.3 What motives decisively influenced your decision to start studying for an MBA? (per cent)

Selected more important motives/ranked	Very important	Rather important	Unimportant
Acquisition of managerial knowledge	97	2	1
Better governance and management	80	17	2
New friends and business contacts	52	41	6
Such knowledge is a precondition for success in the transition process	47	34	16
Improvement in English language skills	47	30	22

at the same time, they do not neglect its significance. A large majority considered the formal title as rather important (61 per cent of respondents) while the proportion of those who chose the other possibilities was low and balanced between the extremes (18 per cent of the sample were for 'unimportant', and 17 per cent were for 'very important'). The common situation of many developed countries with a tradition in MBA education of training future teachers of MBA courses does not exist at present in Slovenia. The quality of the professors, the study mode (concentrated or dispersed in time), the topics covered, and English as a working language have been much more important considerations.

Although most of the MBA graduates concluded their studies quite recently, and it is therefore very early to assess whether their acquired knowledge has been instrumental in improving their managerial performance, the great satisfaction with the courses does demonstrate that they have learned a lot. As many as 71 per cent of respondents claimed that their expectations had been met totally, and 15 per cent that these expectations had actually been exceeded. The quality of programmes is, however, rated differently. One programme proved particularly satisfactory: 17 per cent of its graduates claimed that their expectations had been exceeded and 79 per cent that they had been completely met. Nevertheless, 24 per cent of its graduates said that they would opt next time for a similar programme abroad. In the case of another course, MBA graduates had only been partly satisfied (40 per cent of respondents). On the whole, however, managements of MBA schools or programmes should be very satisfied since their courses received very high marks: 31 per cent of respondents gave them the highest grade (5) and 60 per cent the second-highest grade (4). The overwhelming majority, if asked, would choose the same MBA programme again (see Table 6.4).

As many as 54 per cent of graduates are convinced that they became more efficient after concluding their MBA studies, while 29 per cent of them had to change jobs to make the most of the knowledge they had acquired. The

Table 6.4 If asked, would you again select the same MBA programme?

	Number	Per cent
Yes I would	47	72
I would select studies abroad	13	20
I would take another MBA in Slovenia	4	6
I would not study at all	1	2
	65	100

various MBA programmes in Slovenia have clearly served the needs of students, and also of the economy, therefore, well.

The extent of implementation of the new managerial expertise acquired at MBA courses depends greatly on the position of graduates in firms. The impact of top managers is much stronger than that of the lower echelons of management or experts in general. The majority of MBA students in the survey were from middle management positions (40 per cent) in Slovenia. Those from top management positions, however, did not lag too far behind (34 per cent), in spite of the fact that the average age of the student body was between 30 and 39 years.[21] Clearly, the potential of the participants was still very high. All the respondents had four-year university degrees; some even had master's degrees or doctorates (8 per cent). Men represented 85 per cent of all students, in spite of the very high employment rate of women in Slovenia, and the relatively high proportion of them in middle management (particularly the services).

With the exception of local teachers, who were thought to be only partly adequate, graduates of the MBA programmes considered all the different elements of the courses as satisfactory. This assessment has to be modified by the fact that the influence of a small number of poor teachers on the score was decisive. Moreover, if some local teachers had not been considered as less competitive than foreign ones, they would also have been highly graded.

The positive results, regarding the realization of expectations, are striking (see Table 6.5).[22] However, there are also two important negative results – in the fields of career promotions and salaries. With regard to the former, students did not expect a promotion in their career immediately after completing their studies. Since they had just concluded their MBA studies, this expectation proved correct. Only a few were promoted – a detail that is not entirely explained by the fact that there are not very many managerial posts available. A much better explanation, probably, is still provided by the traditional application of a more negative selection criterion – that is, one which takes job experience into account – rather than a positive one based on training and acquired knowledge. MBA studies are sometimes seen more as the rather curious personal foible of an individual student than as company policy. The situation has recently improved, and more companies have started to consider MBA studies as an instrument for the strengthening of their competitiveness. But the very high proportion of those not expecting job promotion demonstrates that the social climate and the value system are not, in general, in favour of education. Slovenia is certainly not alone in developing a kind of rent-seeking mentality – whereby stock exchange speculators have a higher social standing than innovators. Similar arguments apply to the results on salaries. In as many as one-third of cases, expectations have not been met, and MBA graduates have been disappointed.[23] It is not surprising, therefore, that 29 per cent of them

Table 6.5 Were expectations regarding MBA studies realized? (per cent)

Ranking of selected types of expectations	Yes	Partly	No
Acquisition of managerial knowledge	89	11	0
Better governance and management	84	9	3
MBA title	66	8	20
Self-confidence	64	28	5
Improvement of English language	59	25	13
New friends and business contacts	58	34	9
Higher reputation	50	30	14
Such knowledge as a precondition for success in the transition process	42	42	9
More money	33	33	31
The usefulness of an internationally recognized diploma for jobs abroad	31	39	23
Quicker job promotion	30	39	30

Note: Three answers were possible. Figures do not add up to 100 since some respondents did not answer all questions

changed their jobs after finishing an MBA in order to use their newly acquired knowledge better elsewhere.

The low ranking that is given to any consideration of studying for an MBA abroad does not mean that Slovene MBA graduates are oriented only towards the home job market. International recognition of the diploma was quite an important consideration when choosing an MBA programme. For 31 per cent of respondents it was very important, and for as many as 45 per cent, quite significant. This could also indicate that a number of MBA graduates are thinking of the possibility of working for a foreign firm, or of going abroad to work either for a Slovene or for a foreign company.

Respondents attribute considerable importance to the network of business friends they acquired while studying for an MBA. This aspect has not been explored enough in developing the concept of business education in Slovenia. It means, however, that training abroad should increase in importance, if only because it could provide MBA students with a much better network of friends and potential business partners – extremely important for the needs of a small economy. Clearly this is, in fact, the only real advantage of studying for an MBA abroad – according to the survey (see Table 6.6). Svetličič even claimed that at least 20 per cent of Slovene MBA students should study abroad (Svetličič 1994: 357).

In terms of the potential impact of MBA graduates on the transformation process, another approach is one that is related to the type of knowledge they receive and consider as most relevant (see Table 6.7). The accumulation of practical knowledge was considered to be the least

Table 6.6 What would be the advantages of studying for an MBA abroad?

	Number of respondents	Per cent of the sample
Better network of business friends	42	49
More practical knowledge	12	14
Higher quality of training	9	11
More skills	8	12
More suitable programme	5	6
	86	100

Note: Respondents could have indicated up to five answers so the number of respondents does not add up to sixty five

Table 6.7 Which type of knowledge do you consider as the most useful?

Knowledge type/ranked	Number of respondents indicating the knowledge as useful
Financial	44
Marketing	33
Different skills (negotiations etc.)	31
Interpersonal relations	29
International operations	12
	100

Note: It was possible to indicate up to three answers

effective, followed by different skills such as negotiating ones, and marketing.

Given the predominance of engineers among MBA students, these results are predictable. It is a little surprising that MBA graduates gave such a low ranking to knowledge of international operations since Slovene companies are already very internationalized as compared with others from former socialist countries. The necessity of going beyond 'simple' exporting is not yet fully developed, it seems; consequently there is still a need for specific knowledge about the internationalization of a firm's activities. Existing MBA programmes do not contain many courses specially designed to facilitate the international operations of a firm (e.g. courses on investing abroad, or on the operations of multinational companies, or on strategic alliances, and so forth).[24] Most MBA graduates are convinced that their MBA studies gave them sufficient knowledge of the international operations of companies (74 per cent of the sample). Only 15 per cent would like to have been given more knowledge about such activities and 10 per cent different information. Although there are disparities between the various courses in this regard, the main similarity appears to be that no one single programme helped participants much in this sphere.[25] However, while most participants claim that their MBA programmes were useful, one in particular did not provide enough knowledge about international operations.

In general, it is safe to assume that not enough attention is given to the teaching of international management in Slovene MBA programmes. One reason is that the companies themselves have not yet reached a level of internationalization which would trigger off a greater demand for such courses. Examples provided by foreign companies may not be wholly satisfactory, but, on the other hand, there are almost no local ones. It can therefore be concluded that graduates of MBA courses are not yet fully aware of the kind of knowledge they might need for international operations, because they do not consider the latter to be very important.

Finally, in real life, the impact of the newly graduated MBA students depends to a large extent on their acceptance (or, at least, the acceptance of their knowledge) by the firms within which they had previously been working, and which had sent them to study (see Table 6.8). A great number of MBA graduates claim that they were able to use their newly acquired knowledge and skills at once. In some cases, the education of colleagues and adaptation to the old business environment were necessary preconditions for the effective implementation of such new knowledge.

For the new MBA graduates, then, return to their companies was not always accompanied by 'fanfares' alone. Some of them were even forced to change their jobs because of the gap between their knowledge and that of their company 'environment'. This gap was simply too large.

Table 6.8 Have you utilized your knowledge?

	Number of respondents	Per cent of the sample
Immediately	28	43
There was a need to inform associates about the new knowledge	19	29
Adaptation was necessary	10	15
Gap between MBA knowledge and real life was too great to be able to implement the knowledge at once	5	8
No answer	3	5
Total	65	100

SOME CONCLUSIONS

Management education in Slovenia is not only a phenomenon of the transition. It began much earlier. Thus, it is not surprising that a range of programmes are organized by the two universities, and a number of other, also private, institutions, on a commercial basis. This survey has concentrated on selected, more formal MBA courses. Apart from less ambitious surveys, undertaken regularly by each school, it was the first, more comprehensive attempt to evaluate the opinions of MBA graduates and the effectiveness of MBA programmes for their management activities and for the transition process in general. It is therefore a sound basis for further, more centred, and ambitious research.

The supply of management training programmes is indeed diverse. There is competition among them – which has proved to be useful. Certain complementarities exist that are productive in a small country with limited resources. These are not achieved as a result of cooperation between the programmes, which is almost non-existent, but there is also a lot of overlap. Moreover, it is believed that more cooperation in the future would not hurt the very healthy competition between the different programmes. Such cooperation would be particularly useful in efforts to localize the programmes; to prepare Slovene cases; or, in some narrow areas where the Slovene market is too small to achieve a minimum scale of efficiency, to get internationally competitive results. The participation of foreign experts is another area where there could be greater cooperation among programmes, so that resources can be rationalized.

The very great satisfaction of the MBA graduates indicates that MBA programmes in Slovenia are on the right track. They appear to have achieved an appropriate combination of foreign and local expertise. Further efforts should now be put into strengthening local teaching capabilities, in order to localize the most up-to-date foreign expertise and get local MBA programmes at an internationally competitive level. The results of the survey also suggest that local teachers should have added opportunities for a more regular specialization abroad, and that greater efforts should be made to prepare local case studies.

The smallness of the country, and the very high ranking attributed by MBA graduates to the establishment of appropriate business networks, also indicate that there is a need for a more systematic approach to the sending of students abroad to study for their MBA. Such studies offer better opportunities for the establishment of the international business networks which are such a high priority for companies from small countries, for whom internationalization is a question of 'life or death'.

Although respondents to the survey are generally satisfied with the attention given to the international operations of firms, it seems clear nevertheless that this part of the MBA programmes was not given enough attention in view of both the future needs of Slovene firms and long-term trends in the world economy. Taking into consideration the interrelationship of all the different aspects of the international operations of national or multinational firms, the knowledge students acquired from different functional courses (marketing, finance, and so forth) needs, in future, to be integrated in a special course – such as 'international management'. MBA programmes very rarely embark systematically on 'post-exporting' activities – on investing abroad, strategic alliances, and so forth. Long-term strategic thinking is not their strong suit, although their students do not feel this. Most students rarely think of activities beyond exporting either; they are preoccupied with short-term problems and long-term strategy is no more part of their thinking than it is of MBA programmes. A volatile business environment, so important for a small economy, it is felt, is not given enough attention. One of the most important strategic tasks for managers from a small country is time-based competition and a high level of responsiveness to the impulses coming from the external environment; to try, in other words, to find niches and fill them swiftly.

A strong emphasis on the strengthening of the self-confidence of MBA graduates is a particularly important aspect of MBA teaching in Slovenia. Self-confidence is not a strong part of the Slovene character. It is better, however, that this confidence is based on expertise and not a substitute for it, as is sometimes the case.

NOTES

1 We would like to thank the MBA schools which were kind enough o distribute the questionnaire among their graduates; M. Djurdjević, who conducted ten in-depth interviews with MBA graduates; M. Brglez for his invaluable assistance in computing all the data; and N. Flipović, M. Jaklič, T. Papež, and M. Tavčar for their comments on the first version of the chapter.

2 The Faculty of Economics initiated a special undergraduate programme of business/management education in 1994. Out of the total number of third-year students in that year (specialization in business studies only starts in the third year), as many as 82 per cent enrolled in the business/management programme.

3 The survey, carried out in October 1994, included sixty-five graduates from the following MBA programmes: twenty-nine from the International Executive Development Centre (IEDC) at Brdo near Ljubljana, which undertakes a number of training programmes for managers, including a regular one-year MBA programme (started in 1991) that does not lead to a master's degree; twelve from a special MBA school in the Faculty of Economics at Radovljica, which started in 1993; seven from a second MBA programme in the same Faculty, organized in conjunction with the International Centre for Public Enterprises (ICPE) as the latter's international programme, begun in 1989, in which students from Slovenia also participate (they constitute about 25 per cent of all ICPE's students); nine from the Faculty of Business and Economics at Maribor (which started its MBA programme in 1991); and eight from the Faculty of Social Sciences (FSS), which started its first programme on human resource

management as part of postgraduate studies in sociology in 1988 and its second one in 1992. Organized as a joint venture between the Slovene Institute of Management (established in 1990) and FSS, this latter course specializes in management for 'not-for-profit' organizations. In view of the predominance of graduates from IEDC, the whole survey was largely influenced by their responses.

Three programmes were not included. One was the Faculty of Economics' postgraduate programme in business policy and organization, which had already started in 1969. Another was on entrepreneurship, organized by the Faculty of Economics, and due to produce its first graduates in 1994. The third programme, organized by the *Aktiva* Group and the Consortium of Universities for International Business Studies, IAL-Agenzia Formativa del Friuli Venezia Gulia, was started in 1993.

4 Out of sixty-five graduates, over 50 per cent responded – a much higher percentage than in the case of any similar surveys on different subjects in Slovenia where the response rate is extremely low (sometimes less than 10 per cent). This alone demonstrates that the MBA population is different and more inclined to be socially active. It also shows that they cultivate good relations with their schools since some of the questionnaires were sent out by their respective training institutions.

5 By 1990, Slovene companies had already sold over 58 per cent of the country's exports to the European Union. The market share in 1994 was 66 per cent. Even in the 1970s, this share was not substantially lower. For more on Slovenia's competitive advantages, see Svetličič (1994).

6 One of the MBA graduates, Milan Ambrož, drew attention to the fact that 'management' is not an altogether new concept in Slovenia as the publication *Guidelines for Operations of Department Managers*, which is dated around 1920– 30 (the exact date is unknown), proves. It contains numerous very modern management principles, although labelled rather differently. To mention but a few of these: there is the search for the important, and the distinguishing of this from the unimportant (nowadays this would be referred to as a concentration on core competencies); there is the identification of mistakes, learning from them, and reporting on them; there is the nurture of carefully interpersonal relations; there is consideration of the efficiency of a company's workers and the determination of their salaries accordingly, and so forth.

7 The introduction in 1967 of the first law on joint ventures with foreign partners in former socialist countries was also part of this reform.

8 The Centre for Foreign Trade in Radenci had already been established in 1977, and was organizing up to 150 courses in the different fields of companies' international operations. At least 2,000 experts annually, from different fields of business, participated in specialized courses – mostly of one week's duration.

9 The name of the course was something else but the main themes were the principles of marketing and market research.

10 Iskra had already started its own Foreign Trade School in 1982, and in 1969 it had set up a substantive five-week school of management for all its managerial team.

11 Mayer has stated, for instance, that:

> Young Slovenia imitates too much the developed world and neglects its own intellectual strengths and specificities. Transfer of foreign knowledge is like biological transplantation. The organism has to be carefully prepared for the transplant if it is to integrate well. Think only of failures of foreign managers in our companies or the inefficient training of local managers if trained only by foreign teachers which are not familiar with [the] Slovene development path, organizational or national culture. One's own creativity can not be

substituted by a foreign one. Foreign creativity is not useful if blindly imitated and not fertilized with its own creativity.

(Mayer 1994: 12)

12 Only one MBA graduate had a different opinion.

13 At IEDC Brdo, for example, the MBA course represents only part of all training programmes: functional seminars amount to more than half the latter; then come conferences, in-house company programmes, and strategic leadership seminars (Djurdjevič 1994: 2). In 1993, IEDC Brdo also started the first presidents' MBA programme with seven participants.

14 Undergraduates in Slovenia study for at least five years. They should not, therefore, be compared with college graduates from the United States, with their three-year programme. In the case of Slovenia, it is more appropriate to speak of university graduates and postgraduates.

15 The share was almost identical in all the different programmes evaluated.

16 The Ministry for Economic Affairs received, at the first tender, 136 applications. It approved fifty-one and allocated approximately DM 1.2 million to them. Only two training institutions received funds, the rest went directly to firms. The Ministry estimates that such funds enabled the additional training of 1,300 middle and 150 top managers. Companies had to prepare their strategic development plans in order to qualify for such funds. Therefore, company restructuring programmes are also regarded as a side-effect of this programme.

17 Of ten MBA students interviewed by Djurdjevič, two have been hired by small fast-growing companies, and two by foreign-owned companies.

18 Parliament only passed the law on privatization at the end of 1992, after two years of hectic debate about the concept, with amendments in 1993. According to the law, companies were expected to submit their privatization plans by the end of 1994.

19 MBA fees in Slovenia range from DM 7,000 to DM 20,000, plus another DM 2,000 for a master's degree. Only one programme, not included in the survey, is more expensive. On top of the DM 20,000 fee, participants also have to pay DM 6,000 travel costs for the obligatory training abroad, which is part of the course. The government has so far provided only two scholarships annually.

20 Nevertheless, part of the demand for MBA courses, which also offer master's degrees, should be attributed to title seekers or those wishing to proceed with study towards a PhD degree.

21 Such an age structure can be explained by the study conditions. Apart from university degrees, MBA schools also demand some business experience. At IEDC the precondition is three years of such experience. Other schools have taken a more relaxed position, however. At the Faculty of Economics, for example, the precondition is two years' experience. At ICPE, practical experience is desirable, but not a necessary precondition.

22 It seems that among Slovenes there is a lot of idealism about becoming managers. The most important factors making students decide to study for an MBA are, according to Herzberger's theory of motivation, intrinsic ones. They create satisfaction. However, a very strong egalitarian mentality could also have contributed to such a result.

23 The explanation that they already have a high salary is not a realistic one since only a third of them are among top managers, who are better paid. Others, such as the directors of various sectors, hold middle management positions (40 per cent).

24 The MBA course by BFE at Maribor is the only such course to have a special international management module.

25 Just two programmes, for example, were assessed by their students as being very helpful (by 25 per cent and 21 per cent of them respectively).

REFERENCES

Djurdjevič, M. (1994) 'Does Formal Business Education Matter', Mimeo, Faculty of Social Sciences, University of Ljubljana.

Kraljič, P. (1990) 'The Economic Gap Separating East and West', in *The Columbia Journal of World Business* 25(4): 14–19.

Mayer, J. (1994) *Vizija ustvarjalnega podjetja* [*The Vision of a Creative Enterprise*], Ljubljana: Dedalus, Žalozba IKRA.

Purg, D. (1993) 'Developing Managers for Eastern Europe', in M. Senjur (ed.) *Slovenia – A Small Country in the Global Economy*, Ljubljana: CICD.

Rojec, M. and Svetličič, M. (1993) 'Foreign Direct Investment in Slovenia', *Transnational Corporations* 2(1): 135–53.

Senjur, M. (1993) 'Transition as a Problem for Development Theory and Policy', *Development & International Cooperation* 9(16): 119–37.

Svetličič, M. (1994) 'Njegovo veličanstvo manager(sko) izobraževanje!' ['His Majesty, Management Education!'], *Slovenska ekonomska revija* 45(4): 350–60.

Part II

MANAGEMENT EDUCATION AND BUSINESS

7

MANAGEMENT EDUCATION IN BRITAIN

A compromise between culture and necessity[1]

John F. Wilson

> Business Schools are about as British as drum majorettes: in fields where they believe success depends primarily on experience and instinct, the British only turn to teaching as a last resort.
>
> (Turner 1969: 92)

INTRODUCTION

The principal purposes of this chapter are: first, to provide an insight into the reasons for the establishment of the first business school in Britain, at Manchester University in 1965; second, to explain how up to the mid 1980s it coped with a business culture which, as Turner describes above, was generally loath to accept the need for academic management education (Wilson 1992); and third, to link this story with the performance of Britain's economy. British business and industrial history reveals inherent weaknesses in managerial techniques and structure, and one of the main reasons for these problems must have been the way in which key personnel were recruited and trained. This provides a good reason for tracing the history of Manchester Business School (MBS), because it is possible to demonstrate in graphic form how this environment moulded the methods employed to convince senior executives of the need to change their methods. It is also possible to extend this analysis into a general study of the relevance of management education, because while the British (and American) university system was instructed to provide this form of teaching as a means of improving industrial competitiveness, in Japan no such relationship has been envisaged, begging the important question about the need for management education. American business schools have also recently been heavily criticized for an alleged failure to produce the right type of managers for the competitive challenges of the last generation, pointing to the need for a detailed debate about the role of education and training. In the British context, the establishment of business schools did not solve any of the inherent managerial and organizational weaknesses in the industrial sector, and rather than slavishly imitating the Americans an alternative might have been tried which would have come closer to the Japanese system.

BRITISH BUSINESS AND BUSINESS CULTURE UP TO THE 1950s

The first issue that must be tackled before examining Manchester Business School (MBS) is to outline the main characteristics of the British business culture. It is also important to emphasize that 'British business' means those companies in the manufacturing sector who were based principally in the United Kingdom, rather than the highly successful multinational enterprises (BP, Shell, Glaxo, ICI, and Unilever) which had established a worldwide reputation as first-class managerial organizations. Unfortunately, the latter were very much in the minority, while with regard to the former it has become a commonplace of business history that up to the 1940s (at least) they were dominated by the distinction between 'Gentlemen' (or the owning family) and 'Players' (or salaried managers), and that no divorce between ownership and control had yet appeared (Wilson 1995). Chandler (1990: 235) has coined the term 'personal capitalism' to describe this culture, arguing that as a result, in contrast to their counterparts in the United States, Germany, and Japan, British business generally 'failed' to make the essential three-pronged investments in production, marketing, and management which he regards as 'the logic of industrial growth'. Even the 'Players' who were recruited into British firms had rarely received much more than a basic education, and their training was essentially of a practical, on-the-job nature, while senior managers and directors usually came from the owning families or their close associates. This served merely to perpetuate what Coleman (1973: 101) calls a 'Cult of the Amateur', an ethos which pervaded society as a whole, denigrating the need for professional training in business at a time when the social elite regarded occupations in industry and trade as wholly unacceptable. 'Managers are born, not made' was a common maxim used by businesspeople, and when combined with their highly individualistic approach towards business it prevented the rapid growth of a class of professional managers which possessed the kind of expertise required to improve organizational effectiveness.

Another key feature of the British scene was the attitude of academic institutions towards vocational education. In the first place, given that there was very little demand for professionally trained managers from British business, it is not surprising that universities failed to respond by establishing a steady supply of graduates with degrees in such areas. On the other hand, the situation was by no means as simple as that, because even if a demand had arisen it is not clear whether a supply would have materialized, bearing in mind the antipathy expressed by most universities towards vocational training. As Locke (1989: 58–9) has revealed, the British educational system up to the 1940s was based on a 'Gentlemanly Ideal', with a preference for the liberal arts which arrogantly ignored the practical relevance of the educational system's work. Keeble (1992: 96) has also described how the few management education pioneers who established business-related degree courses (in Birmingham, the LSE, and Manchester) 'had to walk a tightrope between attracting business interest . . . and finding acceptance for the subject as one suitably "liberal" for a university to offer'. Mutual suspicions consequently characterized the relationships between both academics and management education, and businesspeople and formal training, and it could well be argued that until the 1980s this environment hardly altered.

This is not the place to retell the early history of British management education (Keeble 1992: 93–149), but one can only agree with Bowie's (1930: 89) assertion that even by 1930 'Britain is still at the crowing of the cock', compared with the rapid extensions in the United States. Following a reassessment of economic priorities during the Second World War, though, more concerted efforts were made to spread the benefits of the American approach, for example through the work of the government-sponsored Anglo-American Council on Productivity. The Ministry of Education (through the work of its consultant on these matters, Lyndall Urwick) was also responsible for initiating in 1949 the National Scheme of Management Studies, which would be run under the auspices of the newly created British Institute of Management (BIM) and taught in technical and commercial colleges. Urwick's scheme was intended to provide successful candidates with a Diploma in Management Studies, and while this did not quite match an undergraduate degree in status it reflected the state's acceptance of the need to introduce greater professionalism into the occupation of management. Two years earlier, in 1947, the Administrative Staff College at Henley was also created, indicating how while the scale of activity came nowhere near that in the United States at least progress was being made.

During the 1950s, some of this momentum was sustained, although it is important to note that the Diploma scheme only turned out a total of 1,600 awards in twelve years, compared with an *annual* output of 6,000 MBAs from American business schools. Several universities did either expand or initiate management studies courses in spite of the general academic aversion to vocational training, and an Association of Teachers of Management evolved out of an informal grouping of like-minded lecturers in the late 1950s (Wilson 1992: 7–9). On the other hand, this could not be described as the achievement of what Locke (1989: 1159) calls the 'New Paradigm' – the application of science to the solution of managerial problems – and perhaps of greater significance was the increase in in-house training schemes which British firms were setting up from the 1940s. This contrasting approach towards the task of training managers was to persist into the 1960s, and in the debate leading up to the establishment of MBS it was difficult to achieve any consensus, leading to an awkward compromise which materially affected business school finances.

A MOVEMENT FOR CHANGE

By far the most influential body prompting the government into creating business schools was the Foundation for Management Education (FME), an organization created by John Bolton, Sir Keith Joseph, and J.W. Platt in 1960 with the specific intention of expanding this field of studies in universities (Nind 1985). After raising £190,000 from private sources, they managed to persuade the University Grants Committee (UGC) to match this sum, providing a substantial boost to the work already going on in various institutions. As part of the government's planning experiment, the National Economic Development Council (created in 1962) was also arguing for the establishment of an American-style business school in Britain, a viewpoint endorsed by the Ministry of Education in 1963, illustrating how the FME cause was gathering widespread support (Wilson 1992: 1–15).

The main reason why management education was coming to be accepted as an essential feature of economic and educational policy by the 1960s was the general realization that Britain was falling behind her rivals as an industrial and commercial power. This was a cause of great concern among politicians, industrialists, and academic commentators, and in the attempts to focus on the key reasons why Britain was not doing as well as its main competitors – especially the most successful economy in the world at that time, the United States – attention was drawn to the contrasting methods of training managers. At the same time, British business was also changing character, largely as a result of the growing divorce between control and ownership, and a sustained merger process which was converting formerly atomistic market structures into ones dominated by oligopolistic trading practices (Wilson 1995). Indeed, by the 1960s, many of the larger firms were beginning to adopt the multidivisional form, such was their size and complexity after several intense spurts of merger activity (Channon 1973: 50–88).

The dual pressures of greater external competition and increasing business size were prominent features of the economic debates raging from the late 1950s, but it is not apparent that firms were capable of changing their recruitment policies as a means of improving organizational capabilities. The proliferation of in-house training schemes from the late 1940s has already been noted, but it is important to emphasize that these were largely concerned with specific tasks performed internally, rather than acting as a vehicle for professionalizing the general task of management. Indeed, just as in the interwar years, by 1960 'British management was poorly endowed with formal educational qualifications', and industrialists were still arguing that it was easier and cheaper to train people from a young age on in-house courses, rather than try and fit graduates on to their career ladders (Keeble 1984: 266–76). This was symptomatic of the general problem, and contemporary studies provided abundant evidence of the persistent use of 'Gentlemen' from public schools for strategic management posts, while 'Players' moved up from the ranks to act as line managers (Acton Society Trust 1956).

To demonstrate the power of what might be called the traditional approach towards management recruitment and training, it is interesting to see how just at the point in 1963 when the FME seemed to have succeeded in persuading the government to finance the creation of one or more business schools, the Savoy Group demanded a hearing. So called because they met regularly in London's Savoy Hotel, this group of (predominantly engineering) industrialists was not completely averse to new training methods, but above all they refused to believe that university academics had any role to play in fashioning the courses. An *impasse* had been reached, and in time-honoured tradition an arbitrator was required, resulting in the appointment of Lord Franks to provide a basis for future developments in the field of management education. This perhaps might be regarded in retrospect as a missed opportunity, because the government could have decided to ignore the Savoy Group and to institute the plans suggested by the National Economic Development Council. Instead, they allowed Franks the opportunity to draw up a compromise solution, and it will become clear in the next sections that MBS especially suffered as a direct consequence of the severe constraints imposed by Franks on the way business school operations should be financed.

Although the Franks Report (1963) was categorically in favour of establishing business schools, and he specified the Universities of London and Manchester as the two institutions most likely to succeed in this pioneering academic venture, it is also apparent that the protestations of the Savoy Group influenced his decisions. The main problem he identified was 'the uneasiness felt in some academic circles about the intentions of business, and the uneasiness felt in many business quarters about the intentions of the universities', and in order to calm these mutual fears he advised that not only should the business schools be managed by a Council composed of both interests, the initial and operational finance should also be provided in equal proportions. In effect, this meant that the new bodies were dependent to a significant extent on a business community which had pledged its allegiance to the flag of non-academic training courses, providing an enormous challenge which might well have been avoided. To many people's surprise, over £5 million was pledged by British business to the business school appeal launched in 1964, and the FME (1970) described this as a 'most heartening confirmation of the interest of British industry and commerce in management education'. On the other hand, it is noticeable that two-thirds of the donations were for less than £10,000, and the acid test of the sincerity with which this money was given must be the extent to which firms were actually willing to use the schools, a test which we shall see many failed dismally in the following decades (Wilson 1992: 11–15).

THE MANCHESTER EXPERIMENT

This long preamble to the establishment of MBS has been an essential means of explaining the environment into which it was born, and in particular to highlight the widespread suspicion of, and antipathy towards, academic qualifications inherent in the British business culture. Owen (1970: 22) later noted that the two business schools were created 'in a climate where the traditions were against the view that education for business was a respectable subject', and in retrospect any expectations of a 'management education revolution' (Wheatcroft 1970) look naïve and unrealistic. The academics recruited into MBS in the late 1960s were extremely optimistic about their prospects as evangelists of a new doctrine, but they were soon obliged to pursue more market-driven approaches, and within a decade the school's financial position had deteriorated to such an extent that short-term loans from the FME had to be secured in order to balance the books. Perhaps its location in the heartland of Britain's traditional industrial base could well have influenced events (an argument that will be pursued later), but there is little doubt that at first MBS struggled to secure a foothold in the management education world, in spite of considerable support and advice from American practitioners.

Management education had been developing in Manchester since the establishment of a Faculty of Commerce and Administration at the College of Technology in 1904, and after a Department of Industrial Administration had been formed in 1919 (with substantial funds from local textile and engineering businesses) its Director, J.A. Bowie, started the country's first postgraduate management course (Keeble 1984: 67–77). As already noted, relatively few students were recruited on to these courses, and their impact remained marginal, but in the 1950s a small group of academics at the University of Manchester, especially Professors Chester and Williams, were keen to see greater progress in this field. By 1961, apart from a range of general and specific courses provided on an *ad hoc* basis, a Centre for Business Research had been started, with local companies like ICI, Ferranti, Courtaulds, and English Sewing Cotton providing financial support for its work. To coordinate this expansion, the Manchester School of Management & Administration (or Mansma, for short) was created, and Professor D.C. Hague was recruited as its head; and along with enormous support from the Vice-Chancellor, this convinced Franks that Manchester would be a good place for a business school.

Manchester Business School (namely, the Faculty of Business Adminis-

138

tration at Manchester University) opened its doors in October 1965, renting some cramped quarters off the city centre's Piccadilly Square while their purpose-built premises slowly took shape on the main campus. The first director was Grigor McClelland, an appointment regarded as eminently suitable in the circumstances, because, while up to 1957 he had managed his family's business, Laws Stores of Gateshead, thereafter academic research into retailing at Oxford University had taken up much of his time, culminating in 1962 in his appointment as the country's first Research Fellow in Management Studies. The other key members of the early management team at MBS were Professor Hague, the Mansma supremo, Professor Tom Lupton, one of the founder members of the Association of Teachers of Management, and Dr John Morris, a leading behaviouralist thinker who later pioneered important techniques in management education. Together, these four were regarded as the 'founding fathers', and although many other members of staff played crucial roles as course designers and convenors, this small group was primarily responsible for fashioning MBS strategy and structure, or what they liked to call 'The Manchester Experiment' (Wilson 1992: 18–42).

Having consulted, and indeed recruited, many American management education specialists, including Professors Herbert Simon and H.I. Ansoff, on how best to run the new institution, the 'founding fathers' slowly evolved the basic features of 'The Manchester Experiment' in the late 1960s. Its basic characteristics were a multidisciplinary approach to analysing managerial problems based on learning-by-doing, combined with a loose, non-departmental structure which stressed the qualities of teamwork, rather than hierarchical decision making. In theory, the highest level of policy formulation was the Council, on which sat industrialists and academics, but in practice this body became little more than a rubber-stamping mechanism, and the 'founding fathers' retained full control of strategy. The key level of management was course director, because with no discipline-based departments it was up to these individuals to coordinate resources in order to provide all the teaching necessary. In effect, this emasculated professorial authority, and as a result new members of staff often found it difficult to establish a position on courses, because course directors would often stick to the tried and tested. However, in general the loose structure was regarded as a success, and with refinements like the addition of an Operations Group for the overall supervision of programmes, and a Development Group charged with monitoring external attitudes, 'The Manchester Experiment' survived its first ten years intact.

Although one must accredit the 'founding fathers' with an innovatory approach towards organization building, it is not wholly apparent from the first ten years' financial results that 'The Manchester Experiment' was commercially viable. Of course, it is extremely difficult to measure the impact of an academic institution simply by looking at its profit and loss account, and other criteria will be examined later, but one must remember how Franks had laid down the basic principle that the two business schools must raise their operating income from both business and government in equal shares. In effect, this meant that course fees, raised largely from post-experience programmes for practising managers, ought to equate approximately to the amount earned from the University Grants Council (UGC) for postgraduate teaching. However, as Figure 7.1 reveals, the former failed to rise much above 20 per cent of total income in the first ten years.

Furthermore, the initial target for postgraduates was 200 per year (including first and second years), and as Figure 7.2 indicates it took over twenty years to reach this level.

By the time MBS had moved into its purpose-built premises in 1971, and a full complement of sixty staff had been recruited to teach the projected intake, the financial position had deteriorated to such an extent that, as Figure 7.3 illustrates, a substantial deficit of over £72,000 appeared in the accounts. It had been expected that losses would be made in the late 1960s, but for such a heavy deficit to appear in the seventh year of operations, amounting to 11 per cent of total income, was a big shock to MBS and its supporters. Figure 7.3 also shows that the financial position failed to improve much over the next few years, with income levels stagnating badly, and in real terms (with inflation rising to almost 25 per cent by 1975) falling alarmingly. At a time of financial stringency in higher education, the UGC refused to bail MBS out, forcing the director to seek a £50,000 loan from the

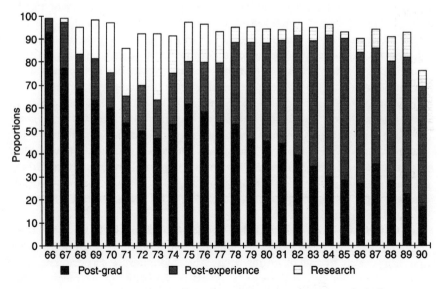

Figure 7.1 MBS income shares (miscellaneous income excluded)

140

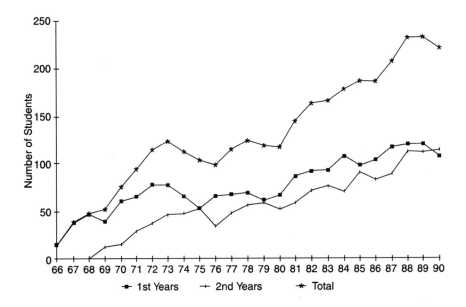

Figure 7.2 MBA intake, 1965–6 to 1989–90

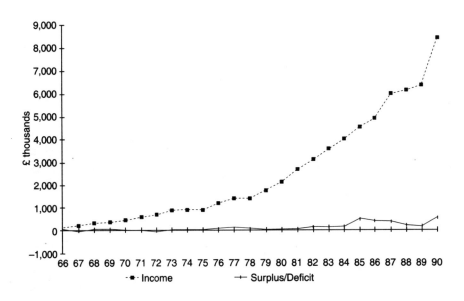

Figure 7.3 Income and surplus or deficit

141

FME, and although this was repaid from the rising income (see Figure 7.3) within a year clearly 'The Manchester Experiment' had not been a commercial success.

Of course, there are other factors to consider when assessing MBS's impact in its first decade, not least its relationship with British business, an issue which will be addressed in the next section. The relative failure of a second appeal for funds undertaken by the FME in 1970 might also be mentioned in this context, because not only did FME have a shortfall of £1.25 million on the target of £7.5 million, it was also decided to use some of the funds to establish new business schools in Scotland and Birmingham. This expansion of management education can only be regarded as a positive move by the FME, but for MBS, given its difficulties in recruiting enough postgraduates and managers to take courses, the extra competition was unwelcome. At the same time, judging from both the appeal's failure and the widespread criticism of business schools generally during the early 1970s (Wilson 1992: 36–8), the attitudes of British business towards management education had also changed little by then. This further illustrates the difficulties these pioneers were facing. The situation required careful thought, particularly as the level of competition continued to increase throughout the 1970s – by 1980, there were fourteen business schools in Britain – and as a result MBS's strategy was modified substantially to cope with the realities of a market which was obstinately slow in accepting the role of academic management education.

ADAPTING TO CIRCUMSTANCES AND INTERNAL CONFLICT

An intrinsic feature of 'The Manchester Experiment' had always been a firm belief in learning-by-doing, and consequently in both postgraduate and post-experience courses students were given projects to complete which were real time and relevant to their problems and studies. Of course, Harvard Business School had been using the case study approach since the 1920s, but this approach is simply an artificial means of examining a situation, while the MBS project casts the student in a specific and actual role, allowing the application of newly learnt techniques or knowledge to the solution of real-time business problems. First used on the MBA second year in the late 1960s, the project became a distinctive feature of all MBS courses thereafter, acting as the foundation stone for a series of innovatory post-experience courses which eventually solved all MBS's financial problems.

One of the more consistent criticisms of business school courses for practising managers was that, while high-fliers were catered for through the long Executive Course looking at general management issues, little attention was paid to the needs of junior and middle managers who would have specific requirements (Mant 1969). In simple terms, business required a more 'proactive' approach towards course design, and in view of MBS's worsening financial predicament Professor Hague was seconded to a role which he described as simply 'filling the gaps in the market'. The first innovation was the Joint Development Activity (JDA), introduced by John Morris in 1969 as a one-off course for Rolls-Royce, but from the early 1970s acting as a blueprint for many similar innovations. As its name implies, the whole purpose of the JDA was for the academics and managers to tackle a specific business problem jointly, developing an educational tool which aroused considerable interest at the time among executives struggling to keep pace with rising import penetration and difficult export markets. The JDA consequently spawned a whole series of imitations within MBS, and courses relating to operational control, corporate growth, and the business environment emerged within a few years, all based on the common theme of listening to customer requirements.

By far the most successful product of this new proactive style was the venture into banking. As with most of the JDA-style courses, this was not a preconceived strategy, because it arose out of a random visit paid by Professor Hague to Barclays Bank International in 1973. However, after fashioning a four-month-long programme based on the customer's specific requirements, efforts were made to sell it to other domestic and overseas banks. By 1976, MBS had formed an International Centre for Banking and Finance, and defying the strongly held notion in banking circles, that non-bankers could never teach them anything useful, this has become the largest generator of post-experience income over the last fifteen years, providing the basis for a period of financial expansion from the mid 1970s (see Figure 7.3).

The expansion of problem-specific courses, on which MBS has since the early 1970s based its post-experience strategy, was consequently a realistic solution to the financial problems and widespread criticisms of the time. It might be argued that the policy was opportunistic, and certainly the academic benefits arising from JDAs were extremely limited. More importantly, though, in demonstrating to practising managers that MBS was willing to listen to their needs, the new programmes provided an opportunity to influence managerial performance and earn more revenue. Initially, because JDAs were time consuming, tying staff up for several weeks, they were incapable of solving MBS's immediate financial problems. However, as Figure 7.1 indicates, by the early 1980s course fees exceeded those earned from the UGC, substantiating the faith placed in this approach by the 'founding fathers'.

Although from the mid 1970s (see Figure 7.3), MBS's financial performance improved, and no more losses appeared in the books after 1975, it is important to stress the degree to which MBS had been obliged to compromise its academic principles in order to achieve this position. Not only were the JDAs of little impact as academic exercises, from the mid 1970s many have argued that research within MBS had been marginalized at the expense of developing customer-specific courses (Wilson 1992: 104–9). Naturally, the 'founding fathers' would counter by emphasizing the need to solve the pressing financial problems of the early 1970s, and under Professor Lupton as director MBS enjoyed a period of considerable growth between 1977 and 1983 (see Figure 7.3). Nevertheless, it is striking that the number of research assistants hired by MBS fell from nineteen in 1972 to just two in 1978, and although more were recruited in the early 1980s this failed to make up the shortfall. Such were the teaching and administrative burdens imposed on a dwindling faculty after the mid 1970s' crises that the value of research grants attracted by MBS staff also fell constantly, hitting a nadir of just £90,000 in 1978, compared with £250,000 in 1973. There was much talk about achieving a balance between the academic values of a university business school and the need to make an impact on managers, who were highly suspicious of such institutions, but financial constraints imposed by the Franks' compromise ensured that the latter would prevail, especially after the losses of 1972–5. One might also mention the conditions imposed by the FME when lending MBS £50,000 in 1975, because it forced the 'founding fathers' to institute severe cuts in staffing levels, demonstrating how financial reality and academic values could never be reconciled easily.

Under Professor Lupton as director, 'The Manchester Experiment' was naturally sustained, resulting in the creation of 'Centres' as a means of focusing activities on the needs of the market. This refinement to the non-departmental structure is an excellent illustration of the market-driven approach which now dominated strategy at MBS, revealing in Chandlerian fashion how structure was adapted to cater for strategic needs. In this system, all staff were made a cost to the Post-Graduate Centre, and the heads of the other Centres (International Banking, Executive Development, New Enterprise, and Language Learning) would negotiate a transfer price for teaching according to budgetary and other resource constraints. A School Management Committee was also created to coordinate the distribution of resources, and a School Policy Group later appeared as a policy-making body. Nevertheless, it is important to stress how the culture remained non-hierarchical, based on the behavioural premise that individuals will develop more effectively when allowed to find their own level and interests. Naturally, many within MBS disagreed with this philosophy because of its inability to bring on young academics, but until the mid 1980s only tinkering changes to the committee structure were effected, and 'The Manchester Experiment' continued.

The key question here, of course, is whether the Lupton strategy and structure was any more effective in dealing with the need to achieve both a balance between academic and functional activities and an impact on British business. As far as the latter is concerned, judging from the evidence in

Figures 7.1 and 7.3, there seems little doubt that income from post-experience courses increased markedly over this period, reaching 62 per cent by 1985 and generating substantial surpluses which were used to enhance the teaching and residential environment within MBS. On the other hand, some feared that MBS was becoming more like a conference centre, and although Lupton talked about achieving a balance between what he called the 'fields of knowledge' (academic disciplines) and 'fields of action' (the business world), by the early 1980s research income accounted for less than 6 per cent of the total compared with over 20 per cent ten years earlier. There is no evidence to support the claim that over that period the 'founding fathers' took a policy decision to reduce the level of research, although they were obliged by financial necessity to reduce the number of research assistants. On the other hand, it can only be concluded that MBS focused its attentions largely on the profitable problem-specific courses for which it was earning a wide reputation.

The debate within MBS concerning the growing imbalance between academic and functional priorities reached a climax in 1983, when as a result of an investigation instituted by the university authorities Professor Lupton was in effect replaced as director, after several of his most senior colleagues publicly derided the now dominant proactive approach (Wilson 1992: 108–23). It actually took the Council over a year to find a successor, during which time Professor Stapleton stepped in as acting director and instituted a fundamental revision of strategy and structure, and when the third director took over in October 1984 significant changes had already been made. The choice of director was particularly interesting, because in contrast to the academic orientation of his predecessors Dr Rab Telfer had spent his entire career in industry, as a divisional manager at ICI and more recently as chairman and chief executive of Mather & Platt. This marked a decisive turning point in MBS's development, redirecting 'The Manchester Experiment' in ways the 'founding fathers' would not have endorsed. A departmental structure was *not* imposed on the academic staff, but the distribution of resources was much more carefully planned, and above all a revival of academic priorities was placed at the head of strategy formulation. Professor Lupton has argued that the surpluses arising from the development of successful customer-specific courses allowed the luxury of refocusing attentions on research, but others have countered that this had been long overdue if MBS wanted to be known as a first-class institution for management education, revealing the fundamental differences of opinion which characterized internal debate from the early 1970s.

IMPACT OF MBS ON BUSINESS CULTURE

Having surveyed the main influences on MBS strategy up to the mid 1980s, it is now necessary to examine the impact this made on a business culture which was, as noted earlier, essentially 'amateurish' in its approach towards management recruitment and training. Judging simply from the expansion in management education – by 1990 there were over thirty business schools or management departments in British universities and polytechnics – one might conclude that, after many decades of mutual neglect, supply was responding to market forces. On the other hand, criticism of academic management education was still a prominent feature of the whole debate relating to whether or not British managers were up to the competitive challenges posed by Japanese, European, and American businesses. Business school staff were, in the late 1980s, still constantly obliged to deal with headlines like 'Why have British business schools failed?' (Wilson 1992: 126–8), while at the same time agreeing with the conclusions drawn up by Handy (1988: 164) that 'in Britain management education and training is *too little, too late for too few*'. Does this mean that little success has been achieved in breaking down the traditional aversion to management education?

Bearing in mind its location, at the centre of a major industrial and commercial region, Manchester Business School might well have been expected to develop a close relationship with north west business. Prior to 1965, Professors Chester and Williams had enjoyed some success in this respect, even managing to convince several local companies to support their Centre for Business Research, and certainly MBS attempted to extend and strengthen this relationship. Initiatives in the field of small business development, a monthly series of lectures by prominent speakers from different sectors of society, and part-time degree courses, were all aimed at drawing the local business community into MBS on a longer-term basis. The significant number of JDAs undertaken with north west companies might also be mentioned, and the intimate consultancy and research relationships forged between the academic staff at MBS and these businesses, demonstrating the degree to which efforts were made in this area. Certainly, when the acute difficulties being experienced by the region's core industries of cotton textiles and engineering from the 1960s are considered, there was undoubtedly a need for fresh ideas on management and competitiveness. On the other hand, success was naturally dependent upon the response of managers to the entreaties made by MBS, and in those industries beset by market challenges of unprecedented proportions rarely was their resolution associated with management education.

It is interesting to note how, in evaluating its role as the north west business school, as well as a British business school, MBS by the late 1970s was beginning to develop a more expansionist thrust in its marketing strategy. In 1965, the two schools in London and Manchester had been seen as British business schools which were to serve the needs of British business, but because the management education market proved too small a stronger international dimension was built into MBS courses. This was manifested particularly in the opening of a language learning facility and the positive encouragement of European, American, and Far Eastern contacts. Of course, this might well be associated with what has become a prominent feature of the economic scene over the last generation, the internationalization of business, but it is also undeniably linked to the need to generate more income, given the limited home market. Even in 1987, a survey of 206 large public and private businesses produced the result that only 29 per cent believed in the value of formal qualifications as an important criterion when recruiting or promoting managers (Constable and McCormick 1987: 85).

There seems little doubt that the Savoy Group mentality of the 1960s debate was still 'alive and kicking' in the 1980s (Wilson 1992: 126–9), but not only is it apparent that a strong aversion to academic management education persisted in Britain, it can also be argued that progress in other areas of recruitment and training had not developed much. It was stressed earlier that British business preferred to train its own managers, and in the postwar period while such an approach proliferated in-house courses remained extremely limited in both nature and impact. Of course, in-house training is the method preferred by Japanese business to develop managerial talent (Nishizawa 1994), but as Handy (1988: 88) argues, in Britain the methods do not compare with the in-depth and cross-functional approach pursued in Japan. Furthermore, in a British government survey of over 2,000 firms, it was discovered that by 1985 56 per cent provided no formal management training at all, revealing a dearth of activity in this field which would be regarded as commercial suicide in other economies. In effect, British business had followed neither the *academic* nor the *corporate* tracks advocated by Handy (1988), inhibiting substantially the attempts made by politicians to improve industrial competitiveness.

This evidence of a persistent aversion to formal training in British business provides further support for the market-led strategy pursued by the 'founding fathers' at MBS. Had they not listened to the requirements of their potential clients, and had substantial efforts not gone into developing a range of project-based, real-time courses, then it can only be concluded that the financial difficulties of the first decade (see Figure 7.3) would have persisted into the 1980s. Over the last twelve years, universities have also been subjected to real cuts in funding, affecting the postgraduate market particularly and again reinforcing the need to build up the post-experience courses in order to provide income for both survival and progress. Financial survival was consequently a matter of adapting to the needs of the market, and even though, in some people's eyes, research might well have suffered at MBS this was an inevitable consequence of operating in an antipathetic business culture. It might be argued that after academic priorities were restored to a more prominent position during the mid 1980s then financial results did not deteriorate (see Figure 7.3), but it is easy to forget that, on average, course fees continued to provide well over one-half of total

147

income, indicating how the revenue earners were by no means ignored. The whole point about giving academic research greater prominence was to utilize the benefits of new insights into the business world to improve the quality of teaching at MBS, strengthening the post-experience courses, rather than marginalizing them. In effect, then, the proactive approach remained at the centre of MBS strategy, reflecting the realities of a business culture which had changed only slightly since the 1960s.

Another aspect of this debate is the growing amount of concern expressed about the effectiveness of the *academic* track (via business schools), as opposed to the corporate track (via in-house training). Aaronson (1992: 172–3) has observed that by the 1980s many were arguing that both the quality and methods of business schools were woefully deficient in preparing managers for Japanese and European competition. In particular, American MBAs were 'not trained to anticipate and flexibly respond to new technologies, production methods, competitors, or markets', while in contrast the 'hands-on, in-house approach to training their future leaders' pursued in Japan and Germany was proving much more successful. Of course, the relationship between management education and economic growth remains unproven, but over the last thirty years a direct correlation between the number of MBAs produced and an economy's deterioration can be traced, and in Britain's case management training (*corporate* or *academic*) has simply never been fashionable among the 'Gentlemen' populating boards of directors. One might well point to a variety of other factors – the inhibiting role of government policy, trade union militancy, the reluctance of financial institutions to provide long-term support to firms – which have contributed to a drastic decline in industrial competitiveness (Wilson 1995). On the other hand, failure at the most fundamental level of training has been among the most damaging obstacles to growth, indicating how British businesspeople have been their own worst enemies. Furthermore, by following the American model, instead of building on the British propensity for in-house training, it might be argued that much public money was wasted, and it is interesting to hypothesize on what would have happened to industrial competitiveness had more effort been put into redesigning the *corporate* track.

NOTES

1 I am indebted to the Manchester Business School, and in particular to two of its previous directors, Professor Tom Lupton and Professor Tom Cannon, for financing this project (intermittently) between 1983 and 1992. Delegates at various conferences in Osaka and Reading have also contributed valuable comments, and I have attempted to modify my opinions with this in mind.

REFERENCES

Aaronson, S. (1992) 'Serving America's business? Graduate business schools and American business, 1945–60', *Business History* 34(1): 160–82.

Acton Society Trust (1956) *Management Succession*, London: Acton Society Trust.

Bowie, J.A. (1930) *Education for Business Management*, Manchester: Manchester University Press.

Chandler, A.D. (1990) *Scale and Scope: The Dynamics of Industrial Capitalism*, Cambridge, MA: Harvard University Press.

Channon, D.F. (1973) *The Strategy and Structure of British Enterprise*, Cambridge, MA: Harvard University Press.

Coleman, D.C. (1973) 'Gentlemen and Players', *Economic History Review*, XXVI: 92–116.

Constable, T. and McCormick, R. (1987) *The Making of British Managers*, London: British Institute of Management.

FME (1970) *Management Education and the Business Schools*, London: Foundation for Management Education.

Franks Report (1963) *British Business Schools*, London: British Institute of Management.

Handy, C. (1988) *Making Managers*, London: Pitman.

Keeble, S. (1992) *The Ability to Manage*, Manchester: Manchester University Press.

Keeble, S.P. (1984) 'University education and business management from the 1890s to the 1950s', PhD Thesis, LSE.

Locke, R. (1989) *Management and Higher Education since 1940: The Influence of America and Japan on West Germany, Great Britain, and France*, Cambridge: Cambridge University Press.

Mant, O. (1969) *The Experienced Manager – A Major Resource*, London: British Institute of Management.

Nind, P.F. (1985) *A Firm Foundation. The Story of the Foundation for Management Education*, London: FME.

Nishizawa, T. (1994) 'Management education in post-war Japan', Paper presented to the Fourth Anglo-Japanese Conference, London.

Owen, T. (1970) *Business Schools: The Requirements of British Manufacturing Industry*, London: British Institute of Management.

Turner, G. (1969) *Business in Britain*, London: Eyre and Spottiswoode.

Wheatcroft, M. (1970) *The Revolution in British Management Education*, London: Pitman.

Wilson, J.F. (1992) *The 'Manchester Experiment': A History of Manchester Business School, 1965–1990*, London: Paul Chapman.

—— (1995) *British Business History, 1720–1994*, Manchester: Manchester University Press.

8

DO THEY MEAN BUSINESS?

An investigation of the purpose of the 'new university' business schools in Britain

Reva Berman Brown, Sean McCartney, and Jeff Clowes

INTRODUCTION

The meanings of the word 'purpose' range from 'a practical advantage or use', through 'a fixed intention that is the object of an action' to the meaning applied here: 'the reason why anything is done, created or exists'. In other words, this chapter reports on research undertaken to answer the broad question, 'What are university business schools for?'

The chapter builds on a study concluded in 1991 concerning the views of academics and directors of university business schools about such topics as the purpose of the university, teaching, research, and the audience for the knowledge which the schools produce. In 1993, a further study was done into the views on these topics of the directors of business schools in the new universities (the former polytechnics), comparing their attitudes to purpose, knowledge, teaching, and research with those of the old university business schools.

The university business school (UBS) under investigation is a department of its parent university, but is itself made up of sub-departments, composed of a variety of disciplines. This chapter puts forward five general models of university purpose, and suggests that UBSs are arenas within universities where contradictions of purpose are evident.

Of course, there are different stakeholders in UBSs, and one can investigate purpose on a number of levels. The level chosen for the research on which this chapter is based is that of the directors of UBSs. To place it in context, a brief overview of management education in Britain is given. 'Business Studies' is the name generally given to the first degree taught at higher education institutions. The MBA is a master's-level degree, and students are assumed either to have a first degree of some kind (not necessarily in business studies) or experience of being a manager for a period of years. As a result, MBA students tend to be in their late twenties or older. In general, business schools are departments of a parent university, with varying degrees of autonomy, though the MBA can be one of the qualifications taught in a department, say, of economics or accounting, by a university which does not have a business school. MBA students in Britain can be full time or part time, or they can obtain their qualification by means of distance learning or in-company, where their organization makes formal arrangements with a business school to create a specifically tailored qualification. Among the various business schools, there is variation between the amount of skills- or techniques-specific 'training' and generalist, theory-imbued 'education' in the composition of the MBA programme which they deliver.

In the main, part-time MBA students tend to receive financial support from their organizations, while full-time students tend to pay for themselves, having left their jobs in order to study full time. Most full-time courses last a calendar year (from October to September), while part-time courses are delivered over two or three years. The specific point to bear in mind when reading this chapter is that for all the business schools in the sample, the MBA is a postgraduate qualification, distinct from post-experience management education, which tends to be delivered as short courses that do not earn a formal qualification. Lower-level business or management qualifications are also provided at the new universities, as well as in colleges. For instance, a qualification in management is currently provided in a range of ways.[1] The management (or business) education (or training) asked about in the research concerns, in the main, the first degree or master's degree provided by UBSs.

The directors of UBSs in Britain tend to have the status of professor. They share many of the 'job attributes' of the dean in the United States and elsewhere in Europe. The 'regulations' governing the way a UBS operates are the same as for the parent university, although funding comes from both governmental and commercial/industrial sources. A crude distinction can be made: the first degree in business studies is meant to train young people for their first job, while the MBA is meant to make managers into better managers (however 'better' is defined). Both qualifications serve the wider social purpose of raising the status of the person involved in commerce or industry above those employed at the lower levels of the organization.

And a final comment on the 'new' universities: the polytechnics were created in the late 1960s out of the merging of several types of colleges – of technology, of art and design, of commerce, and of building – into one higher educational institution. Initially, thirty polytechnics were proposed by means of a government white paper in 1966, creating a binary division in higher education, with both the polytechnics and the universities able to bestow degrees on qualifying students. For Halsey (1990: 17) writing in the *Times Higher Education Supplement*,

Any notion that the universities are confined to scholarly 'uselessness'

151

or to basic science and scholarship, while the polytechnics pursue the application of science and letters to the vocational needs of an industrial society, founders on the facts. . . . The reality of the binary system is a blurred division of quality and not a horizontal division of educational function.

The binary divide has now been abolished and the polytechnics (together with a number of colleges of higher education) are now universities. From the late 1980s, many of the polytechnics created business schools out of their separate departments of business, management, economics, accountancy and finance, and law. The major difference between these business schools and those of the 'old' universities is that the latter have always had a greater degree of autonomy from their parent institution, while the polytechnic business schools seem to have come into existence for 'brand value' or administrative purposes.

This chapter takes the following form: in the first section, the origin and conduct of the research is put forward, and in the next, the five models of university purpose are discussed. The third section looks back to the creation of the 'old university' business schools (in 1965) and posits that the original purpose of these schools has not, in the authors' opinion, been realized. Then, by way of contrast, a view of the 'new university' business schools is presented and it is argued that they have, in fact, fulfilled the functions allotted to the 'old university' schools more effectively than the 'old university' schools did themselves. This view is supported by the research findings which are presented in the next section. Finally, it is argued that the abolition of the binary divide may undermine the success of the 'new university' business schools.

RESEARCH DESIGN

As part of a larger doctoral research project, conducted from 1988 to 1991 (Brown 1991), the purpose of university business schools was investigated (reported in Brown 1993). The UBSs in question were those situated in the 'old universities'; the polytechnics (the 'new universities') had not yet received university status. Two years later, in early 1993, the research was extended to include 'new university' business schools (NUBSs), the results of which are reported here.

The 'old university' business schools (OUBSs) were chosen to suit the purposes of the doctoral research. The seven OUBSs in England fulfilling the following criteria were selected: they run degree programmes for undergraduates and postgraduates, cater for doctoral study, and also provide post-experience/executive development courses. What was required were academic institutions which are involved in the entire range of management education provision. In an attempt to answer questions concerning the purpose of the UBS, a questionnaire was sent to the directors of the seven OUBSs which fitted these criteria in January 1990, requesting their opinions. While the views of seven people are unlikely to provide statistically significant confirmation of the information required, these seven are the people whose job it is to guide, or lead, their UBS in its management of knowledge. The questionnaire was therefore sent on the assumption that the directors' views would, at the least, give interesting insights into and, at best, provide useful views of knowledge and purpose in the UBS. In the event, six out of the seven directors filled in the questionnaire and returned it; the seventh director wrote a letter to say that he was 'too busy' to respond, giving a response rate of 86 per cent.[2]

In January 1993, the directors of the NUBs were sent the same questionnaire as had been sent to the directors of the UBSs in January 1991, and their views as to the purpose of their UBSs were elicited. In this case, the status of the institutions being new, the stringent requirement of the provision of the entire gamut of management education was not deemed appropriate in the sample selection. As a consequence, the directors of all the business schools situated in the former polytechnics were sent the questionnaire (totalling thirty-three) and nineteen were returned, a response rate of 57 per cent.

Strict one-to-one comparison is thus not possible between the OUBSs and the NUBSs, there being three times as many NUBS replies compared with the OUBSs, but each sample set is representative of UBSs, and it is suggested that what has been lost in rigour has been compensated for by the sharpness of the picture which has emerged. The limitations inherent in the approach, however, are apparent – one of the 'benefits' of hindsight.

The usual inadequacies of a questionnaire also apply: an overall, measured picture has been achieved, but it is somewhat thin and lifeless. Also, the first part of the research into the old universities was conducted two years before the second part into the new, so that the 'snapshots' are separated in time. An even greater 'own goal' is the fact that this work isolates the UBS and is based on very few institutions.[3] The directors were not asked to consider the environment in which their UBS is placed, and were not asked about the UBSs' competitors within higher education or outside it. What can be said, in defence of the thesis here, is that it has uncovered some perceptions about the purpose of UBSs that are of interest to a number of constituencies, and that they are worth thinking about.

THE MODELS OF UNIVERSITY PURPOSE

A review of academic, governmental, and social opinion on university purpose shows that the literature is replete with opposing views and controversies. The five models summarized below provide a broad answer to the apparently simple question, 'What are universities for?'.

Model 1: A university is an institution whose purpose is the search for knowledge for the sake of its intrinsic value (RESEARCH). This model is the basis of the view of the university as an ivory tower, untouched by the complexities of 'real life'. The proponents of the research model include Flexner (1930) and Truscott (1943).

Model 2: A university is an institution whose purpose is the dissemination of knowledge (TEACHING). In modern times, this view of the university extends back as far as 1852 when Cardinal Newman (1959) suggested that teaching should take primacy over research.

Model 3: A university is an institution the purpose of which is the training of skilled labour in fields of need that are relevant to the society in which the university operates (VOCATIONAL). It is this view which has enabled the introduction of university degree courses in areas such as engineering and accounting. Proponents of this view range from Roger Ascham (Green 1969) in the sixteenth century to Ishaya Audu (1977) in the twentieth.

Model 4: A university is an institution whose purpose is to serve the aspirations and aims of a particular society in which the university operates (SOCIETAL). This view holds that the role of a university is to serve a particular society. For their functions to be relevant, universities must involve themselves in the aims and aspirations of the particular society in which they are placed, in order to benefit the community which created and maintains them (Searle 1972).

Model 5: A university is an institution whose purpose is the simultaneous pursuit of research, teaching, vocational, and societal purposes (PLURALISTIC) (Kerr 1963). While the pluralistic model of university purpose is flexible and comprehensive, a source of conflict is that, as a result of prevailing circumstances, the university may emphasize one or more of these models to the neglect of others. Logically, such differing emphases are present (to differing degrees) in the various university departments, of which the business school is one.

The five models are not, of course, the only way in which university purpose can be categorized. For instance, a three-category model could be considered, divided into (1) research, (2) teaching and education, where the vocational is subsumed into the educational dimension, and (3) societal, subsumed into the pluralistic model that emphasizes the wider purpose of universities.

A distinction also needs to be made between 'purpose' as used here ('Why do university business schools exist?') and 'function' ('What are university business schools intended to do?'). For instance, the functions of selection, screening, and gatekeeping – or of legitimization and the provision of credentials – could be regarded as part of their overall purpose, or could be viewed as parallel purposes, different but equal.

THE OLD UNIVERSITY BUSINESS SCHOOLS

Management education is a relatively recent addition to the curriculum of British universities: the first business schools were established in the mid 1960s. This is in stark contrast to the situation in American universities, where management education dates back to the nineteenth century. The Wharton School of Finance and Commerce was started at the University of Pennsylvania in Philadelphia in 1881. By 1914, there were thirty-one business schools in existence (Simpson 1983), and by the 1950s, when concern about the lack of such facilities was beginning to be voiced in Britain, there were 166 business schools, departments, or colleges teaching business at university level in the United States.

This lag (of nearly seventy-five years) seems traceable to deep-rooted cultural factors in both academic and business communities in Britain. The universities in Britain are traditionally seen as repositories of the strong anti-industrial, anti-enterprise, or anti-business strands in British culture (Weiner 1981). British universities were long reluctant to concede that business or management studies were suitable subjects for university education. Wheatcroft (1970: 3) summarized the universities' main objections to business and management studies as follows: first, management had no academic content which could be taught; second, business subjects were vocational training and, hence, not the proper function of a university, which exists to develop its students' minds and to give them a critical and analytical approach rather than a 'professional' one; and third, the aim of business is to make money, and this was not considered an objective which academic education should encourage.

For their part, managers in British industry have traditionally been suspicious of, if not hostile to, universities and academics, as a result of a deeply rooted empirical and anti-intellectual attitude. This empiricism, and the conservatism which went with it, were long recognized as a serious weakness of British industry (see Balfour Committee 1929: 245–6).

One aspect of this attitude was a disdain for higher education, and indeed theories and ideas of any kind. Before the Second World War, British industry had very little use for higher education (other than the technical). Many industrialists were of the opinion that university training was irrelevant to business life, considering that it was more beneficial for a manager to have derived training from years of practical experience with the firm, earning promotion on the job. Even in the 1970s, a report on the need and demand for management education could comment that for many of the firms surveyed education was:

an ivory-tower activity pursued by academics unrelated to business and directed towards a different end, whereas training with its respectable industrial history smacked of the real world of solid practical work.

(Leggatt 1972: 3)

The first business schools in the mid 1960s were set up as a response to the perceived decline in Britain's economic fortunes. In 1963, the recently established National Economic Development Council (NEDC) produced a report entitled *Conditions Favourable to Faster Growth* which argued that education was crucial to improving Britain's economic position, and in particular emphasized the importance of skilled management. Business schools were suggested as a source of such skilled management, although the report did not go into the question of where, how, and by whom such schools should be established, or how they should be financed.

Before 1965, the gap left by the universities was, to some extent, filled by the technical colleges where many courses were developed – mainly at the instigation of professional or semi-professional institutes concerned with the interests of members such as personnel and purchasing officers, production managers, or cost accountants. The general course in management provided by some colleges subsequently developed into the Diploma in Management Studies, which was established in 1961. Students were, in the main, middle managers, and studied mostly part time.

Given the entrenched attitudes of industry and academics, the vocationally orientated technical colleges might have seemed the obvious choice to house the new business schools. But here is a striking paradox: it seems to have been taken for granted, even by business leaders themselves, that the new business schools must be set up as parts of existing universities. In 1953, the Federation of British Industry (the FBI, later renamed the Confederation of British Industry, or CBI) produced a Handbook entitled *Education and Training for Management*, which argued the necessity of more extensive and better management education. If this was to happen, it argued that 'the universities must be persuaded to give their wholehearted assistance' (FBI 1953: 13).

The establishment of the first university business schools had to wait another twelve years, however, until two years after the study conducted by Lord Franks, whose *British Business Schools Report*, sponsored and published by the British Institute of Management, was published in 1963. Franks recommended a partnership between universities and business, involving joint control of the two basic instruments of management: policy and money. He proposed the establishment of two business schools, each part of a university (London and Manchester were suggested), but enjoying considerable autonomy as a partnership between the university and business, and offering courses for both postgraduate and post-experience students (but not undergraduates).

156

From the outset, the relationship between the business schools and their parent universities was recognized as problematic. It was the *purpose* of the UBSs to be the institutions where the management elite would be educated (or trained). This would lead to improved economic performance by British industry generally. Yet the UBSs were placed inside institutions which regarded such a pragmatic purpose as entirely beyond their remit and indeed antithetical to their academic function. This tension was the reason why the business schools were set up as autonomous organizations with a degree of private funding. From their inception, however, the UBSs have been the target of persistent criticism to the effect that they are too close to academia and too remote from business to fulfil their original purpose. For example, during the 1960s and 1970s, the National Economic Development Office (NEDO) published a series of reports about management education. A recurrent theme in these reports is contained in the comments about, and criticisms of, the academic emphasis of the programmes provided by UBSs. One reason advanced for the overacademic emphasis of courses was the lack of teachers with sufficient management experience. Too many teachers were professional academics with no actual managerial experience at all:

> Organizers of management education and training would probably have a better understanding of industrial problems if more had practised in industry at managerial level.
> [Verbatim quotation from an unattributed respondent] (NEDO 1965: 26)

This theme concerning the inappropriateness of academics, with little or no practical managerial experience, being the people who teach management (and thus define what 'management' might be and what a 'proper' manager needs to know) has continued to the present day. The current requirement for academic employment at a university is at least a master's degree, and preferably a doctorate. Few senior managers possess this, and even if they did, they would be unwilling to take the large drop in salary that moving to the university sector would entail. As one NEDO report put it:

> The nature of management education, with its considerable emphasis on teaching experienced managers in mid-career, places special demands on teachers who must be credible in the eyes of their students and *not merely academically competent.*
> [Emphasis added] (NEDO 1971: 10)

Unfortunately, as another NEDO report (*Management Education in the 1970s: Growth and Issues* – the Rose Report) pointed out, the supply of teachers with these qualities was outstripped by demand. Interviews with businesspeople made it clear that the shortage of teachers had created dissatisfaction with the quality of teaching and course design:

> What was evident was a shortage of ideal teachers who can convince

the experienced manager-student that an analytical approach can help solve the problems of industry and also bring a sufficient level of practical experience to his [sic] postgraduate course.

(NEDO 1970: 58)

Another report, *Education for Management: a Study of Resources* (NEDO 1971: 72), stated, in its survey of teachers, that only one-third of teachers at the universities had entered the profession with management experience. Overall:

it was generally believed that there were insufficient 'good' *management* teachers who could teach the subject in an integrated manner, particularly to experienced managers.

[Original emphasis] (NEDO 1971: xiii)

Complaints in reports and from students about the relevance of the curriculum have continued throughout the 1970s and 1980s into the present day. The results of the study by Porter and McKibbin (1988) on the status of American business schools have relevance for British schools. The findings conclude that:

1 Young faculty members are too narrowly trained in their specialities.
2 Research is too heavily oriented to the academic community.
3 There is insufficient contact with real managerial problems.
4 The curriculum currently lacks meaningful integration across functional areas.

The 1980s saw a number of academic papers on the question of management education, as well as reports from NEDO, BIM, the DES, and so forth (Cooper 1981; Griffiths and Murray 1985; Kakabadse and Mukhi 1984; Rogers 1988). And what emerges here in the criticisms are the ambiguities about the nature of the business school/parent university relationship and the ambivalences present in the business school/business community interaction. Lupton (1981: 72) pointed out that the greatest stumbling block to the erosion of discipline boundaries in business schools is the dilemma that in the discipline/faculty organization of a university, the best business school teachers (in the sense that what they are doing is both intellectually exciting and practically useful professionally) are unlikely to get preference in promotion against candidates who have produced scholarly work in research central to a known discipline.

What is identified here is a conflict in UBSs between attachment to discipline and the world of scholarship and scholarly values, and attachment to the school and its commitment to improve professional performance in management and to increase professional knowledge. Given that most teachers in the UBSs are in any case discipline specialists who do not have management experience, and that rewards (promotion, status, and so forth) go to those who adhere to university values, Lupton found it possible make the following assertion:

158

It would not be putting it too strongly to say that the degree of prestige of a School is in direct proportion to its supposed 'distance' from the professional activity of managing, and the prestige of a teacher in a School in direct proportion to his [*sic*] lack of practical concern for the profession his [*sic*] School exists to serve.

(Lupton 1981: 62)

Thus Lupton acknowledged the clash between traditional academic criteria (emphasis on individual scholarship leading to publication in prestigious journals) and pressures to engage in group activities of joint problem solving which are professionally valuable, but not productive of the kind of articles that learned journals publish. In short, the business schools have been absorbed into the culture of their parent universities to such an extent as seriously to vitiate their original purpose.

Later, in the 1980s, Griffiths and Murray (1985) made the following criticisms of the UBSs. They were too academic, excessively restricted, remote from business, buttressed by academics' lifetime security of tenure, and not market determined. Griffiths and Murray suggested that these faults or weaknesses stemmed from the original, flawed conception of business schools as substantially publicly funded and part of the university industry, which they described as a closed cartel. Moreover, the faults could all be corrected by removing the 'university' connection from UBSs. Griffiths and Murray suggested a radical solution – that UBSs be privatized. Underlying their analysis appears to be the notion that the faults are the result of bad organizational design, rather than incorrect usage of what the schools have to offer.

THE NEW UNIVERSITY BUSINESS SCHOOLS

The story of the 'new university' business schools (NUBSs) offers an interesting contrast to this. The British polytechnics were established in the late 1960s and were always intended to have a different mission from the universities. In a sense, the polytechnics were another reaction to the traditional anti-industrial culture with which the universities were seen to be imbued. The Robbins Report (1963) had suggested the expansion of higher education by upgrading technical colleges into universities. Anthony Crosland, when Secretary of State from 1964, rejected this approach on the grounds that the colleges would inevitably be assimilated into the culture of the existing universities (a process referred to as 'academic drift'). The pressing need, Crosland felt, was for:

institutions which cater not only for the traditional full-time degree course, but for the part-time student, the sub-degree course, and the kind of education which has its roots in the technical college tradition.

(Kogan 1971: 195).

Hence the decision to establish a separate higher education sector which would be more concerned with teaching, more vocationally oriented, more responsive to the needs of employers, and so on. In short, the polytechnics created in the 1960s from former college-level institutions were intended to fit the 'Teaching' and 'Societal' models as opposed to the 'Research' model of university purpose. The polytechnic sector tended to pride itself on the quality of its teaching, and the vocational and practical orientation of that teaching, whilst there was a widespread view, amongst officials at the Department of Education and Science for instance, that the universities were neglecting their teaching responsibilities (Kogan 1971: 129). This had an impact on the polytechnics' prestige and 'pulling-power' with potential students.

The business schools of the polytechnics, as distinct from their parent bodies, were mostly established in the 1980s, although their provision of management education predated this.[4] There was no national debate before this happened, and no weighty reports by committees of the great and the good. The business schools were set up as the results of decisions taken by the individual polytechnics (as most of the new universities then were) to expand provision in the management/business area, and to reorganize themselves accordingly. These business schools had no special constitutional status within their institutions, and were usually the result of straightforward 'organizational carpentry', if not a simple change of name for 'branding' purposes.

The development of the NUBSs has been a reflection of that of their parent institutions, which gradually acquired the ability to offer more and more degree programmes, postgraduate programmes, and so on. By the end of the 1980s, MBA programmes were commonplace in the NUBSs: demand was growing all the time and every institution wanted to offer an MBA as a flagship programme – proof that they were a 'real' business school.

With the abolition of the binary divide in 1992, the former polytechnics and universities are now of equal status, and so are their business schools, although, as explained above, their history has been rather different. The research project described in the next section was intended to clarify the purpose of the NUBSs, and to contrast them with the OUBSs.

RESEARCH FINDINGS

The model of university business school purpose – research or teaching?

For the purposes of the research, the five models described above were conflated into three: research, teaching, and a combination of these. It was taken as read that, by their nature and operation, UBSs express both the vocational and societal models, the nature of management containing both concepts. The directors were asked to express their opinion of the model of university purpose demonstrated by their UBS. The questions were so phrased as to elicit the actual model and the ideal model. The range of possible responses was from 1 (not at all) to 5 (to a great extent) (see Table 8.1).

What the responses in Table 8.1 indicate is that research, where the prime concern is knowledge acquisition, is valued as a model of UBS purpose in the OUBSs to a great extent, while the NUBSs have not yet shifted their ethos from being teaching oriented. None of the NUBS respondents considered that research is an actual model of purpose in their institution to a great extent; indeed, such value as this model has for them is only to a little extent.

The view of teaching highlights the original aim behind the setting up of the polytechnics – that they should teach to degree standard. It would seem that the ethos (established in the old universities, but new to the former polytechnics) of the importance of research for a university has apparently not yet been accepted by NUBS directors (or, it can be assumed, their

Table 8.1 The model of university business schools

UBS model	Not at all	A little extent	To some extent	A great extent	Very great extent	Total no.
Research:						
Old universities						
Actual	–	1	2	3	–	6
Ideal	–	1	1	3	1	6
New universities						
Actual	1	12	4	–	–	17
Ideal	1	1	9	5	1	17
Teaching:						
Old universities						
Actual	–	1	4	1	–	6
Ideal	–	–	5	1	–	6
New universities						
Actual	–	1	–	11	7	19
Ideal	–	2	4	8	5	19
Combination of research and teaching:						
Old universities						
Actual	–	1	2	3	–	6
Ideal	–	–	–	3	3	6
New universities						
Actual	–	4	8	4	1	17
Ideal	1	–	2	4	11	18

academic faculty). While twelve NUBS directors consider that research is actually a model of purpose in their UBS to a little extent, eleven acknowledge that it is the teaching model which exists in their UBS to a great extent.

To a degree, the responses indicate the difficulty of creating and maintaining a balance of emphasis on both research and teaching. This is, of course, not a problem confined to UBSs, but extends throughout all university departments. Where UBSs are concerned, this 'both/and' view of the primacy of both research and teaching contributes to the mixed message of purpose coming from them into the business community.

What kind of research?

Research has always been seen as an important activity in a business school. Why this should be so is not immediately obvious, if one starts from the premise that the object of the exercise is to improve the quality of British management. A number of reasons could be posited for the importance of research. First, teaching needs a basis of research. This is not, however, supported by the experience of the binary divide. Many would argue that the teaching in polytechnics is superior to that in universities precisely because they have a teaching rather than a research mission. Second, the research conducted would be relevant to business, developing techniques or generating insights which would then be passed on to real-world managers. In fact, one of the constant criticisms of the UBSs is precisely that their research output is so academic and remote from the actual concerns of management, as to have no value in the eyes of the latter. The nature of the research which is conducted in a business school is considered below. Third, research is necessary for the credibility of the schools and the academics who staff them. Without research, management teachers will simply not be taken seriously, by academics in other disciplines or by business leaders.

It is this last view which really seems to underlie the push for research in the nascent business schools in the 1960s.[5]

The common denominator definition of research is that it is a systematic investigation to establish facts or principles, to collect information on a subject, or to acquire knowledge about it. The research model of the purpose of UBSs was further investigated by means of two questions about the wider purpose of research undertaken in UBSs: to provide knowledge for knowledge's sake, or to provide practical help for management (see Table 8.2).

One could conclude from these responses that where research is undertaken in UBSs, for the OUBSs, 'knowledge for knowledge's sake' is an ethos actually endorsed to a great extent, whereas in the NUBSs, one-third of the directors consider that this ethos does not apply at all, and for the majority of the remaining two-thirds, it applies only to some extent.

Table 8.2 Research in university business schools

Research	Not at all	A little extent	To some extent	A great extent	Very great extent	Total no.
Knowledge for knowledge's sake:						
Old universities						
Actual	–	1	3	1	1	6
Ideal	–	–	2	3	1	6
New universities						
Actual	6	7	4	1	1	19
Ideal	1	8	7	2	1	19
Knowledge for practical help for management:						
Old universities						
Actual	–	3	2	1	–	6
Ideal	–	–	3	2	1	6
New universities						
Actual	–	1	12	6	–	19
Ideal	–	–	3	7	9	19

The two questions posed concern knowledge acquisition (knowledge for its own sake) and knowledge dissemination (the provision of help to managers). That is to say that it is not so much the research itself that is to be disseminated, but those results of research which are likely to provide practical help to managers. What this response appears to indicate is that, where research is concerned, it is 'teaching' value (knowledge dissemination) that is of more importance than research for its own sake.

What kind of teaching?

Where teaching is concerned, there are also discrepancies between the ideal situation and that which actually exists in the UBSs. Three questions were asked concerning the purpose of teaching: whether it was to provide theoretical knowledge of management, practical knowledge, or practical skills (see Table 8.3).

These responses indicate that, in the 'new universities', not only is an emphasis on theory not an actual purpose of the NUBSs to any great extent, but it tends to be an ideal only to some extent. If this view continues to predominate, it would seem that the content of teaching of the NUBSs will have a less theoretical orientation than that which already exists in the OUBSs.

Where the teaching of practical knowledge of management is concerned, from the NUBSs' point of view, the actuality matches up with the ideal to be aimed for; in the OUBSs, however, more teaching of practical knowledge of management goes on than should ideally be the case.

Table 8.3 Teaching in university business schools

Teaching	Not at all	A little extent	To some extent	A great extent	Very great extent	Total no.
Teaching of theoretical knowledge of management:						
Old universities						
Actual	–	1	2	3	–	6
Ideal	–	–	3	1	2	6
New universities						
Actual	–	4	11	4	–	19
Ideal	1	6	8	4	–	19
Teaching of practical knowledge of management:						
Old universities						
Actual	1	2	3	–	–	6
Ideal	1	1	2	2	–	6
New universities						
Actual	–	2	8	7	2	19
Ideal	–	4	6	6	3	19
Teaching of practical skills of management						
Old universities						
Actual	–	2	4	–	–	6
Ideal	–	3	3	–	–	6
New universities						
Actual	–	5	10	3	1	19
Ideal	–	8	7	3	1	19

When it comes to the teaching of the practical skills of management, the responses indicate that the actuality exceeds the ideal to some extent and falls short of it to a little extent. It would seem that the teaching of management in the NUBSs concerns the practicalities of management (the tools and techniques) and this is also the ideal to be aimed for; while in the OUBSs, the ideal of such teaching taking place to a little or some extent is met in actuality. It seems a reasonable inference that courses (such as MBAs) in the NUBSs will be more practically orientated, and less academic, than those in the OUBSs.

Education or training?

An ongoing discussion in the area of management education is whether this should be a matter of education (providing a person who is well educated in a general sense) or training (providing a person with specific skills in management). Questions concerning the part that the UBS plays in the education and/or training of managers were included in the questionnaire

Table 8.4 Education and training in the university business school

	Not at all	A little extent	To some extent	A great extent	Very great extent	Total no.
The UBS provides an integral part of a manager's all-round education:						
Old universities	–	–	1	4	1	6
New universities	–	2	–	10	7	19
The UBS solves immediate problems facing companies who are sponsoring students at the UBS:						
Old universities	1	2	2	–	1	6
New universities	–	4	11	4	–	19
The UBS contributes to the long-term performance of companies which are sponsoring students at the UBS:						
Old universities	–	1	2	2	1	6
New universities	–	5	8	6	–	19
The UBS is concerned to enhance the career prospects of students:						
Old universities	–	1	1	3	1	6
New universities	–	3	4	10	2	19
The UBS informs managers of new techniques and developments in management:						
Old universities	–	2	–	3	1	6
New universities	–	3	4	10	2	19

because attitudes about education and training feed into the overall purpose of UBSs (see Table 8.4).[6]

The questions to which the directors responded concerned, as seen in Table 8.4, the degree to which the various educational and training purposes of the UBSs are:

- to provide an integral part of a manager's all-round education;
- to solve the immediate problems facing companies which are sponsoring students at the UBS;
- to contribute to the long-term performance of companies which are sponsoring students at the UBS;
- to enhance the career prospects of students;
- to inform managers of new techniques and developments in management.

The issues which emerge here are those of long-term or short-term perspective. The UBS deals, according to the directors, with knowledge in the long term, while the business community has a shorter time horizon. This discrepancy of outlook adds to the organizational problems of the UBSs. The UBS also focuses on the all-round education and career of the individual manager/student rather than on the needs of industry *per se*. There is no apparent difference, however, between the 'old' and 'new' business schools in this area.

CONCLUSION

Unlike most other departments in its parent university, where work is judged by peers using the standards of the discipline, the business school is subject to two sets of judgements, reflecting the views of its two constituencies – one in the university, and the other in professional practice (Cheit 1991: 208). Thus the inward orientation of the UBS is to theory and scholarship; the outward orientation is to applied problems and operations. The result of this double orientation is that very often the UBS finds itself in the position of being able to satisfy neither of its constituencies.

Folk wisdom used to have it that the OUBSs would provide a prestigious MBA degree, the contents of which would tend towards the 'airy-fairy', while the polytechnic's business schools could be relied on to have their feet on the ground and to provide an MBA more concerned with the tools, techniques, and practical aspects of management. The findings presented above certainly support this view.

The story of management education in Britain in the last thirty years is full of ironies. Until the 1960s, management education was rather undeveloped for two reasons, both of them reflections of deeply rooted cultural values. On the one hand, there was the disdain of universities for anything which smacked of commerce, and on the other, the contempt of the 'practical' people of business for anything emanating from the ivory towers. Yet when business leaders (such as members of the old FBI or the BIM) were persuaded of the need for a more educated managerial cadre in British industry (for entirely pragmatic reasons, of course), they saw no alternative but to call on the universities to do the job. The technical colleges which had hitherto filled the gap left by the universities were relegated to the role of second-rank providers of training to the lower levels of management, a division of labour symbolized by the MBA (for 'officers') and the DMS (for 'other ranks').

By having the capacity to define management, the universities 'took it over', and turned it into another academic discipline. 'Management' and 'Business Studies' are now established subjects, and the latter is even taught in secondary schools.[7] But this process has been at the expense of the practical purposes for which the UBSs were first established.

Referring back to the models of purpose of the universities outlined in the first part of this chapter, although British universities may be pluralistic, engaging in research, teaching, and societal functions, there is no doubt about what *drives* (the 'old') universities, gives them prestige, and makes them 'excellent' (or not) institutions. It is research. The same is true of the

166

individual academics who work in them: prestige, promotion, careers, are all built on research, and research only. This inherent tension between the original (stated) purpose of the UBSs and the culture of the institutions in which they were placed was recognized at the outset and explains a number of the features of the original business schools – for example, their quasi-autonomous status. The original concentration on post-experience courses, to the exclusion of undergraduate programmes, also distanced the business schools from the culture of their parent universities.

But this is precisely what has gone wrong. In all respects save one (the lower level of public funding), the UBSs have been gradually captured by academia. The schools have concentrated on research rather than teaching. The research itself has become more and more academic, research *about* management, to be read by other academics, published in academic journals which managers never read (Griffiths and Murray 1985; Lupton 1984).

Only a minority of the academics in the OUBSs have ever had any management experience (Brown 1991), and the subject of the first degrees of OUBS academics (Brown 1991) gives little indication that they will end up in a business school. The trend has been to recruit academics rather than practising managers who wish to enter academia (unlike the NUBSs, where anecdotal evidence supports the view that they were more willing to recruit managers who wished to become educators).[8] Brown (1991) reports that first degrees include such diverse areas as theology, philosophy, geography, history, medicine, education, ecology, languages, biology, zoology, and aeronautical engineering. Faculty have, however, subsequently also qualified in the areas more relevant to their careers in a business school: accounting, sociology, psychology, economics, computing. It is likely that they did not enter commerce or industry after graduating, but went straight into academic work after acquiring the appropriate qualifications to lecture.

What the academics teach tends to be academic and theoretical, ill suited to the practical day-to-day problems of the managers for whose benefit the institutions were set up. And the courses they teach conform more and more to university norms. In the 1970s, there was actually a debate over the question of whether UBSs should offer first degrees in management, the original UBSs being postgraduate or post-experience/executive development institutions.

Anecdotal evidence suggests that the latest development is the increasingly common phenomenon whereby newly graduated students enrol on a full-time MBA, turning the MBA into a postgraduate degree like any other master's degree, where the criteria for enrolment are academic, rather than practical knowledge and experience. The purpose of a first degree in business studies is to provide commerce and industry with people who have the knowledge to fulfil their potential and, with appropriate experience on the job, to become managers. A student who goes straight into an MBA degree after graduation undermines the purpose of that degree, which is to improve the performance of existing managers.

In the meantime, the technical colleges, having become polytechnics, set up their own business schools, which are far closer to meeting those needs which the UBSs were originally supposed to address. Paradoxically, although chronologically first, the OUBS is, in fact, an imitation: it is the NUBS which is nearer the real thing – if we define 'the real thing' as the business school envisaged by those who first suggested it, for example Lord Franks (1963).

It might be interesting to speculate on what would have happened to management education if it had simply been left alone, and the 'old' universities had never become so deeply involved. Dominated by the polytechnics/'new' universities, it might have been much more useful (although far less prestigious). But that is the point: for all the contempt professed by managers for the ivory towers, management education had to be placed inside academia before managers would take such education seriously.

Now the wheel has turned again, and the abolition of the binary divide puts the NUBSs, in theory, under the same pressures as the OUBSs. The research findings suggest that, so far, they have kept their distinctive ethos. Whether they can do this and stave off 'academic drift' remains to be seen. It would be the cruellest irony of all if the pressures of the academic market force the real things to imitate the imitations.

NOTES

1 For example, National Vocational Qualifications (NVQs) and General National Vocational Qualifications (GNVQs) which are intended to be alternatives to certificates and diplomas can be obtained from colleges and even the Open University.
2 Obviously, it is possible that the interpretation of the purpose of directors of UBSs may or may not be the same as their faculty – and the earlier research (Brown 1991) elicited faculty opinion. The resulting comparisons and contrasts are tangential to the aims of this chapter, and are not referred to here. Research is currently being undertaken to elicit the views of NUBS faculties in order to compare them with the OUBS data.
3 With university status granted to the polytechnics, there are now around 100 UBSs in the Britain.
4 The polytechnics had, in their previous incarnation as technical colleges, been the main providers of such education prior to the establishment of the OUBSs, as explained above.
5 For example, in 1966, when the first two UBSs were only months old, a conference was held at Ditchley Park to consider 'The Place of a Business School in a University'. Speakers at the conference expressed the conviction that research should be a major activity for first-rate business schools, to which one-quarter to one-third of the schools' budget should be devoted: 'When our

business schools come to be judged, they will stand or fall on the quality and quantity, above all the quality, of the research they have done' (Ditchley Foundation 1966: 13).

6 These questions were not split into an ideal and actual purpose. When the questionnaire was designed, it was taken as read that the major function of any academic institution is the education or training of students.

7 There is a Business Studies GCE A-level, for example.

8 This aspect of NUBS academics is the subject of further research currently being undertaken by the authors.

REFERENCES

Audu, I. (1977) 'Ahmadu Bello University, Nigeria: The Agricultural and Educational Role of the University', in K.W. Thompson, B.R. Feigel, and H.E. Danner (eds) *Higher Education and Social Change in Developing Countries, Vol. 2: Case Studies*, New York: Praeger.

Balfour Committee (1929) *Final Report on Industry and Trade*, London: HMSO.

British Institute of Management (1963) *British Business Schools Report* (The Franks Report), London: British Institute of Management.

Brown, R.B. (1991) 'The Knowledge of Business and the Business of Knowledge', unpublished PhD thesis, University of Bradford.

—— (1993) 'The Purpose of University Business Schools', *Journal of Further and Higher Education* 17(2): 14.

Cheit, E.F. (1991) 'The Shaping of Business Management Thought', in D. Easton and C.S. Schelling (eds) *Divided Knowledge: Across Disciplines, Across Cultures*, Newbury Park, CA: Sage.

Cooper, C.L. (ed.) (1981) *Developing Managers for the 1980s*, London: Macmillan.

Ditchley Foundation (1966) *Management Education*, Ditchley Paper No. 8, Oxford: The Ditchley Foundation.

Federation of British Industries (1953) *FBI Handbook: Education and Training for Management*, London: Federation of British Industries.

Flexner, A. (1930) *Universities: American, English, German*, London: Oxford University Press.

Franks Report (1963) *British Business Schools*, London: British Institute of Management.

Green, V.H.H. (1969) *The Universities*, Harmondsworth: Penguin.

Griffiths, B. and Murray, H. (1985) *Whose Business?: A Radical Proposal to Privatise British Business Schools*, Hobart Paper No. 102, London: Institute of Economic Affairs.

Halsey, A.H. (1990) 'Slow Blur of the Binary Line', *The Times Higher Educational Supplement* 26 January.

Kakabadse, A. and Mukhi, S. (eds) (1984) *The Future of Management Education*, Aldershot: Gower.

Kerr, C. (1963) *The Uses of the University*, Cambridge, MA: Harvard University Press.

Kogan, M. (1971) *The Politics of Education*, Harmondsworth: Penguin.

Leggatt, T. (1972) *The Training of British Managers: A Study of Need and Demand* (The Leggatt Report), London: HMSO.

Lupton, T. (1981) 'The Structure and Functions of Business Schools in the 80s', Working Papers Series No. 68, Manchester: Manchester Business School.

—— (1984) 'The Functions and Organisation of University Business Schools', in A. Kakabadse and S. Mukhi (eds) *The Future of Management Education*, Aldershot: Gower.

National Economic Development Committee (1963) *Conditions Favourable to Faster Growth*, London: HMSO.

National Economic Development Office (1965) *Management Recruitment and Development*, London: HMSO.

—— (1970) *Management Education in the 1970s: Growth and Issues* (The Rose Report), London: HMSO.

—— (1971) *Education for Management: A Study of Resources*, London: HMSO.

Newman, C.J.H. (1959) *The Idea of a University*, New York: Image Books.

Porter, L.W. and McKibbin, L.E. (1988) *Management Education and Development: Drift or Thrust into the 21st century?*, New York: McGraw-Hill.

Robbins Report (1963) *Higher Education*, Cmnd 2154, Committee on Higher Education, London: HMSO.

Rogers, J. (1988) *MBA: the Best Business Tool? A Guide to British and European Business Schools*, London: Economist Publications.

Searle, J. (1972) *The Campus War*, London: Pelican.

Simpson, R. (1983) *How the PhD came to Britain: A century of Struggle for Postgraduate Education*, Guildford, Surrey: Society for Research into Higher Education.

Truscott, B. (1943) *Redbrick University*, London: Faber.

Weiner, M.J. (1981) *English Culture and the Decline of the Industrial Spirit 1850–1980*, Cambridge: Cambridge University Press.

Wheatcroft, M. (1970) *The Revolution in British Management Education*, London: Pitman.

9

THE INSTITUTIONALIZATION OF INDUSTRIAL ADMINISTRATION IN NORWAY 1950–90

Consequences for education in business administration of domination by engineering

Haldor Byrkjeflot and Tor Halvorsen

INTRODUCTION

It has now become common wisdom that there is a link between management practice and the culture of a given society. There have, however, been few studies that deal with the way in which educational institutions shape industrial administration (Fligstein and Byrkjeflot 1996). This may be due to the strong influence of neo-classical economic thought, in which the education system in itself does not matter because, in the last instance, it is shaped by the economy. Managers are understood to be calculators responding to market stimulus, and also in their search for new managerial recruits and their demand for education. In the current wave of cross-national cultural studies, on the other hand, managers and educational systems are presumably pre-programmed by a given society's culture (Hofstede 1993; Lessem and Neubauer 1994). This sudden jump from economic determinism to culturalism seems unfortunate. In the authors' view, there ought to be a relationship between the patterns of recruitment and qualification in management – what managers actually do, and what kind of industrial structures and strategies emerge in a given geographical area. Knowledge-producing institutions matter because they influence and shape the groups and personalities that are recruited to the executive positions; because of their impact on the way in which they interpret their own activities; and thus also how they legitimate what they do when confronted with opposition or insecurity.

171

THE MODERN HISTORY OF INDUSTRIAL ADMINISTRATION

The institutionalization of industrial administration

The modern history of Norwegian industrial administration, from about 1950 to about 1980, is the history of change within a tradition of strong continuity. During this period, the Norwegian system of industrial administration, for which the foundation was laid in the previous period (1900–50), was institutionalized. This institutionalization was due to a particular configuration of actors and ideas within the firm, the pattern of industrial relations, the professions, and the educational system.

All these actors have to be taken into account in a fully fledged account of the history of Norwegian business administration. In this connection, stress will be put on forms of learning and possible types of education. However, in this period, there was no development of educational institutions for management education as such. The only private business administration school of any importance – the Norwegian School of Management (NSM) – focused primarily on practical economic administration and techniques for middle management (Amdam 1993). The major public institution for private business education in Norway – the Norwegian School of Economics and Business Administration (NSEBA) (Jensen and Strømme Svendsen 1986) – also leaned more towards teaching administrative techniques and economics than general management and leadership-oriented subjects.

However, the decisive point as far as the Norwegian system is concerned, was the historical domination of engineers in management positions, and the importance of engineering education in the production of managerial knowledge. In comparison with technical education, business education came very late, and its influence has to be considered against this background. Most positions above the level of supervisors that contain managerial obligations are strongly dominated by one type of engineer or another. Even though engineers have to acquire new types of knowledge in order to improve their chances of advancement as managers, they seldom lose their primary industrial/technological identification. This is, of course, due to their historical heritage – namely, that engineers were the dominant professionally educated group in industry during the process of indus-trialization – and, more specifically, to the way this heritage is currently being reproduced by established institutions (Halvorsen 1993).

Norway has a strong polytechnic educational tradition (Halvorsen 1993). This is considered to be the basic type of education – to which any managerial knowledge has to be added. Thus management and technology seldom lose contact. The educational system is linked to a hierarchy of all levels of administration within the firm. This hierarchy does not, however, create strong lines of demarcation between the different sorts of engineer, making, for example, the most prominent kind of engineering education a type of management education. Managerial careers may also emanate from lower-level types of education, even though civil engineers dominate this area and sooner or later more than half of them end up in executive positions. Some of the reasons for the strong organizational domination of the engineering profession will be illustrated below, and suggestions made as to how this is related to the shaping of management.

Between the United States and Germany?

As a gross simplification it may be indicated that the Norwegian system developed as an unstable compromise between the American and the German systems. On the one hand, the strong German tradition within the engineering profession, and on the other, the powerful leaning towards the West with regard to business relations and social orientation, represented alternative structures and positions that had to be united. After the Second World War, 'a wave of Americanism' came to dominate on the level of language, ideology, and social identification, but did not manage to change German practices which were already entrenched (Hartmann 1963; Ermarth 1993). No consensus as to what management is was established. Two major elements accounted for this relative instability: first, the entrenched position of engineers in Norwegian industry; second, the particular compromise reached in the early 1950s between the macro-governance of markets and financial systems and meso-management in industries and firms, which left the task of macro-governance in the economy to the national economists, and management, leadership, and administration in the firm to the engineering profession.

Before embarking on the historical account, however, it is useful to specify the comparative background against which changes in the Norwegian scene are analysed. The success of the American management tradition is due to the fact that it has effectively combined the functions of leadership and administration in the idea of *general management*. Within an organizational unit, the terms leadership and administration may be used to distinguish between the need for motivation and innovation, on the one hand, and control and coordination, on the other.[1] This means that people in formal authority positions at all levels of the organization are responsible for leadership as well as administrative functions. The major distinction, then, is not between leadership and administration, but between general and specific management. Leadership is believed to be a necessary activity in all parts of the system, particularly where managers have to manage other managers. The American general management tradition, which emerged as a fully fledged idea and practice in the interwar period, was constructed by innovative business practitioners and consultants such as Alfred Sloan, Chester Barnard, and Peter Drucker (Barnard 1938; Drucker 1949, 1954; Sloan 1963).

The ideal was not the public administrator nor the owner-entrepreneur nor the technical director, but the general manager. The higher up the hierarchy, the more leeway there was for fulfilling this ideal; but in order to advance to such a level the specific manager would have to demonstrate leadership abilities. The logic of the whole system, therefore, was more attuned to leadership than to administration. This logic was supported by an industrial relations system, which had a sharp distinction between the managerial and labouring classes, and an educational system, which separated education for manual and management functions. In the long run, according to such a philosophy, engineers could not occupy major positions in industry. It was a system that was much more open to dispute among the various professions presenting alternative leadership models. The theory of decentralized control and management by objectives, as introduced by Sloan and Drucker between the wars, and the steadily increasing influence of an economic and financial way of understanding leadership, have to be understood in such a perspective.

Then there is the type of business administrative system which is found in Germany. The German *Unternehmer* is even better educated than the American top executive, although more often in a technical discipline. The German's leadership function is more constrained by family heritage, public administration, and a cartel type of governance structures (Byrkjeflot 1993a, 1993b). The continental leadership/administration tradition (*Führung/ Leitung* in German) puts less emphasis on leadership and more on administration in the lower managerial positions. The leadership dimension is taken for granted to a much greater extent; in the career system, therefore, most emphasis is put on administration, and thus education in the appropriate administrative techniques. The idea is that leadership should not be thought of in relation only to specific educational programmes for business, but has to be developed and preserved within other spheres, such as the state, the family, or professions and occupations.

It is claimed that the technical, engineering-dominated, and patriarchal family-dominated systems have each made their impact on the Norwegian management tradition. However, the suspicion is that, in general, the technical element is even more important in Norway than in Germany, which comes closest among the larger nations to the technical ideal. In Norway, the patriarchal system predominates within some networks of small firms in the regions, whereas the technical system is most firmly entrenched on a national level. Because there is often a missing link between regional and national industry, however, the engineering dimension is the key source of identification for actors in the field of industrial administration.

The new system of business administration education, which was established in Norway in the early 1950s, contained an unstable compromise between the different actors: the owner–executives, the employer associations, the unions, the professions, and the politicians and administrators involved in the educational system (Halvorsen 1982, 1993). They all contributed differently to the evolution of business administration and had varying opinions on how managerial strategies and practices were to be developed. They were, in different degrees, leaning on either the new Americanism or expressing established traditions.

Trends and movements, 1950–90: an overview

The Norwegian field of business administration in the postwar era has been constituted by four epistemological trends and social movements. These are the post-Taylorist, socio-technical, industrial democracy, and managerial trends.[2] It is in the interaction of the systems of ideas, the actors who pick them up and give them new meaning, and the merger of these ideas and actors into social movements that the meaning and importance of epistemological trends may be grasped. These trends are constant only in an analytical way, however, because new forms of knowledge and actor constellations emerge and create new ideologies and practices on the basis of the same systems of knowledge. Moreover, they do not just combine the same basic ideas in new ways, they also create new kinds of knowledge and accumulate new types of experience. Managerialism, as it emerged in the United States from the 1930s on, and was disseminated to the rest of the world after the Second World War, may have been exactly such a new combination of ideas and actions crystallizing into new kinds of social movements and social structures (Enteman 1993; Ringer 1992: Swidler 1986).

It is not thought, however, that managerialism existed as anything other than a sub-current in the Norwegian field of industrial administration in the immediate postwar era. Four epistemological traditions have been identified – that is, trends in the Norwegian context to which most actors had to relate. Some actors, of course, were more likely to link up with one trend rather than another. The trends were interdependent, which means that, in a field of knowledge, each developed partly as a response to another (Ringer 1992). However, the actors did not make entirely independent choices as to which ideas to pick up and respond to. Certain trends caught on more than others owing to economic, political, and social circumstances.

The four trends were both cumulative and conjunctural. The socio-technical trend and the industrial democracy movement were closer to thinking of the human relations type than that of the more rationalistic and bureaucratic post-Taylorist kind. Managerialism in the Norwegian context, where the organic way of conceptualizing society was firmly ingrained, was a difficult programme of governance for anything other than the firm – at least before the 1980s when managerialist governance of the whole of society emerged as a possibility.

The post-Taylorist trend in the 1950s

The emphasis in the 1950s was on administration and efficiency, rather than on leadership and effectiveness, which later emerged, along with the socio-technical and industrial democracy movements, as the more important themes in industry. On the whole, however, the field of industrial administration was getting increasingly complex and involved a growing variety of actors (Gulowsen 1984, 1987).

A compromise between an industrial relations system of joint management and a post-Taylorist type of internal administration was developed. The basis for this compromise was a deal, in the early 1950s, between government and industrialists, on the one hand, and economists and engineers, on the other. According to this deal, it was government's task, with the help of national economists, to devise the overall economic framework in which industrial actors could operate (namely, macro-economics), whereas the development of technology and business organization was left to the engineers in alliance with the owner–managers. This meant that a major part of the leadership element in management was left to the government, and that, accordingly, the emphasis within the firm was on administrative tasks and product development. The tradition of post-Taylorism was both encouraged and advanced by this system of joint administration and division of labour between the professions and actors in government and business.

The deal was a setback for the managerial trend, which was being revitalized throughout Europe, partly as a result of direct American intervention. The golden era of post-Taylorism in Norway was in the immediate postwar period, and then again in the 1980s. However, when it reappeared in the latter period, it was in a new and more mature – and perhaps also a genuinely innovative – form: managerialism. Post-Taylorism was always the sub-current against which other more significant trends and actors defined their positions. Elements from this philosophy were institutionalized at several levels within the field of business administration: at lower levels through the training-within-industry (TWI) courses for middle and lower managers, and at higher administrative levels through the Norwegian Productivity Institute (NPI), which was established in 1952 with funds from the Marshall Aid programme. Between 1953 and 1958, 6,000 workers and supervisors went through the TWI programme. The purpose of the programme, which was initiated by the Norwegian trade unions, was to qualify union leaders for supervisory positions within industry (Gauslaa 1993; Utnes 1993).

After the Second World War, then, several institutions were established with the explicit purpose of transmitting knowledge of American business administration to Norwegian firms, but the emphasis was more on specific techniques than on managerialism as a philosophy and governance model.

The leading group within the field of industrial administration was an alliance between representatives of the joint management type of programmes and the engineering profession. The latter had a technically competent and politically neutral image that fitted well with the agenda of the major owner–entrepreneurs in Norwegian industry in the 1950s, as well as with the consensus-oriented and technocratic governmental agencies. The major threat, in the perception of the owner–entrepreneurs,[3] came from the strong labour unions. They themselves probably preferred the macro-governance of industrial development promoted by the national economists with the support of the social democratic government to industrial self-government in the economy, which they feared might leave an opening for a union takeover and thus intervention in so-called managerial prerogatives.

So the compromise that was struck was not only between management and labour, and government and industrialists, but also between economists and engineers. It was envisaged that the economists would concentrate their efforts on economic macro-governance, whereas macro-innovation and industrial administration would be left to the engineers. In this last task, however, the engineers were very much constrained by the joint management idea. A system for labour representation was developed within the firm, as well as on a societal level. The major consequence of this was a further strengthening of the culture of cooperation, consensus making, and continuous bargaining between representatives of the workforce and the managers.

The socio-technical trend in the 1960s

The predominant trend of the 1950s was challenged in the 1960s by the socio-technical trend. The movement forming around this trend introduced a human relations type of management, and contributed strongly to the development of human resources administration as a major strategy. The first major alternative to the engineering tradition in industrial administration was thus introduced – namely, social science, primarily in the form of psychology. However, it was still not introduced as an attempt to challenge the engineering profession, but rather as a means of supplementing its knowledge and ability to manage (Lundberg 1991).

During the 1960s, engineers, still the predominant recruits to managerial hierarchies, saw the demand for new managerial techniques of the types the social sciences provided. The socio-technical movement also challenged and partly changed the industrial relations arrangements initiated in the wake of the joint management deal struck in the 1950s. It supplemented the Taylorist tradition by adapting elements from the particular Norwegian joint management tradition. The new compromise was an abandonment of wage systems and systems of reward based on the traditional Taylorist system of measurement (work and time studies) and the introduction instead of trust-building agreements based on productivity and fixed wages for all categories of workers. The idea was to pass over the zero-sum power ideology, and show that both parts could increase their power through new forms of participation. This led, on the one hand, to an increased legitimization of the administrative system of the firm, bringing in types of knowledge from outside the engineering professions. On the other, the strengthening of the bargaining power of the leaders of the workforce at the firm level increased the legitimacy of the local union, at the same time as the union at national level had its position boosted. More aspects of the work situation now came under the joint management system. Engineers were able to adapt to this new situation and could therefore continue as the core group in the industrial administrative system.

The industrial democracy trend in the 1970s

The joint management type of administration of the firm came to a peak in the 1970s. It was during these years that the firm-based union administration developed several types of shop stewards (*tillitsmenn*) who not only defended the workers' immediate interests but were also involved in the firm as such – that is, in the development of policy relating to technology, marketing, and human resources. Moreover, a number of new positions were established as a result of the new laws for industrial democracy, the industrial environment, and health care (Hagtvedt and Lafferty 1984). The firm was increasingly managed from the top down by the senior executives and the union representatives, leaving middle management in a crisis.

The managerial trend in the 1980s

This crisis of middle management continued into the 1980s, which was a decade of strong ideological and political change. The Norwegian system of industrial administration now faced several major challenges, among them the revival of post-Taylorism as managerialism. This movement was associated with a strong belief in economics as an instrument of governance, mainly on the organizational level, and a frontal attack on the Keynesian ideology which had been the basis of the Norwegian compromise between economists and engineers, and workers and managers.

This perceived failure of planning and macro-governance gave an impetus to the new managerial movement. The firm as an organization became the central unit of interest for the managerial revival, because it focused on the need for autonomous management strategies at the firm level. The deepening economic crisis supported this fixation on the firm, since it was diagnosed as having been caused by 'Eurosclerosis' – namely, too much emphasis on macro-regulation, public administration, and privileges for special interest groups in the private economy. The firm had been incapable of reacting appropriately to market demands owing to the joint management tradition and the heavy domination of engineers and macro-economists in the administrative system. This development posed a challenge to the actors within the industrial relations system, who based their legitimacy precisely on a belief in joint management and the macro-regulation of relations within the firm. In addition, it was a major blow to the socio-technical traditions which, in Norway, had been successfully adopted by the engineers. The new managerialist movement was gaining support within the engineering profession as well, but its primary protagonists were graduates from the business schools. Support for the post-Taylorist model of industrial administration was clearly in decline. This was also due to increased complexity in the economy, the rise of the new educated middle classes, and the educational revolution.

New types of positions and organizational forms had been developed within the education system of business administration, and new ways of interpreting the purpose and strategy of the firm were introduced as a result of increased professional diversity. Innovative conceptions of industrial administration emerged among groups outside the engineering professions. New cooperative ventures between blue- and white-collar workers and management were launched – kinds of cooperation that connected the firm to the societal and political scene in other ways than the earlier joint management tradition.

To summarize this overview: the 1980s represented a major challenge for the Norwegian system of industrial administration. But this challenge did not result in a fundamental change of the system. The diversity has increased; moreover, during the 1990s a revival of the trends associated with the other major movements in the postwar era has been experienced, together with a partial rehabilitation of the engineer who, in Norway, has demonstrated a remarkable ability to adjust to new trends in industrial administration. However, in the long run, the managerialist challenge of the 1980s may turn out to be a serious blow against the predominance of engineers in the management of industry. A new type of discourse has been established around 'the flexible firm', in which industrial relations and industrial democracy are considered as obstacles to change (Reve 1994). The diagnosis is that the social and political constraints on the autonomy of the firm have to be leavened so that the process of decision making relates more strongly to its market aspect. Its human resources aspect has not lost importance; on the contrary, it is seen to be more important than ever. However, this aspect is perceived to be important for a different reason. The emphasis is now more on the formation of skills, individual performance, and adaptability, in contrast to the previous emphasis which was on the design of the job itself, the internal career system, and so on. Macro-governance of the development of human resources is promoted at the same time as macro-governance of the economy and of the firm are being abandoned as a strategy for change.

Different trends and types of education for management

How the different trends and movements stimulated different types of training and education for management is the next thing to be discussed. At one end of the spectrum, the most formalized and institutionalized sort of programmes come to mind – programmes that contribute to the formation of the professional system and positions within the industrial administration system. At the other, the more informal and *ad hoc* types of education, in which practitioners try to preserve their established position through the enlargement of their knowledge base, need to be included. The next section of the chapter will discuss how the system of education for management, which was established in an era of engineering dominance, has influenced the position of various groups in industry, and how management in general is to be conceived of in Norway.

The educational system may be studied as an agent of change in the field of business administration, as will become apparent. Changes in the educational system in one period affect the interactions between those involved in the next. There is a continuous time-lag. Initiatives and ideas from peripheral and non-hegemonic groups are activated within institutions of learning and counselling; they then blossom when the 'time is ripe' – namely, in conjunction with political and ideological changes in society. The movements described in the previous section may have strengthened certain epistemological positions, and affected thereby the attention these trends were given within the education system. Furthermore, various groups in the professions and the educational system react against the predominant trends within industry. Such groups develop programmes and institutions that may influence the system for industrial administration in a major way. In the long run, too, the educational system is the primary means of bringing new actors and conceptions of industrial administration on to the scene. If managerialism is indeed a new ideology, its emergence, diffusion, and possible downfall cannot be understood independently from development trends generally within the education system.

EDUCATION AND MANAGEMENT IN THE POST-TAYLORIST PERIOD

The struggle between different actors and ideas

In the immediate postwar era, there was a struggle between two sets of actors and ideas. On the one hand, there were those who were primarily oriented towards the Anglo-Saxon kind of management thinking, and on the other, there were those who emphasized instruments for macro-governance along with joint administration at the shop-floor level.

The post-Taylorist tradition was boosted by the Marshall Plan in particular, and the strong links between the Norwegian leaders and those of Britain and the United States during the war. A cluster of managerial ideas, inspirations, and traditions in Norway, which are hard to separate, are embraced by the post-Taylorist period. It might be said that what, in all probability, separated managerialism from Taylorism was the 'general management' idea. However, as George Kenning, an American consultant working in Norway, emphasized, it was difficult to get top Norwegian executives to adopt a generalist attitude (Kalleberg 1991; Schjander 1987). This was because Norway was part of the continental European tradition, in which the distinction between 'general' and 'specific' management has not been emphasized.

In the Norwegian context, the managerial task was to administer a system on the basis of premises established elsewhere, whereas the Anglo-Saxon generalist manager was a less constrained specialist in the task of setting a purpose and then getting others to do the work necessary to arrive at this purpose. It was much more difficult to emphasize the need for strong leadership at the firm level in the Norwegian context, since the demand for such leadership was not strong among owners and workers owing to belief in macro-governance and the joint management method of running the firm. There is also, for several reasons, a general scepticism among Norwegians of authority, which makes it difficult for managers to establish legitimacy for decisive action (Andersen 1988; Sejersted 1993). This may be the reason why it was easier to transfer the leadership function to national economists and the social democratic state, which had acquired its legitimacy in democratic elections and in its resistance to the German occupation. In the local business system, the causes of the limited success of managerialism may have been different again. The leadership function in small firms was less problematic, since it was often taken for granted that someone in the owner–entrepreneur's family would take on this role. The family and the regional context were more important than the belief in industrial administration or the government as such.

Internal recruitment

To specialize in general management, then, was not an appropriate career strategy in a country with a legacy of public administration, joint management, and a predominance of small family firms. To the extent that management was separated from ownership at all, in Norwegian firms around 1950, managers were primarily recruited internally (Halvorsen 1983). This gave them a double identification: with their occupation and with their firm. Their occupational identification could not be separated from the firm since their skills were both based on experience and socially embedded in the context of a firm. The educated engineer also had to start in a lower position in the firm, and go through the same sort of career moves as other workers; it was difficult, therefore, to distinguish the professional from the managerial career.

In other words, there were no established separate career tracks for general managers and professionals, as was usual in the United States and Britain (Goldner and Ritti 1967). The advantage of this type of recruitment was that it contributed to a high level of trust between upper- and lower-level positions. The engineer–executives knew the capabilities and tasks of the professional and managerial people below them because they had worked their way up through the same positions and had developed a network of social relations in the firm. Thus it was possible for them to allow the people beneath them to solve their own administrative and technical problems. As a result, the relatively untrusting Anglo-Saxon tradition of management thinking was not implemented in Norwegian firms in the 1950s, even though its success at the ideological level was apparent (Fox 1974; Kalleberg 1991; Schjander 1987). In the main, this new managerial orientation established a position outside of the firm, within the growing number of consultancies. In the increasing, though still not very developed, process of separation between owners and managers, the latter companies played an important part. Consultancy was an engineering activity at this time – a leading position that only lessened slightly during the 1960s, as first business school graduates and then social scientists began to enter the arena.

Training and educational institutions

These management consultancy firms were backed by factions within the industrial organizational networks who, in accordance with new ideas emanating from the liberated West, hoped to get rid of some of the forces constraining management action within the firm. Many members of these factions had been educated in the United States, on management courses. Both people and organizations had strong links to the Taylorist movement; indeed, some of the organizations were actually installed to advance Taylorist management techniques. The most important of these was IR, later IRAS (Industriforbundets Rasjonaliseringsgruppe), established in 1936. The groups that pushed to have this division established were central to driving forward the neo-Taylorist techniques and services that now started to flood the market. This was done through the use of and backing from private consultancy firms, but more importantly still through particular organizational settings within the established industrial associations. To a large extent, the aim of these institutions was to transfer information to the general public about new ways of managing. IR, for example, started its own bulletin on management and rationalization within the national journal on industry (*Industri*).

The actions taken by the network of management-minded industrialists were often closely coordinated with those of a number of rationalization agencies established by the engineering profession.[4] All together, they represented a substantial attempt to advance post-Taylorist strategies within business administration. These groups were all dominated by engineers, and the most active and energetic among them established a tightly linked network of institutions and persons, which was the core of the post-Taylorist movement in Norway.

Nevertheless, this movement was unable to establish any form of regular education for management within the established educational institutions, even though it may be regarded as a breakthrough that the Norwegian Institute of Technology (NTH) decided, after about thirty years of discussion, to establish a professorship for industrial economics and organization (Halvorsen 1982; Hanisch and Lange 1985). When the professorship became effective after five years of planning, the curriculum consisted of a combination of subjects, from labour law and industrial relations matters to techniques from the Taylorist 'cookbook'. Demands, from management circles within the Norwegian Association of Industry, that NTH should create a whole division for studies on management were not granted owing to the strong polytechnic tradition. The purpose of the school was to educate engineers not managers.

There were courses in company management at some of the lower-level technical colleges at this time. However, they seem to have vanished during the 1940s and 1950s, basically because the engineering elite was trying to establish the discipline of business administration as a monopoly for the top echelons of the profession. The courses that had been initiated on a local basis at the technical schools lost their place in the system, therefore, and the support of planners of the education curricula. It is only recently that these schools have again become arenas for systematic managerial and organizational training.

The Taylor tradition also had some representatives at NSEBA in Bergen, mainly thanks to a Swedish professor, but it dwindled at this school too (Halvorsen 1983; Jensen and Strømme Svendsen 1986). The social network of organizationally oriented engineers was tight-knit and their strategy was to establish business administration as a high-status field of knowledge within the engineering profession. This group provided an important link between the activities of the various types of interest organizations, which gave an impetus to a strong post-Taylorist movement in Norway. Nonetheless, the achievements of the movement were limited. In the long run, the professorship at NTH may actually have turned out to be an obstacle to the establishment of a more broadly based education in management and organization.

The post-Taylorist movement, then, was most successful at the ideological and cultural level. It was met with resistance by owners of firms and among some labour leaders. An agreement between the social partners in industry – the so-called agreement on work evaluation and time studies – established a structure that gave the engineers room for action within the post-Taylorist framework. This agreement, reached in 1947, the same year as the professorship was established at NTH, represented the beginning of the post-Taylorist phase. It meant that the post-Taylorists were established across organizations that combined the engineering profession with managerial interests and positions. They contrived to create pressure groups – the so-called committee for cooperation between NTH and industry amongst others – but did not succeed in establishing higher education for management. They only succeeded in implanting managerial knowledge within the established professional education system.[5]

EDUCATION AND MANAGEMENT IN THE SOCIO-TECHNICAL PERIOD

The success of the post-Taylorists was not total, leaving room for both supplementary and complementary types of management practice and thought. In this period, therefore, institutions and types of education were created on the basis of alternative traditions that had emerged during the 1950s. These traditions later developed a more permanent and penetrating influence on company practices and management cultures. The established post-Taylorist institutions also became more diversified in terms of their knowledge orientation. Consultancy firms, for example, introduced new management techniques both in commercial fields and in human resources administration and development.

It was appropriate that the first challenge to the post-Taylorists should come in Norway, as in other countries also, from the psychology-inspired 'human relations' tradition. Einar Thorsrud, a psychologist, had already come on the scene in 1950. In 1953, he launched his frontal attack on the Norwegian Taylorists' most cherished progeny: the Method, Time, and Measurement (MTM) programme. This was a continuation of Taylorism, and closely associated with the ideas underpinning the Marshall Plan. Due to Thorsrud's intervention, however, and a general resistance based on values deeply ingrained in Norwegian culture, the MTM programme was never allowed to take off. Rather, the standards that had been developed became an export product, which turned out to be particularly useful for the Swedes (Volvo).

Thorsrud established an alliance with leading industrialists and managerial groups that wanted to push forward various types of human resources management. In 1958, his work was rewarded when the Institute for Industrial Milieu Research (IFIM) was established at NTH in Trondheim. At the same time another institution, the Seminar on Industrial Administration, was established at NTH. This traditional technological centre was thus enlarged by two institutions which were directly concerned with the organization of the firm. The Seminar on Industrial Administration was later able to establish its own department as a result of several years of discussion about the relationship between engineering and management, and the need for specialization or generalization in administration. The department was established after pressure from the engineers, who sought to secure and advance their managerial positions in the firm, positions that were challenged essentially by the owner–managers, and only marginally by other educational groups at that moment in time.

The new institutions at NTH represented alternatives to the essentially engineering way of thinking and the focus on administrative techniques of the post-Taylorists. From 1952, a further alternative – the 'Solstrand courses' – came to be located at NSEBA in Bergen. While the new institutions at NTH were oriented towards the internal problems of the firm, the purpose of the Solstrand courses was to broaden and enlarge the perspectives of top managers. However, the leader of the programme, a psychology-oriented engineer called Rolf Waaler, also had a long career in vocational planning and the teaching of supervisors. These courses did not therefore become the basis of an entirely 'general management' type of institution, but one based, rather, on a hermeneutical philosophy. The fundamental learning process consisted of collective reflections around own practices. Overall, this movement boosted the socio-technical programme that was formulated during the early 1960s, and activated as projects the so-called experiments in 'industrial democracy' from 1966. These work-organization-centred projects came to dominate the period, creating fresh space in the next phase for the development of both industrial relations and industrial democracy.

A new dimension had now been institutionalized within the Norwegian system of industrial administration – the socio-technical, practice-oriented, and shop-floor-centred tradition of managerial thinking. It was primarily scholars at NTH who were active in this field, while the main business school (NSEBA) maintained a rather low profile. Thus the idea of 'general management' became more distinctly associated with the engineering profession than with business school graduates.

EDUCATION AND MANAGEMENT IN THE PERIOD OF INDUSTRIAL DEMOCRACY

The 'general management' trend developed among groups identifying with the post-Taylorist position at the same time as the socio-technical tradition was appearing as a movement. By the 1960s and 1970, however, it was far less influential than the socio-technical trend and the joint management movement.

The 1970s represented a breakthrough for regulation of the managerial function, through agreements, tariffs, laws, and other so-called constraints on the freedom of the top executive. Many of the traditional institutions got involved in this process, and a new psychological research institute was established – the *Arbeidspsykologisk Institutt* (API). This institute was located in Oslo, and was able to gain the initiative in the field of industrial administration, which meant that the centre of the socio-technical tradition moved from Trondheim to Oslo.

In some ways this period represented a return to the post-Taylorist debates: what types of incentives to use, how the degradation of work could be avoided through processes of rationalization, and so forth. The socio-technical tradition of the 1960s had developed into a movement for the reinterpretation of the old Taylorist devices as they had been developed within a Norwegian system of bargaining. Even though it was possible, in this period, to see a growing number of schools and courses claiming to do training and education for general management (Amdam 1993), the real content of these new initiatives was rarely anything other than various techniques within the discipline of business administration. The need for these kinds of courses was obvious: the relative weight of administrative personnel within the hierarchy of the firm had grown fast. The proportion of white-collar workers, for instance, had increased from about one-sixth in the 1950s to one-third in the 1970s (NAF funksjonærstatistikk 1982). On the whole, the field of industrial administration was now thoroughly regulated and there was a variety of institutions and organizations which based their activities on the need for interpretation and defence of established positions within this field. The role of shop stewards in local bargaining on social- and health-related matters, as well on issues of wages and technology, had been emphasized in the new labour law. Worker representation on boards and new types of joint internal control systems were also established.

EDUCATION AND MANAGEMENT IN THE PERIOD OF MANAGERIALISM

In the 1980s, the increased power of the upper-tier executives and union representatives in the field of industrial administration was met by resistance from lower managerial personnel. Middle management was tired of being excluded from both industrial democracy and the new staff departments. Lower managers linked up with educators in a movement which sought to establish the need for new managerial knowledge and possibly to professionalize. This is particularly reflected in the jargon of the Norwegian School of Management, but also in the various initiatives for the revival of managerial education at the technical colleges. The middle managers' union developed courses on management and administration that were quite demanding. The schools for business administration and technology experienced a boom in interest, and they now also had to relate to a demand for more systematic education for practising managers. Many of the institutions which had been established in the previous periods became much more active – for example, the Norwegian Institute for Human Resource Management (NIPA). This was the case with most institutions, save for the North European Management Institute (NEMI), which did not survive intact for the glorious years of the 1980s, but, as discussed in Chapter 2 above, faded away after a short period.

Even though money was wasted on NEMI, in general experience was accumulated. Some of this was applied to the new Norwegian Institute for Leadership and Administration (NILA), which was a joint venture between those who now felt the need for more systematic support for the managerial interests within industry. The professional organizations of the business school graduates and the engineers were involved, as well as industrial relations and business associations.[6] NILA represented the sorts of groups that would establish a leading position in the 1980s. It emerged as a central meeting place for the business-oriented circles within the professions and the owner interests. All kinds of problems relating to management were discussed. On the personnel side, there was continuity from the post-Taylor period. Those who had been active in the 1950s now participated in the new 'general management' campaign, although they were now more attuned to social science terminology. But NILA never became much more than a talking shop, and a coordinator and initiator of activities in other organizations.

Perhaps the most lasting contribution was the new management education programmes within the professional organizations. Quite a few leaders were drilled in management techniques by these professional associations or by the independent agencies sponsored by NILA. By far the greatest energy was shown by NIF, the civil engineers' association, particularly in the so-called OLUF programme. Business school graduates were more dependent on their parent educational institutions for the transmission of this kind of knowledge. NSM now started to play a more important role in the development of management as a separate type of epistemology – an alternative to the predominant emphasis on the economic 'theory of the firm'.[7]

The managerial period represented a revival of interest for the executive function and the strategic importance of managerial hierarchies. Earlier periods had been more concerned with how the structure of the firm influenced productivity, improved democracy and working relations, and provided beneficent constraints on managerial activities. Now, 'to manage' was considered an activity that could change structures as well as develop new ideals and goals, and this meant that the emphasis was put more on leadership than administration. Or to quote Enteman:

Whether the organization behaves in an organic way is, to an important extent, a result of the management's efforts, and the direction of that organic force is something over which management attempts to exercise control.

(Enteman 1993: 164)

This ideological shift was of course related to an international ideological trend, but it was also linked to a change in the power structure of the firm. The unions lost power owing to economic setbacks, and the state could no longer subsidize industry for social and long-term economic reasons. Managers both attained more internal power and were also given greater responsibility for their own survival in the market. Managerial decisions about investment and market strategies emerged increasingly as a central focus. The 'general management' idea was something increasingly greater numbers of Norwegian managers were attuned to, and, as a result, consultancy firms and educational institutions now found a growing market for their services.

CONCLUSION

After this broad overview of groups and institutions that were involved in movements and practical experiments about training and education in management, it may be concluded that these movements were not very successful in establishing business administration as a formal discipline in Norway's educational system. Educational planners still have not put this field of education on their agenda, in the same way as, for example, with engineering or the social sciences. Management has always been a supplementary field of knowledge for the established professions, and not a requirement for advancement into the top executive positions. Engineers may now specialize and write their diplomas within the ORAL programme, which combines thinking on post-Taylorism, industrial relations, and general management. But this is as far as development within the traditional Norwegian system can come. Even graduates from the Norwegian School of Management (NSM) seek an identity as economists, not managers (although they are opposed to macro-economics) (Lidtun 1996). The emphasis is on the administrative and theoretical dimension, and also on how economic activities are influenced by the organizational setting called the firm. The focus has been quite narrowly centred on issues of interest for practising executives in industry, which had often to be put on the agenda in specific interest organizations before anything happened. The professional organizations were the most important, in this context, but organizations of owners and business entrepreneurs, in which full-time executives were represented, also sometimes put forward demands for more management education. But while the professions wholeheartedly tried to increase their influence as managers within industry through forms of self-development and various courses in administrative techniques, scepticism among owner–entrepreneurs towards any kind of professionalization that might threaten their social position has been a constant feature.

The central argument in this chapter has been that, in the postwar era, the engineering dimension has been of primary importance in the emergence of a structured field of industrial administration. The lack of general management as an autonomous type of knowledge, profession, or career type is explained by the influence and shape of the engineering profession. This profession has had a strong influence over the shaping of the industrial structure because it has been able to combine substantial knowledge on technology and industry with experience-based knowledge of organizations. In an industrial structure where ownership interests have been reluctant to withdraw from administrative positions, and with strong unions, scepticism of 'general management' and professional staff is a significant phenomenon. General management has been welcomed as an ideology, as a tool, and as a criterion of identification for social movements, but not as a holistic and systematic type of knowledge that could be formalized within the education system nor a specific job category nor career track in the firm.

The joint management tradition is an important background for understanding the relative stability within the field of industrial administration. Joint management meant that the function of production was granted primary status within the business system. Even the economic crisis towards the end of the 1980s did not change this orientation. The engineering profession still provides a coordinating mechanism at the organizational level, linking a technology-oriented small-firm-dominated business system to technology-oriented public administration systems of research and innovation. The ongoing internationalization process, represented by increasing capital flows across the borders, and the international restructuring of production processes and technologies, might seem to threaten stability in the Norwegian field of industrial administration. Currently, however, this does not appear to be the case. Even though there have been some major changes in the 1980s, the suspicion is that the engineer–managers are still firmly in charge.

These generalizations have implications about how to theorize about management and education. First of all, they show that the executive function needs to be underpinned by a particular kind of division of labour in order to make it possible for industrialists to create the image of the 'general manager' and venture into the process of professionalization. The educational system may push forward this type of division of labour, but cannot create it. The long-term development of interfaces between such unwieldy institutions as work organizations and the educational system cannot be changed overnight. These institutions even heavily influence the conception of the firm in itself in a society. Managerial hierarchies cannot be studied separately from the cultures and institutions in which they are embedded. 'General management' is a programme for leadership as well as administration. The core of the idea is lost if management is understood either as a bundle of administrative techniques or as an ideology, as has often been the case in Norway in the postwar period. The original idea of general management itself puts a great deal of emphasis on leadership, more than is common in European managerial hierarchies, but there is of course no escape from administration. If one is a general manager then one is responsible for leadership as well as administration. There has also been much dissension recently over the tendency in the American field of business administration to put all emphasis on administration, leading to a 'collapse in leadership morality' and an 'exhaustion of managerialism' (Scott and Hart 1991: 46; Scott 1992).

It is argued that 'as management education grew, it increasingly divorced itself from its humanist background and pretended to be applied economics' (Enteman 1993: 168). In Norway, management education never had a humanist background, and the present trend in management education may represent an attempt to establish such a background. However, the Achilles' heel of managerialism in Norway may not lie in the lack of a humanist background. Rather, the problem may be that managerialism in itself is fundamentally undemocratic:

> managerialism presents a lethal challenge to democracy, because it discounts the importance of the individual in general and, more specifically, discounts the importance of voting in regard to the social choice.
>
> (Entemann 1993: 157)

The idea of general management as a guiding ideology for societal development and governance may be difficult to sell in Norway precisely for this reason. But the idea is also in conflict with Norway's continental heritage, with its stricter separation between administration and leadership. If one is a German *Unternehmer*, one may blame those below one who are responsible for an administrative failure. The reason for this, according to Hartmann (1959), is that the right of a German *Unternehmer* to exercise leadership is not questioned. In the American setting, on the other hand, the top executive's right to lead is continually questioned. This means that he or she has to prove his or her right to lead – and also to take charge of administration – and demonstrate such ability.

In the egalitarian and democratic Norwegian tradition, it seems difficult to legitimate managerial power – or the need for educational institutions for general management – in either the German or American way. Perhaps the more traditional type of family and state authority, especially if supported by political discourse, votes, and opinion polls, is the most promising alternative. What is wanted is a general administrator and a democratically elected leader, not a general manager. The era of engineers and public administrators, then, may not be over.

NOTES

1 When the term 'general management' is used in this chapter, the specific American tradition of business administration is meant. When the general term 'management' is used, however, it encompasses the executive function and the personnel engaged in activities related to 'management'.

2 The distinction between trends and movements is an attempt to keep separate the ideas themselves and their use by the actors. The institutionalization of a field of industrial administration, from this perspective, is an outcome of the constant interaction between systems of knowledge, and actor constellations crystallizing around these as social movements.

3 It is hard to estimate from available information the numerical strength of different types of ownership within industry. Owing to the importance of small-scale industry, Norwegian owner–entrepreneurs also played a comparatively big role as a collective social actor.

4 Among the agencies in question were *NIFs rasjonaliseringsgruppe* and *Polyteknisk Forenings Rasjonaliseringsgruppe*. The last agency was an old and distinguished institution containing an amalgamation of the industrial- and the national/industrial-oriented educational bourgeoisie factions.

5 The major achievement of the post-Taylorist movement was at the level of propaganda and consultancy. Two establishments need to be mentioned in particular: *Norsk Produktivitetsinstitutt* (NPI: Norwegian Productivity Institute) and *Produksjonsteknisk Forskningsinstitutt* (PROFO: Institute for Technical Productivity and Research). PROFO was established in 1950 by the leading American-educated Taylorists, and soon acquired a reputation as far as consultancy was concerned. The aim of this institution was to merge microeconomics and knowledge of the technology of production into a specifically Norwegian tradition of rationalization. See also Carew (1987) and Yttri (1993).

6 *Norske Siviløkonomers Forening, Norske Sivilingeniørers Forening, Norsk Arbeidsgiverforening, Norges Rederforbund,* and *Norges Industriforbund.*

7 The theory of the firm is genuinely anti-managerialist since one manager must easily substitute for another. The operation of the firm thus cannot depend upon the insight or wisdom of specific managers. By introducing 'the concept of the corporation' instead, to use the title of Drucker's book about General Motors, business schools also had to abandon the notion that the corporation exists to maximize profits (Enteman 1993, Drucker 1949).

REFERENCES

Amdam, R.P. (1993) *For egen regning: BI og den økonomisk-administrative utdanningen,* Oslo: Universitetsforlaget.

Andersen, S. (1988) 'Seks teser om organisasjon og ledelse i norske bedrifter', *Working Paper* No. 20, Oslo: Norwegian School of Management.

Barnard, C. (1938/1968) *The Functions of the Executive,* Cambridge, MA: Harvard University Press.

Byrkjeflot, H. (1993a) 'Hvorfor har ikke det Amerikanske ledelses ideal fått gjennomslag i Tyskland?', *Working Paper* No. 57, Bergen: LOS.

—— (1993b) 'Engineering and Management in Germany and the USA: The Origins of Diversity in Organizational Forms', dissertation proposal.

Carew, A. (1987) *Labour under the Marshall Plan: The Politics of Productivity and the Marketing of Management Science*, Manchester: Manchester University Press.

Drucker, P.F. (1949) *The Concept of the Corporation*, New York: John Day.

—— (1954) *The Practice of Management*, New York: Harper & Row.

Enteman, W.F. (1993) *Managerialism: The Emergence of a New Ideology*, Madison, WI: The University of Wisconsin Press.

Ermarth, M. (1993) *America and the Shaping of German Society 1945–55*, Providence, RI: Berg.

Fligstein, N. (1990) *Transformation of Corporate Control*, Cambridge, MA: Harvard University Press.

—— and Byrkjeflot, H. (1996) 'The Logic of Employment Systems', in J. Baron, D. Grusky, and D. Treiman, (eds) *Social Differentiation and Stratification*, Boulder, CO: Westview Press.

Fox, A. (1974) *Beyond Contract*, London: Faber.

Gauslaa, S. (1993) 'Norge vraket verdiskapning i 1952', *Dagens Næringsliv*, 29 April.

Goldner, F.H. and Ritti, R.R. (1967) 'Professionalization as career immobility', *American Journal of Sociology* 72: 489–502.

Gulowsen, J. (1984) 'Arbeiderkontroll og vitenskapsbasert produksjon', in H.W. Andersen and G. Stang (eds) *Studier i teknologihistorie*, Trondheim: Tapir.

—— (1987) *Kvalifikasjon og arbeidermakt: Samlet og sterk eller splittet og svak*, Oslo: Universitetsforlaget.

Hagtvedt, B. and Lafferty, W. (1984) *Demokrati og demokratisering*, Oslo: Aschehoug.

Halvorsen, T. (1982) 'Profesjonalisering, Taylorisering – Ingeniørar mellom leiing og arbeidarmotstand', Thesis, University of Bergen.

—— (1983) *Kunnskapsformer og profesjonelle yrker vitskapsgjeringa av norsk foretaksorganisasjon*, University of Bergen, Moral-prosjektets skriftserie No. 6.

—— (1993) 'Profesjonalisering og profesjonspolitikk. Den sosiale konstruksjonen av tekniske yrker', unpublished Dr Polit. Dissertation, University of Bergen.

Hanisch, T.J. and Lange, E. (1985) *Vitenskap for industrien*, Oslo: Universitetsforlaget.

Hartmann, H. (1959) *Authority and Organization in German Management*, Princeton, NJ: Princeton University Press.

—— (1963) *Amerikanischer Firmen in Deutschland*, Köln: Westdeutscher Verlag.

Hofstede, G. (1993) 'Intercultural Conflict and Synergy', in D.S. Hickson (ed.) *Management in Western Europe: Society Culture and Organization in Twelve Nations*, Berlin: Walter de Gruyter.

Jensen, O.H. and Strømme Svendsen, A. (1986) *Norges Handelshøyskole 50 år*, Bergen: NHH.

Kalleberg, R. (1991) 'Kenning-tradisjonen i norsk ledelse', *Nytt Norsk Tidsskrift* 3: 218–44.

Lessem, R. and Neubauer, F. (1994) *European Management Systems,* London: McGraw-Hill.

Lidtun, V. (1996) 'Ledelsesteori som profesjonsstrategi: Forming ar den norske siviløkonomprofesjon etter 1945', in H. Byrkjeflot (ed.) *Fra styring til ledelse*, Bergen: Fagbokforlaget.

Lundberg, S. (1991) *Personalledelse*, Oslo: Bedriftsøkonomisk forlag.

NAF funksjonærstatistikk (1982) Oslo.

Reve, T. (1994) 'Skandinavisk organisasjon ogledelse', *Tidsskift for samfunnsforskning* 4: 568–82.

Ringer, F. (1992) *Fields of Knowledge*, Cambridge: Cambridge University Press.

Schjander, N. (1987) *Hvis jeg bare hadde en bedre sjef, George Kenning om ledelse*, Oslo: Hjemmets Bokforlag.

Scott, W.G. (1992) *Chester I. Barnard and the Guardians of the Managerial State*, Lawrence, KS: University Press of Kansas.

—— and Hart, D.K. (1991) 'Managerialism Exhausted', *Society* 28(3): 39–48.

Sejersted, F. (1993) *Demokratisk kapitalisme*, Oslo: Universitetsforlaget.

Sloan, A.P. (1963) *My Years with General Motors*, Garden City, NY: Doubleday.

Swidler, A. (1986) 'Culture in Action: Symbols and Strategies', *American Journal of Sociological Review* 51: 273–86.

Utnes, G. (1993) 'de Lange griper roret', *Dagens Næringsliv* 27 July.

Yttri, G. (1993) 'Pris og rasjonaliseringslova – ordskiftet i og ikring DNA-regjeringa 1952–53', Cand. philol. Thesis in history, University of Oslo.

10

MERCURY'S MESSENGERS
Swedish business graduates in practice

*Lars Engwall, Elving Gunnarsson,
and Eva Wallerstedt*

INTRODUCTION

In the National Gallery in London, visitors can admire a painting by the Flemish painter Peter Paul Rubens representing Paris's choice. In the picture, to the left, there are three sparsely dressed women – the Roman goddesses Juno, Minerva, and Venus. On the right stand Paris and the messenger of the gods, Mercury. In fact this appears to be one of the few occasions in Roman mythology when Mercury, god of merchants, and Minerva, goddess of wisdom, arts, and sciences, were seen close to one another. In modern times, however, their relationship has become more profound. As shown by Engwall (1992), through the development of contemporary academic management education they have progressed to a state of cohabitation. In turn, this implies that Mercury, messenger of the gods, has gained a large number of messengers of his own – that is, academic business graduates. Needless to say this has not been a rapid development but a step-by-step process. For quite some time, resistance to these messengers was considerable, both from academia and from practitioners. One example of the negative attitude of university professors can be found in the statement made in 1918 by the famous American economist and social theorist, author of *The Theory of the Leisure Class*, Thorsten Veblen (1918: 209–10) that:

> A college of commerce is designed to serve an emulative purpose only
> – individual gain regardless of, or at the cost of, the community at large
> – and it is, therefore, peculiarly incompatible with the cultural purpose
> of the university. It belongs in the corporation of learning no more than
> a department of athletics.

And the attitude of the business community was equally sceptical. In the late 1950s, Fritz Redlich noted that:

194

there could be no growth of academic training for business as long as businessmen insisted that would-be merchants must become apprenticed at an age of fourteen or fifteen years and stay in business thereafter.

(Redlich 1957: 45–6)

Thus, the provider of a business education – an Odysseus caught between the dangers of Scylla and Charybdis – faces the difficult task of finding a balance between academia and the world of practice. The dilemma can be further illustrated by postwar development in the United States. In the 1950s, the Carnegie Commission and Ford Foundation set up committees to work for the improvement of business education. These committees presented reports suggesting that business studies in the United States should be more scientifically oriented (Pierson 1959; Gordon and Howell 1959). This scientific orientation not only came to pass, but led, in the late 1980s, to the opinion that business studies had become *too* scientific: in other words, professors of business administration were considered to place too much weight on theoretical research and to have lost touch with the realities of the business world (Porter and McKibbin 1988).

Nevertheless, business graduates were quite successful in penetrating commercial corporations and later even public organizations. Fligstein (1990: 282) reports that while, in 1959, only two of the presidents of the hundred largest corporations in the United States held an MBA, the number had risen tenfold in 1979. However, these company presidents constituted only the tip of the iceberg of a large population of business graduates in the United States. Similarly, this chapter will show how business graduates have been successful in the Swedish context. This will be done by following up a study of top managers in large Swedish companies done fifty years ago by Sune Carlson (Carlson 1945). Moreover, before turning to the penetration of business graduates in Sweden, an important prerequisite for this process will be examined – the mechanism of supply and demand.

THE SUPPLY AND DEMAND FOR ACADEMIC BUSINESS EDUCATION

Academic business education is far from a normal consumer good. First of all, the demand comes from a number of different sources: the industrialists and politicians who for various reasons promote such an education, the students who enrol for it, and the employers who hire the graduates. The first of these sorts of demand is particularly important for the establishment of new institutions, while the second and third constitute responses to an existing supply. Basically, the three types of demand are hierarchically dependent on each other. The first constitutes a prerequisite for the second, which is, in turn, necessary for the third. What is seen, in studies of the

195

penetration of graduates, is thus just the last link in this chain. This final demand then appears to be reinforced by two kinds of forces – one technical and the other social.

The *technical force* is a result of the emergence of an increasing number of large enterprises. Their mere size has led to a need for the division of labour and specialization (Chandler 1962, 1977, 1990), which, in turn, has implied a need for sophisticated internal and external economic control systems. Needless to say, this development has increased the demand for business graduates. Similarly, growth aspirations have resulted in the emergence of marketing functions, which have also provided a job market for business graduates. Thus such graduates have the opportunity of reaching top management positions and challenging thereby the two types of graduates who earlier dominated large companies – engineers and lawyers. Of these two, lawyers are the most likely to lose, since they, like business graduates, work mainly in administrative functions. However, engineers also face the risk of losing, even if their risk is less than that of lawyers because their competence is more difficult to challenge. In consequence, business graduates should be expected to be more successful in non-manufacturing areas – such as trade, finance, and so forth.

The *social force* is grounded on the fact that, to an appreciable extent, consumption is a social process. This means that the demand of one individual or group is influenced by the demand of other individuals or groups. Another way to express this phenomenon is that demand is socially constructed (Berger and Luckmann 1966). If this observation is applied to recruitment, it may be expected that certain practices are developed within an organization or organizational field. These practices in turn are likely to be governed by the values of the dominant actors of that organization or organizational field. An important basis for these values is the educational background of the dominant actors. This can even be expected to constitute a significant factor in screening job applicants and to provide an important barrier to entry for applicants with a different educational background to that of the dominant actors. So, in the same way as new consumer products have difficulties during an introductory phase, new types of education can be expected to have similar problems of acceptance. However, as such kinds of education successfully penetrate an organization or organizational field to some extent they are likely to attract increasing numbers of similar people. Furthermore, in a sense, this growth process has features in common with such communications systems as mobile telephones, fax, and electronic mail: that is, in order for consumption to take off, there is a need to reach critical levels. For example, it is difficult to be an early user of a communication system if one has nobody to communicate with. Similarly, it is difficult to introduce single graduates of a specific sort into an organization; but as the process becomes easier, and they multiply, they can develop a communications system through the language of concepts,

which gradually takes over earlier practices. Thus business and management concepts have had a tendency to take over in the organizational
language, just as English has taken over in the language of international
communication. Both these tendencies are part of a modernization of
society (see, for instance, Giddens 1991), which is manifested through
rationalization and marketization. This in turn has implied tendencies for
isomorphism, implying that business organizations tend to imitate each
other and that public organizations such as hospitals, universities, and
schools tend to follow suit (DiMaggio and Powell 1983; Meyer and Scott
1992/1983). Against this background, the purpose of the chapter is to
investigate how academic management education has succeeded in
Swedish industry from the Second World War on.

It should of course be expected that the growth of academic education
will be reflected among top managers, to the extent that an increasing
proportion of them will have academic degrees. This is then likely to have
an effect on mobility: the more managers there are with a general education,
the less they will be attached to a particular company. In due course,
therefore, top managers may increasingly be expected to have been
employed by more than one company.

The above reasoning implies that academic business education can be
expected to exhibit first a slow development and then a considerable
growth, as a result of both the emergence of large corporations and the
social interaction of actors in the field. Another implication is that business
graduates are likely to outnumber law graduates, in particular, but also
engineering graduates, to a certain extent, in top management positions.
Finally, the increasing proportion of academic graduates in business can be
expected to reduce the number of executives who have a single-company
career. These expectations should be kept in mind as the empirical results
are now examined.

THE SUPPLY AND DEMAND OF BUSINESS
GRADUATES IN SWEDEN

The supply of graduates

In terms of supply of Swedish academic business education, five major
epochs can be identified (Table 10.1).[1] The first of these was characterized
by efforts which did not result in long-term success. However, it also
included the creation at Uppsala University – as early as 1741, in a
mercantilist spirit – of a chair entitled *jurisprudentiæ, œconomiæ et
commerciorum*. In this sense, Sweden was second only to Germany, where
chairs were created about a decade earlier in Halle, Frankfurt an der Oder,
and Rinteln. By the end of the century, the Swedish chair had lost its
orientation towards the economic sciences, and commercial education had

become instead the preserve of the grammar schools of the various commercial centres in Sweden. Efforts to introduce accounting to the university curriculum were met with criticism.[2]

The second epoch implied a breakthrough for academic business education in Sweden, through the foundation of the Stockholm School of Economics in 1909. This event was preceded by a number of study visits, particularly to Germany, to find appropriate models for a Swedish school. At the time, The Wharton School in Philadelphia and École des Hautes Études Commerciales had been operating for more than a quarter of a century. They had also gained followers in various universities in the German-speaking world (Aachen, Leipzig, St Gallen, and Vienna in 1898; Cologne and Frankfurt am Main in 1901; Berlin in 1906; and Mannheim in 1907) and in the United States (University of California and University of Chicago in 1898; Dartmouth in 1900; Columbia University and Harvard University in 1908).[3]

Members of the Wallenberg family, a financial dynasty in Sweden, were significant supporters of the business school in Stockholm. However, their motives for the latter's foundation seem to have been governed more by an interest in raising the status of businesspeople, than by the institution's educational content. The early years were difficult for the school, in terms of both the hiring of competent professors and the labour market success of the graduates.

The second period also saw the creation of a second business school in 1923 in Gothenburg, the commercial centre on the west coast of Sweden.

Table 10.1 Five epochs in Swedish business administration

Epoch	Characteristics of the epoch
pre-1909	Attempts to introduce the discipline into the university with only short-term success. Resistance from the academic community
1909–32	*An epoch of commercial techniques*: establishment of the discipline, with the successful foundation of two business schools on private initiatives. Only one professor in each department. Accounting predominates
1933–56	*An epoch of consolidation*: addition of chairs to the established schools and to specialized institutions. Increasing demand for business education. Attacks on the duopoly, which fights back. Financial support from the government
1957–68	*An epoch of entries*: support from the government creates departments of business administration in all universities. The number of chairs more than doubles. Gothenburg School of Economics is taken over by the state
1969–	*An epoch of expansion*: great expansion of research and teaching of business administration. The introduction of new PhD programmes. Expansion of business administration into local colleges

Source: Engwall (1992: 41)

Plans for this project went back to the last century but nothing had materialized, most likely because there was already non-academic education of a high standing in Gothenburg. When it was finally established, the business school in Gothenburg went through a similar development process, with similar problems, to the one in Stockholm. In both schools, accounting dominated and the German influence was considerable.

The interwar period and years up to the mid 1950s – that is, the third epoch in Table 10.1 – constituted a period of consolidation for the two first business schools. Additional chairs were created in business administration, in addition to those being created at such specialized institutions as the Royal Agricultural College (1931), the Royal College of Forestry (1933), and the Royal Institute of Technology (1939). In addition, an increasing student demand for academic business studies led to a government proposal to introduce them into university programmes. However, this was resisted until 1957, when chairs and departments were created in Lund and Uppsala. In terms of curricula, a gradual transition from a strong emphasis on financial issues may be observed, with administrative and marketing issues being given increased attention. The first defence of a doctoral dissertation in business administration (1950) also belongs to this period.

In the fourth epoch, chairs and departments were created in all universities. This considerably increased the capacity to offer an academic business education. The period was also notable for the fact that one of the private schools, the Gothenburg School of Economics, was forced, for financial reasons, to give up its private status and become integrated with Gothenburg University.

Finally, the fifth epoch saw a considerable expansion in the number of business graduates, as the departmental expansion of the previous period now bore fruit. In addition, the discipline was introduced into local colleges. Today, business administration is one of the largest disciplines of Swedish post-secondary education. Parallel to this development, considerable growth in terms of research can be observed.

The demand for graduates

The development described meant a rather slow growth in the numbers of departments, chairs, and graduates until the 1950s. The capacity then increased drastically, particularly in the 1960s, through the creation of departments and chairs. As a result, there was a real take-off in the numbers of business graduates in the 1970s and 1980s, which meant that their share of the labour market increased. If business, law, and engineering graduates are considered as belonging to the same cohort of job seekers, therefore, the market share of business graduates rose from 13.5 per cent in 1911–15, to 40.1 per cent in 1980–5. This growth occurred predominantly at the expense of law graduates, whose market share for the two periods mentioned fell from 36.9 per cent to 16.2 per cent. The figures for engineering graduates remained stable, at about 50 per cent (Engwall 1992: 99–101).

In terms of industries, it is clear that the manufacturing industry has been the major recipient of business graduates. Data reported by Engwall (1992: 106–7) show that before the war about a quarter of graduates went into manufacturing, and this rose to a third after the war. Moreover, in a broad definition of 'industry', it appears that business graduates have been particularly successful in the engineering industry – that is, in the stronghold of engineers. Finally, both during the war and in 1980 large numbers of business graduates entered the public sector, which at these times attracted as many as one-quarter of all graduates.

Upon analysis of the jobs of business graduates, marketing and economic control have been found to be the major functions. For the period 1931–50, about one-quarter of the first jobs of graduates were in marketing, and about two-fifths in economic control (Engwall 1992: 105). Interestingly enough, figures regarding the functions of business graduates in 1966, 1970, and 1974 are very similar (Engwall 1992: 108).

Concluding remarks

The evidence provided above implies that, before the Second World War, academic business education in Sweden was on rather a small scale, but that it has grown considerably in the postwar period, particularly since the 1960s. This has had effects on both the absolute number of business graduates and their position – especially in relation to law graduates. Despite the fact that the supply of business graduates has increased considerably, a high level of demand has been maintained. The majority of business graduates have been working in the areas of economic control and marketing. There is also evidence that, in the Swedish commercial community, business degrees have been important vehicles for careers. This topic, the main focus of the current chapter, will now be examined.

THE PENETRATION OF TOP MANAGEMENT

The founding fathers of the Stockholm School of Economics really did have ambitions beyond the education of merchants. In an article in 1907, the renowned Swedish professor of economics Gustav Cassel argued against those who were in favour of the school offering a strictly commercial education. He declared that 'the Stockholm School of Economics must have as its mission the education of those *who eventually will become the leaders of our economic life*'.[4] To find out to what extent this ambition has been fulfilled, the results of three earlier studies and a current study by the authors of this chapter, which examine the educational background of top managers in Sweden, will be compared.

Earlier studies

The point of departure is a 1944 study conducted by Sune Carlson. In this study, Carlson investigated the background of 200 presidents and vice-presidents of the then most prominent Swedish trading and industrial companies, evenly distributed amongst ten different lines of business. The names of these executives were taken from official publications such as *Who's Who in Trade and Industry* (*Vem är vem inom handel och industri*), *Who's Who* (*Vem är det*), and various other sources. The variables considered in the study were the formal education of the presidents, their careers inside and outside their companies, and their international experience.

Carlson's study was replicated on two other occasions. The first occasion was in 1956, when Fred Ohlsson carried out a follow-up study using references similar to Carlson's in order to define a total of 100 presidents and vice-presidents. Ohlsson also investigated the same characteristics as Carlson had. The second replication was undertaken sixteen years later, in 1972, by Erik Bolin and Leif Dahlberg, who studied the top managers in the 200 largest companies, fifteen largest banks, and ten largest insurance companies in Sweden. Since two of the subjects held CEO positions in two companies, the Bolin and Dahlberg sample contained the 223 presidents of 225 companies. Information about these individuals was collected through a mail survey, which when completed showed a 70 per cent response rate.

In addition to the three studies mentioned above, which will be used in comparison with the situation in 1994, there are a number of other studies on the education of top managers. In the 1950s, Hökby (1950) and Malmenström and Wiedenborg (1958) as well as Ohlsson carried out work in this area. However, since their populations differed considerably from that of Carlson, they have not been used in the present study as major sources for comparison. The same is true of a study on the top managers of the 1,000 largest Swedish companies presented in the business magazine *Ledarskap* in 1987. Similarly, a very recent study on the top management of the seventy-six largest Swedish companies (listed as well as unlisted), presented in *Affärsvärlden* (1994), has been difficult to use for comparison as it takes a somewhat different approach and looks at a greater number of members of the top management group.[5]

The design of the present study

In the present study, the authors have chosen to look at the presidents of the 105 Swedish companies listed on the Stockholm Stock Exchange. The survey also included chairpersons, but data for them are not included here. The names of these people were provided by the Stock Exchange in the first instance: information was then solicited from those subjects with addresses in Sweden, through a short questionnaire to be returned by fax. Respondents were asked to state their educational background (school, year, and so forth), and their career path inside and outside the company. Despite several reminders, some respondents have not returned the questionnaire. Even without these replies, however, the response rate was 94 per cent – there were six missing answers out of the total of 105.

The overall development

In his study Carlson (1945) argued, as did Berle and Means (1932) and Burnham (1941), that the character of the company president had changed since the turn of the century. In the early 1940s, top managers had become employees and their jobs had gradually become a special occupation – a new 'profession'. This change was also reflected in the educational background of presidents. While, in the early 1900s, an academic degree was an exception among chief executives, in 1944, more than half of them had such a degree. For the age group containing executives younger than 55, academic education was even more common: almost two-thirds had a degree. And as is shown in Table 10.2, this trend of the increasing importance of academic education for top managers has continued. Presidents without academic degrees have become progressively less frequent. While 52 per cent of the managers in 1944 had an academic degree, the corresponding figure for 1994 was 84 per cent. However, Ohlsson could report that, as early as 1956, the dominance of academically trained top managers had already increased since 1944. In his total sample, 72 per cent had academic degrees; while for those under 50 years of age the proportion was even higher, at 77 per cent. In the Bolin and Dahlberg study, which took place in 1972, the proportion of academic graduates had reached three-quarters of the whole sample. And in the 1990s, it is fair to agree with the conclusion of the business magazine *Affärsvärlden* that 'an academic degree is not a must, but not to have one is becoming more and more rare' (our translation).

In contrast with the increasing share of academic graduates in top management positions, the tendency between 1944 and 1994 to have more than one academic degree does not seem to have changed much. In 1944, this figure was 4.5 per cent and in 1994 it was 6.1 per cent. The latter is also very close to the figure reported in 1956 (6 per cent).[6] The most common combination is engineering and business administration.

It is reasonable to expect that the penetration of business graduates will differ in different lines of business: namely, that engineering graduates will be more successful in manufacturing, and business graduates more common in trade, finance, and shipping. This certainly turns out to be the case for both 1944 and 1994 (Table 10.3). But it is quite evident that the formal education of those occupied in industry, as well as in trade, finance,

202

Table 10.2 Background of top managers in Sweden – 1944, 1956, 1972, and 1994 (per cent)

Year	1944	1956	1972	1994
Business	12	20	27	37
Engineering	21	22	25	28
Law	13	20	7	7
Other academic degree	6	10	16	12
Total academic degrees	52	72	75	84
Grammar school	30	17	19	16
Other	18	11	6	0
Total	100	100	100	100
Sample size	200	100	157	99

Sources: Carlson (1945), Ohlsson (1957), Bolin and Dahlberg (1975), and the present survey (1994)

and shipping, has increased considerably in the last half century. In 1944, 58 per cent had an academic degree in industry; in 1994, this figure was 84 per cent. The same trend can be found with those occupied in trade, finance, and shipping. The major part of this increase comes from people holding degrees in business administration. In industry, 10 per cent of the sample had a degree in business administration in 1944; in 1994, this figure had more than tripled to 34 per cent. The corresponding figures for trade, finance, and shipping are 14 per cent and 43 per cent respectively.

An expected effect of the increased level of education among top managers would be increased mobility. A higher education might be expected to facilitate movement between jobs. Furthermore, there is evidence for this (Table 10.4). In 1944, 61 per cent of the top managers had made their career within one and the same company. This figure has gradually fallen and the present study shows that a mere 10 per cent of the presidents had been with the same company for the whole of their professional career.[7]

The three main roads to the top

It is evident from the previous section that academic graduates have become more and more numerous among Swedish top managers. Among these

Table 10.3 Educational background of top managers in 1944 and 1994
in different industry sectors (per cent)

Sector	Manufacturing		Trade, finance and shipping	
Year	1944	1994	1944	1994
Business	10	34	14	43
Engineering	31	31	7	22
Law	9	7	20	5
Other academic degree	8	12	2	13
Total academic degrees	58	84	43	83
Grammar school	29	16	38	17
Other	13	0	19	0
Total	100	100	100	100
Sample size	118	63	82	36

Sources: Carlson (1945), and the present study (1994)

Table 10.4 Proportion of top managers making their career in a single company –
1944, 1956, 1972 and 1994 (per cent)

Year	1944	1956	1972	1994
Share	61	42	11.5	10

Sources: Carlson (1945), Ohlsson (1957), Bolin and Dahlberg (1975), and the present survey (1994)

graduates, three degrees clearly dominate: business, engineering, and law. Even at the time of Sune Carlson's study, these disciplines could be identified as providing the most common academic backgrounds for top managers. Together they accounted for 46 per cent of the total sample. In the later studies, this proportion became even more significant: 62 per cent in 1956, 59 per cent in 1972, and 72 per cent in 1994 (Ohlsson 1957; Bolin and Dahlberg 1975; and the present survey). There can be no doubt that graduates with these degrees have been very successful in penetrating the top management of large Swedish corporations. These three areas will therefore be concentrated on in the following analysis.

Limiting the population to the three categories mentioned, and looking at

Table 10.5 Proportion of Swedish top managers with business, engineering, and law degrees – 1944, 1956, 1972, and 1994 (per cent)

Year	1944	1956	1972	1994
Business degree	25	31	47	52
Engineering degree	47	35	40	40
Law degree	28	34	13	8
Total	100	100	100	100
Actual number	92	62	109	71

Sources: Carlson (1945), Ohlsson (1957), Bolin and Dahlberg (1975), and the present survey

Note: In cases where an individual holds more than one degree the percentage has been divided between the groups

the market shares within this area (Table 10.5), we find that the business graduates have been quite successful. Their share has more than doubled – from 25 per cent in 1944 to 52 per cent in 1994, a change which, to a large extent, had been accomplished already by 1972 (47 per cent). Those displaced were primarily holders of law degrees, whose share, after peaking at 34 per cent in the 1956 study, fell from 28 per cent in 1944 to a mere 8 per cent in 1994. The proportion of engineering graduates has remained fairly constant, with a small and oscillating decline from 47 to 40 per cent. This is also consistent with the overall pattern for the three degrees reported above.

In order to get a fairer comparison of the relative success of holders of these three degrees in reaching top management positions, the numbers of candidates for these positions who held one or other of the three degrees must also be considered. As, for many years, there have been greater numbers of persons with engineering rather than other degrees, if holders of that degree are to be regarded as equally successful in reaching top positions, there should be a correspondingly greater proportion of engineers already at the top.

Thus to arrive at an estimate of the relevant populations of persons with one or other of the three degrees from whom top managers could be selected, the age at which the degrees are obtained has to be assessed, and the age period between appointment to and retirement from top management positions. Based on information presented in Bolin and Dahlberg (1975: 102), the age of graduation has been estimated as 25 years. Both in this study and the 1994 one, it can be seen that top management positions are held by persons from 35 to 65 years of age, with a concentration between the ages of 40 and 60. The latter core group has been chosen as the focus for this chapter.

Table 10.6 Relative success of graduates in top management –
1944, 1956, 1972, and 1994

Year	1944	1956	1972	1994
Total number				
Business degree	1,079	1,754	3,263	15,248
Engineering degree	3,742	4,746	8,198	26,216
Law degree	2,503	3,442	4,184	9,426
Top managers/1,000 degrees				
Business degree	21.3	10.8	14.9	2.6
Engineering degree	11.5	4.6	5.1	1.1
Law degree	10.4	6.1	3.4	0.7
Index				
Business degree	185	234	294	236
Engineering degree	100	100	100	100
Law degree	90	132	66	64

Sources: Handelshögskolan i Stockholm (1909–1959), Carlson (1945), Ohlsson (1957), Bolin and Dahlberg (1975), Utbildningsstatistisk Årsbok (1978), Markgren (1981), Engwall (1992), and the present survey

In Table 10.6, the analysis of success in the top management core group for the three degree bands has been extended by taking into account the numbers of degree holders who fall within the relevant age group (between 40 and 60 years). For instance, the figure 1,079 for the total number of business degree holders in 1944 represents those who had graduated from the Swedish business schools in the period 1909 to 1928.

As the average for the engineering band seems to have maintained a leading position, especially in competition with the business band, the engineering degree has become the basis for an index of relative success.[8]

Table 10.6 demonstrates that the number of top managers per 1,000 graduates has decreased for all three bands: those with business degrees from 21.3 in 1944 to 2.6 in 1994; those with engineering degrees from 11.5 to 1.1; and those with law degrees from 10.4 to 0.7. The decline can be explained by the explosive growth in the number of candidates for top management positions from 1944 to 1994 who held degrees. In 1944, there were 7,324 graduates (1,079 in business, 3,742 in engineering, and 2,503 in law), but in 1994, there were 50,890 – almost seven times the 1944 figure. The decrease in graduates in top management also depends to some extent on the differences in the sample sizes – 200 in 1944 and ninety-nine in 1994 – but this is of only minor importance.

The most interesting conclusions to be drawn from Table 10.6 appear to be found in the index figures. Particularly striking is the success rating of the business graduates, who, with their lowest index of 185 in 1944 and highest of 294 in 1972, do more than twice as well as the engineers over the entire period of the four studies. Taking into account the fact that the business education of the period studied was about one year shorter than the duration of the two competing degrees, it could be argued that the business degree, in terms of academic studies, has served as a shortcut to top management positions in Sweden.

In order to investigate relative success in different sectors of private enterprise, the 1994 figures have also been compared with those of the Carlson study of 1944. Carlson divided private enterprise into two groups – one consisting of industry, and the other of trade, banking, insurance, finance, and communications. Indices for these groups have been calculated as in Table 10.6 above, and then compared to the corresponding figures for 1994 (Table 10.7).

Table 10.7 shows that business graduates have been more successful than engineering graduates even in the industrial group. However, as expected, the difference between business and engineering is still more obvious in the trade- and finance-oriented sector. It is mainly in this sector, too, that the law degree has had any significance, though its importance dramatically declined between 1944 and 1994.

The reported results seem consistent with those of other studies on Swedish top management. Thus the mid 1980s study, presented in *Ledarskap* (1987), related that business graduates had taken over the lead in the population of top managers in the 1,000 largest Swedish companies. Of these managers, 32 per cent were found to be business graduates, 22 per cent engineering graduates, and 9 per cent law graduates; 27 per cent had some other academic education; and only 10 per cent had no academic degree whatsoever. In certain areas, engineers held on to their lead over business graduates – for instance, in manufacturing (34 as against 31 per cent) and consultancy (30 as against 21 per cent).

Table 10.7 Relative success in top management for business, engineering, and law graduates in two sectors of Swedish private enterprise – 1944 and 1994

Year	1944		1994	
Sector	Industry	Trade, etc.	Industry	Trade, etc.
Business degree	112	636	188	344
Engineering degree	100	100	100	100
Law degree	36	399	63	70

CONCLUSION

The present study seems to provide a number of important conclusions regarding Swedish senior managers. First, the tendency identified by Sune Carlson fifty years ago – that an increasing number of top managers held academic degrees – has been confirmed. However, there are still managers who have a successful career without an academic education (e.g. Volvo President Sören Gyll, and SE-Banken Vice-President Anders Hedenström), though they are becoming increasingly fewer. One important reason for this tendency is probably the use of academic degrees as a first screening device in recruiting. Related to this, also, is the fact that people are apt to prefer to employ those who are similar to themselves: in other words, academic graduates are likely to hire academic graduates.

Second, it is quite clear that academic business education has experienced considerable success since the start of the Stockholm School of Economics in 1909, thereby providing firm evidence that this school and its followers in the field of academic business education have flourished. It seems justifiable to say that Gustav Cassel's vision of an education for 'those who will eventually become the leaders of our economic life' (Cassel 1907: 208) has to a considerable extent come true. In the postwar era, the likelihood of a business graduate becoming a top manager has been more than double that of an engineering graduate, and, in 1972, close to three times as high. This also accords with expectations. An important reason for this development is that business graduates have been appointed to strategic positions in companies: namely, in the areas of economic control and marketing. Both of these activities involve the management of critical relationships between companies and their financiers and customers. Such links to crucial resources may in turn create important power bases in the development of companies (see, for example, Pfeffer and Salancik 1978). Needless to say, the personal networks established both during studies and early in a person's career also play important roles. In this context, it is not unreasonable to expect that graduates from the oldest of the Swedish business schools, the Stockholm School of Economics, have had certain advantages over graduates of other schools as a result of their school having been on the market longer, and having thereby more people placed in influential positions in Swedish companies. The extent to which this is true will be a topic for future research.

In conclusion, it is also appropriate to try to see the results of the present study in a wider context. In fact the results reported here belong to the general issue of the selection of business elites. This, too, is definitely a question that calls for thorough comparative research. A first step in that direction is offered in a recent volume by Engwall and Gunnarsson (1994), in which evidence regarding academic management studies in various countries is presented. The study observes interesting differences, not least between Japan and Western countries, and should lead to more cross-cultural research regarding top management recruitment. This would then lead to the question of how behavioural rules are developed in different business systems (Whitley 1992). Perhaps such studies would illuminate interactive processes, through which actors in different organizational fields adapt to each other in a 'copy-cat' manner. Business education is one factor in these processes, and may facilitate communication between actors and thus reduce uncertainty. Another important factor, for both the structure of business education and business behaviour, is the industrial structure – that is, the orientation, ownership, company size, and so forth – of a particular country.

NOTES

1 This section is based mainly on Engwall (1992) and sources referred to therein, particularly Gunnarsson (1988) and Wallerstedt (1988).

2 For treatment of the first Swedish chair in economic sciences, development in the nineteenth century, the preparation for the first Swedish business school, see Gunnarsson (1988).

3 For further discussion and sources, cf. Engwall (1992, Section 1.3).

4 Our italics and our translation from the Swedish text, which reads as follows: 'Men handelshögskolan måste ställa som sin uppgift att utbilda dem, som en gång skola bli ledarne af vårt ekonomiska lif' (Cassel 1907: 287).

5 In this study, sixty-one of the seventy-six companies responded to the questionnaire. It reports that the typical top management team in Swedish companies in early 1994 consisted of seven to eight members, a president, two or three vice-presidents leading the most important business areas, a financial director, a controller, a personnel manager, and a company lawyer. They are all men, most of whom are 53 to 55 years of age.

6 An exception during the period seems to be 1972, when as many as 16.5 per cent were reported as having more than one degree. However, as the Bolin and Dahlberg analysis, in contrast to the other studies, considered further education within the same discipline as more than one academic degree, their figure is not comparable.

7 This does not exclude the possibility that they have been with their company a long time. According to the study presented in *Affärsvärlden* (1994), it is very common for the top managers in large Swedish corporations to have been with their company for many years.

8 The numbers of degree holders after 1937 have been taken from the official educational yearbooks, *Utbildningsstatistisk Årsbok* (1978: 412–14, 446–7, 502–3; 1980: 284–5, 332–3; 1986: 362–3). Prior to 1937, Swedish education statistics were not collected systematically. Source material has, however, been obtained from *Utbildningsstatistisk Årsbok* 1978, *Handelshögskolan i Stockholm 1909–1959*, Markgren (1981), and Engwall (1992). For the few years before 1911, it has been estimated that the number of law and engineering degrees was the same as for the five-year period beginning 1911. For some years between 1911 and 1937, where only five-year totals are available, those totals have been divided equally among the five years.

REFERENCES

Affärsvärlden (1994) 'Ledningsgruppen kartlagd. Håkan, 53, styr svenskt näringsliv', 15: 28–9, 31, 34.
Berger, P.L. and Luckmann, T. (1966) *The Social Construction of Reality: A Treatise in the Sociology of Knowledge*, Garden City, NY: Doubleday.
Berle, A.A., Jr and Means, G.C. (1932) *The Modern Corporation and Private Property*, New York: Macmillan.
Bolin, E. and Dahlberg, L. (1975) *Dagens storföretagsledare*, Stockholm: SNS.
Burnham, J. (1941) *The Managerial Revolution*, New York: John Day.
Carlson, S. (1945) *Företagsledning och företagsledare*, Stockholm: Nordisk Rotogravyr.
Cassel, G. (1907) 'Den högre undervisningen för handel och industri', *Ekonomisk Tidskrift* 9: 286–304.
Chandler, A.D., Jr (1962) *Strategy and Structure: Chapters in the History of the American Industrial Enterprise*, Cambridge, MA: MIT Press.
—— (1977) *The Visible Hand: The Managerial Revolution in American Business*, Cambridge, MA: Harvard University Press.
—— (1990) *Scale and Scope: The Dynamics of Industrial Capitalism*, Cambridge, Mass.: Harvard University Press.
DiMaggio, P.J. and Powell, W.W. (1983) 'The Iron Cage Revisited: Institutional Isomorphism and Collective Rationality in Organizational Fields', *American Sociology Review* 48(2): 147–60.
Engwall, L. (1992) *Mercury Meets Minerva. Business Administration in Academia: The Swedish Case*, Oxford: Pergamon Press.
—— and Gunnarsson, E. (eds) (1994) *Management Studies in an Academic Context*, Uppsala: Acta Universitatis Upsaliensis, Studia Oeconomiae Negotiorum 35.
Fligstein, N. (1990) *The Transformation of Corporate Control*, Cambridge, MA: Harvard University Press.
Giddens, A. (1991) *Modernity and Self Identity*, Cambridge: Polity Press.
Gordon, R.A. and Howell, J.E. (1959) *Higher Education for Business*, New York: Columbia University Press.
Gunnarsson, E. (1988) *Från Hansa till Handelshögskola. Svensk ekonomundervisning fram till 1909*, Uppsala: Acta Universitatis Upsaliensis, Studia Oeconomiae Negotiorum 29 (thesis).
Handelshögskolan i Stockholm 1909–1959 (1959) Stockholm: HHS.
Hökby, B. (1950) 'Om företagsledare i storindustrin', *Balans, 2*, 2: 97–103.
Ledarskap (1987) 'Ekonomerna styr företagen', 6(11): 45–6.
Malmenström, G. and Wiedenborg, B. (1958) *245 svenska storföretagsledare*, Stockholm: SNS.
Markgren, B. (1981) 'Forskningens och undervisningens effekter på praktisk verksamhet', in L. Engwall (ed.) 'Företagsekonomiska utgrävningar', *Working Paper* 1981/3, Department of Business Administration, Uppsala University, 37–51.
Meyer, J.W. and Scott, W.R. (1992/1983) *Organizational Environments. Ritual and Rationality*, Newbury Park, CA: Sage.
Ohlsson, F. (1957) 'Företagsledarnas utbildning', *Ekonomiskt forum* 20: 17–21.
Pfeffer, J. and Salancik, G.R. (1978) *The External Control of Organizations*, New York: Harper and Row.
Pierson, F.C. (1959) *The Education of American Businessmen*, New York: McGraw-Hill.
Porter, L.W. and McKibbin, L.E. (1988) *Management Education and Development: Drift or Thrust into the 21st Century?*, New York: McGraw-Hill.

Redlich, F. (1957) 'Academic Education for Business: Its Development and the Contribution of Ignaz Jastrow (1856–1937) in Commemoration of the Hundredth Anniversary of Jastrow's Birth', *Business History Review* 31: 35–91.

Utbildningsstatistisk Årsbok (1978, 1980, 1986) Stockholm: SCB.

Veblen, T. (1918) *The Higher Learning in America*, New York: B.W. Huebsch.

Vem är det (1943) Stockholm.

Vem är vem inom handel och industri (1944) Stockholm.

Wallerstedt, E. (1988) *Oskar Sillén – Professor och praktiker. Några drag i företagsekonomiämnets tidiga utveckling vid Handelshögskolan i Stockholm,* Uppsala: Acta Universitatis Upsaliensis, Studia Oeconomiae Negotiorum 30 (thesis).

Whitley, R. (ed.) (1992) *European Business Systems*, London: Sage.

11

DINOSAURS IN THE GLOBAL ECONOMY?

American graduate business schools in the 1980s and 1990s

Susan Aaronson

INTRODUCTION

American graduate schools of business are peculiar academic animals. They do not really resemble either of their parents – the business world or the ivory tower. Their faculty must find a delicate balance between research that advances learning and knowledge and research that serves the interests of capital. As a result, each graduate school of business has evolved its own mix of academic and business culture.

Although each school is unique, many graduate schools of business in the United States share an approach to education that is different from other professional schools. Until recently, few of these schools emphasized practice, focusing more on theory or replication of practice in the classroom.

This chapter surveys the state of American business schools, focusing on research, curricula, and the interaction between business and business schools. In an earlier study of business education after the Second World War, it was found that students were neither educated by doing (by performing as managers) or by doers (those who had succeeded at managing). The conclusion was that by delegating such training to an outside supplier, many American companies showed an amazing lack of interest in the preparation of a key factor of production – people (Aaronson 1992b).

Today loyal, productive, and 'entrepreneurially skilled' employees are even more important in a world where technology, labour, and capital are global. As United States President William Jefferson (Bill) Clinton has noted, 'investing in people' is key both to corporate and national competitiveness. Thus, this chapter assesses whether changes in the world economy have altered the relationship between American business and American graduate schools of business, as they have altered the relationship between business and government in the last decade (Krugman 1994: 28–44).

AN OVERVIEW OF GRADUATE BUSINESS EDUCATION IN THE UNITED STATES

Since the postwar period, American business has relied on business education as a sifting device. Corporations abdicate to business school admissions offices the responsibility for selecting young managers. With the added wrapping of an MBA degree, young men and women were made acceptable to corporate recruiters. Companies saved money on their pre-selection and training costs by hiring students deemed fit for corporate management (Aaronson 1992b: 172).

MBA-educated executives were a rarity in American business until the middle of the twentieth century. But during the fifteen years following the Second World War, corporate recruiters increasingly turned to graduates of American business schools to staff their flourishing operations. American graduate business schools grew in influence at the same time that American business experienced twenty-five years of enormous growth (both in national and international markets) followed by dramatic decline (Aaronson 1992b: 160).[1]

Because so many American premier companies continue to recruit their next 'whiz kids' from the latest crop of shiny new MBAs, young men and women flock to these schools. In 1963, universities granted only 5,787 MBAs, but by 1991, this had increased to some 78,700. The number of MBAs as a percentage of all master's degrees granted grew from some 6.3 per cent in 1963 to some 23.3 per cent in 1991, while the number of accredited MBA programmes increased from fifty-three in 1963 to 273 in 1993 (Edelstein 1994: 12–13). However, the growth in MBAs appears to be levelling off, although applications remain at high levels (AACSB Newsline, Spring 1993: 11).

Despite the stakes for the national economic interest, these schools are not controlled or assessed by the federal government – whether public (financed through the states) or private. American graduate business schools are accredited by teams composed of academic experts organized under the aegis of the American Assembly of Collegiate Schools of Business (AACSB). In accrediting an institution, AACSB teams look at curricula, faculty qualifications and research, student admission standards, and library and instructional resources.

Most MBA programmes require students to take two years of study, although there are part-time programmes, intensive programmes, and executive programmes, which require students to attend weekend classes for several years. According to Richard Edelstein, Director of Professional Development and International Affairs at the AACSB, 'the academic program usually includes study of economics, finance, accounting, marketing organizational behavior, and . . . business strategy'. In the second year, students may often specialize in one of these disciplines or take courses in other areas – such as manufacturing, technology management, business/

S. AARONSON

government relations, information systems, or leadership and supervision skills (Edelstein 1994: 1, 6, 7, 12, 13). The scope of the curriculum is not very different from the 1950s, when the Ford Foundation encouraged schools to eliminate industry-specific electives and required a 'comprehensive core of basic business courses' including rigorous analytical, quantitative, and behavioural components (Porter and McKibbin 1988: 56–7).

EVALUATING BUSINESS EDUCATION

There are many ways to evaluate how well American graduate schools of business serve American business. For example, many students rely on three publications, *Business Week, U.S. News and World Report*, and the *Princeton Review – Student Access Guide to the Best Business Schools*, to assess how a particular programme might 'jump-start' their career. These surveys rank business schools by a wide range of factors including conveyance of specific skills; student selectivity; placement success; graduation rate; reputation; quality of faculty; best skills; alumni network; and student diversity. To attract the best and most ambitious candidates, school bulletins highlight their placement services. For example, in its efforts to market its MBA programme, the University of Maryland devotes several pages to its placement services, stressing both the prominent companies that recruit at the school and its graduates' salaries by job function and industry (University of Maryland *Bulletin* 1994: 12–15; see also Stern School of Business *Bulletin* 1994: 138).

But American graduate schools of business can also be judged by other criteria. Like other forms of professional education, business education can be evaluated by how well it provides knowledge that is useful (values, skills, and information) to business practitioners, from trainees to corporate presidents, throughout their careers (Locke 1989: 212). However, graduate business schools differ in how they convey such 'useful knowledge'. In contrast with other professional schools – like law, engineering, education, or medicine – graduate business schools do not rely principally upon practitioners to teach business nor do they teach business through practice, in clerkships or internships. According to Charles Hickman of the AACSB, although some schools do have executives in residence, they rely more on part-time or adjunct faculty to expose students to current business practice. His best 'guestimate' was that no more than 10 per cent of graduate business school faculty were practitioners; about 90 per cent of permanent full-time faculty had a terminal degree – a PhD or a DBA (Hickman Interview, 1 December 1994). Thus future managers were not taught by experienced managers – their education was twice removed from real-world experience.

Graduate business education can also be assessed by how well this training prepares managers to make a wide range of decisions. In *Strategy and Structure*, Alfred D. Chandler, America's pre-eminent business

214

historian, noted that the role of managers is to plan and direct the use of corporate resources to meet short-term (operational decisions) and long-term (entrepreneurial decisions) developments in the markets. When managers responsible for entrepreneurial decisions concentrate on short-term activities to the exclusion or detriment of long-range planning and coordination, they have failed to carry out effectively their role in their enterprise and in the economy. This is called vision; over the long term, those executives who fail to develop an entrepreneurial outlook hamper their companies' performance (Chandler 1962: 11–16, 383, 396).

An earlier study of business education in the years between 1945 and 1960 found that American graduate business schools trained students to make operational decisions, but these schools were less successful in helping their graduates develop an entrepreneurial outlook (Aaronson 1992b). According to Alfred D. Chandler, business paid a high price when managers made the mistake of listening to academics who told them management was a general skill. Chandler believes business education gave these managers a sense of arrogance and presumption that they could succeed in almost all industries (Chandler 1992: 37–8; Chandler Interview, 1 October 1989). Equally importantly, American business leaders were uninvolved in developing the curricula at American premier business schools. Hence the reliance of American business upon graduate business schools may have had consequences for American business and the American economy (Aaronson 1992b: 161).

In the late 1980s, as in the postwar period, business school deans and faculty admitted that they were very good at preparing students for an operational perspective. But they did not know quite how to prepare students for an entrepreneurial perspective (Porter and McKibbin 1988: 99).

AN OVERVIEW OF THE CRITICISM OF MBA PROGRAMMES

Criticism of business education is not new. Since the first days of graduate business education, analysts have questioned whether management can be taught in the classroom, without 'getting one's hands dirty'. There have been three periods of radical curriculum change: in the immediate postwar period, when demand for men in grey flannel suits first boomed; in 1959–60, when the Ford Foundation and Carnegie Commission issued two reports showing how business education could be improved; and more recently, in 1989–91, when members of the AACSB developed new accreditation standards to meet the changing needs of business schools and business. However, these 'revolutions' did not alter the basic strategy of business education: teaching business without practice or practitioners (Aaronson 1992b: 172–3; Porter and McKibbin 1988: 132; Schlossman and Sedlak 1988, 83–95).

Many of the problems of postwar business education are still problems today. According to Wickham Skinner, Professor Emeritus at Harvard Business School, 'many faculty people are so removed from industry that they have no idea what they are really preparing their students for' (Sheridan 1993: 11).

In the postwar period, business school faculties rarely performed leading-edge research; they were often insular and inbred. The bulk of faculty involvement with business was as consultants, not as 'hands-on' managers. With some prominent exceptions, business school research had little impact upon practice (Aaronson 1992b: 165–7). Today, these problems continue. In 1990, *Business Week* magazine reported that the top twenty business schools spent nearly $240 million annually on research. Business faculties, however, admit this research is of little use to managers in their daily work (*Business Week*, 29 October 1990: 52–8). So what are these academics researching and writing about? A *Harvard Business Review* article described two typical (although make-believe) titles: 'An Approximation Algorithm of Space-Optimal Service Queues' and 'A Convergent Gambling Estimate of Market Place Entropy' (Linder and Smith 1992: 16–33). Even someone with English as his or her native language will probably have no idea what they are talking about. Such articles have little relevance to managers as they go about their daily tasks (*Business Week*, 29 October 1990: 53). Not surprisingly, with the exception of *Harvard Business Review* and the *California Management Review*, most managers in the real world do not read business school research publications.

Yet faculties cannot be blamed for their focus on academic business research. They are doing what they are supposed to do in an academic institution. The only way to encourage applied research relevant to business needs is to reward such research. One solution is to adopt a two-track research approach, one for applied and one for basic research (Hickman Interview, 1 December 1994). However, most business school faculties are still promoted on the basis of academic publications. Teaching and real-world experience are less important (Sheridan 1993: 12). Until business schools really make it clear that applied business research is worthy of tenure, faculties will continue to publish for a small audience of their colleagues.

As in the postwar period, those teaching business to MBA students tend to be scholars of business rather than business practitioners. A survey of AACSB members of some 23,351 faculty members in 1993 found that 21,661 (or 92 per cent) had some sort of doctoral degree (Gust Interview, 1 December 1994). According to Porter and McKibbin, many of these faculty members know very little about how issues and problems play out in the hurly-burly of the workaday business world. If it is assumed that direct experience helps faculties teach business effectively, reliance on scholars of business deprives 'students of insights and perspectives that will be necessary when they graduate and go out into the practice of management' (Porter and McKibbin 1988: 132).

Although business schools have adopted the mores of the academy for promotion, they rarely interact, team-teach, or collaborate with their colleagues in other divisions of their universities. Business schools tend to hire their own business school economists, ethicists, and sociologists. Cross-disciplinary and intra-university interaction is not a priority (Porter and McKibbin 1988: 193). Yet within most corporations, assignments require a cooperative effort among employees from many different divisions. Whether designing a new product or preparing the annual report, managers must learn to work in a cross-functional setting. Again, business education is removed from business reality.

From a review of the literature and interviews with AACSB officials, it seems clear that a greater number of executives today participate in business education by serving as guest lecturers, as mentors, as alumni advisers, as students, and as administrators. But as noted above, their involvement is often part time (Porter and McKibbin 1988: 138–47, 335–41; Hickman Interview, 1 December 1994).

One of the most vociferous critics today is Peter Robinson, who was a speech writer in the Reagan White House. Robinson left the 'corridors of power' to enter the 'ivy halls of academia' in 1988. He decided to go to Stanford University Graduate School of Business, one of the most prestigious business schools in the United States. Robinson completed his MBA and lived to tell his story in a new book, which he aptly titled *Snapshots from Hell: The Making of an MBA* (Robinson 1994). He concluded that it is almost impossible to translate practical tasks into academic disciplines. He quotes one of his professors (of ethics, no less) who has proposed an experiment. In this experiment, Stanford Business School would admit two identical classes of students. Members of one class would do the work; members of the other 'would not do a damn thing, just play golf and throw hot tub parties'. Both groups would be given MBAs. 'It is my contention', said that professor of ethics, 'that five years after they graduated, you wouldn't see a didly squat's worth of difference between the two groups' (Lewis 1994: 6–7).

Robinson is not alone in criticizing this reliance on the classroom rather than the 'school of hard knocks'. Since the 1980s, these critics have alleged that management education is too removed from the real world. Consequently, it has not been responsive to the wrenching economic changes the American economy has undergone in the last twenty years, such as the globalization of business and technology; the increase in minorities, the disabled, and women in the workforce; and the rise of small business (AACSB 1992, 1–11; Sheridan 1993: 12; Porter and McKibbin 1988: 3–18; AACSB Newsline, Summer 1993: 17). In the hope of learning from these 'market'-based criticisms, in 1988, the AACSB commissioned a study of business education by two prominent business school professors, Lyman W. Porter and Lawrence E. McKibbin. The two analysts were also charged with finding a better way to educate American future business leaders.

Porter and McKibbin found that business schools are generally criticized for insufficient emphasis on generating 'vision' in students; insufficient emphasis on cross-functional integration between disciplines; too much emphasis on quantitative skills; insufficient attention to managing people; inadequate emphasis on the international dimension of business; insufficient attention to the external environment of business; insufficient attention to ethics; and poor communication skills (Porter and McKibbin 1988: 64–6). They also reported that these critics believe MBA graduates have overly high expectations for their careers; are more loyal to their careers than to a company; have poor communication and interpersonal skills; and lack leadership training and skills (Porter and McKibbin 1988: 79, 81, 98–9, 116, 122, 129).

CHANGES IN AMERICAN BUSINESS EDUCATION

Business schools heard these criticisms. In glossy brochures, bulletins, and pamphlets, American graduate business schools trumpet how they are changing. Many proudly proclaim the 'internationalization of their curriculum', their receptivity to 'the challenge of change', or their technological 'savvy' (Stern School of Business *Bulletin* 1994: 3; University of Maryland 1994: 5, 40; Lubin School of Business 1994: 5). According to Dick Edelstein of the AACSB, Case Western, Duke, the University of Michigan, The Wharton School, Columbia, Southern Methodist, Indiana, Tennessee, Penn State, Carnegie Mellon, and the University of Denver have already radically reformed their curricula and approach to business education. At the time of writing, Harvard and the University of Texas are beginning curricular reform (Edelstein Interview, 7 July 1994). Those schools that did not radically revise their curricula have added a new emphasis on integrative courses or themes (Sheridan 1993: 12).

From the author's research, American graduate business schools were found to have adopted seven approaches to revamping their curriculum in the 1990s: this was corroborated in an interview with Dr Milton R. Blood, Director of Accreditation at the AACSB, and a former business school professor and administrator (Blood Interview, 7 July 1994).

The first strategy calls for the reorientation of business education to respond to the direct needs of local companies. This makes business education closer to executive education, where companies even sponsor research or demand specific courses to meet their particular needs. Lehigh University seems to have followed this course (Aaronson 1992a: 334–5). But focusing on the needs of local companies may decrease enrolments because the school in question may seem too narrowly concentrated. Moreover, faculty may be reluctant to follow this strategy, as it means education could be biased to serve the 'dirty hand' of the market, rather than the 'genteel hand' of the academy.

Another strategy calls for thematic reorganization: reordering the business school curriculum around themes that today's managers must cope with, such as global competition, leadership, ethics, and technology. This strategy also allows business schools to differentiate themselves from their competitors in the market. For example, The Wharton Business School at the University of Pennsylvania asked executives, futurists, and corporate recruiters how the curriculum could be changed to meet future business needs. Their suggestions led to a revised curriculum that emphasizes ethics, leadership, and international business. Columbia and Georgetown made similar changes. Harvard returned to its roots by emphasizing leadership. At Babson, the curriculum has been reoriented around total quality management. At the Darden School of Management at the University of Virginia, all first-year students take courses in ethics, strategy, leadership, and change. As part of the course, students play the Oriental game of 'Go', which requires participants to think in non-traditional, non-Western ways – thus cultivating new ways of thinking (AACSB Newsline, Spring 1993: 3; and Blood Interview, 7 July 1994).

But focusing the curricula around a theme is hard to do. For example, leadership means different things to different people. Schools as diverse as Harvard, the Darden School, New York University, Stanford, Chicago, Michigan, and Carnegie Mellon say they are educating business leaders, not mid-level managers. However, there is no consensus on how to teach leadership, if leadership can be taught, or even what leadership means (AACSB Newsline, Spring 1993: 1; Edelstein Interview, 7 July 1994). Does it mean taking charge of people, resources, products, and ideas or does it mean entrepreneurial management (Aaronson 1992b: 161)?

In the belief that the customer is always right, the University of Tennessee's College of Business Administration took a different approach. Faculty conducted a survey to find out what business and industry wants in the graduates it hires. Based on the survey findings, this school completely scrapped its first-year MBA curriculum and replaced it with a single integrated course, team-taught by fourteen faculty members. Its faculty tried to develop courses based on what executives said they needed to know. Thus, faculty members proposing content for the course had to stand before the other thirteen members of the teaching team and convince them that the material was something that every manager should know. This forced the academics to differentiate between what managers need to know and what their subordinates need to know (Sheridan 1993: 13).

The University of Michigan Business School decided to give students the opportunity to learn by doing – representing a fourth approach. But the students were not required to take internships or apprenticeships. Instead, they spend time at a company studying a specific business process such as inventory management and then present recommendations to company representatives and faculty. This situation does not quite replicate real-world experience, for students cannot be fired or promoted on the basis of their answers. In contrast, Southern Methodist University established a leadership centre, which teaches leadership as a skill and encourages students to learn leadership through internships (AACSB Newsline Spring 1993, 3; and Blood Interview, 7 July 1994).

The fifth approach stems from problems in the United States in producing competitive quality products on a timely basis. Georgia Tech, Stanford, Michigan, and Carnegie Mellon, schools with strong engineering programmes, have redesigned their curricula to enable their graduates to straddle business and technology management. These programmes will teach managers about engineering and engineers about managing. Proponents believe such programmes are necessary, because there is a wide gap between industry's technological problems and the business school curriculum (AACSB Newsline, Spring 1994: 6–7).

A sixth approach, exemplified by Northwestern, is to balance the theoretical and the applied in research and in the curriculum. Thus, the school has come closest to the medical school model with a bifurcated faculty: a clinical faculty (with business practitioners) and a research faculty (Hickman Interview, 1 December 1994). For the last few years, this balance has been seen as particularly effective by students, faculty, and business recruiters. Northwestern almost always ranks among the most admired business schools for its approach to education and its placement success.

A seventh approach recognizes that the United States needs leaders who can move in the three different types of institutions of the political economy: the public, private, and non-profit sectors. Each sector needs individuals that can manage ideas, products, people, and money. Although this approach was recently abandoned by Yale School of Management, it has been adopted by the University of California at Irvine (Blood Interview, 7 July 1994; Porter and McKibbin 1988: 318).

In addition to these seven approaches, some twenty schools – including Northwestern, University of Georgia, and University of Pittsburgh – have adopted one-year MBA programmes. The AACSB described these programmes as a response to new market conditions. But their advent raises two questions – what do future managers need to know and what specifically should they learn in the classroom (AACSB Newsline, Summer 1993: 14–15)? Can this be learned in one year?

Even the association that accredits business schools is changing. In 1991, the AACSB leadership decided the organization needed to encourage greater flexibility among business schools in curriculum development, in hiring faculty, and in sponsoring research. They devised a new approach to accreditation, which allowed business schools new freedom to be creative in developing MBA programmes. According to Charles Hickman, a school must provide 'a clear, unambiguous mission statement that defines who its customers are and how it intends to serve them' (Sheridan 1993: 15). But this process will be slow, since American business schools must renew their accreditation only once every nine years.

Impediments to change

American graduate schools of business have made important changes to their curricula, but these changes are incremental. Moreover, it is thought that these changes have not resulted in a more 'real-world' approach to business, nor have they led to greater business involvement in business education.

In May 1994, a computer search of articles on graduate business education published in 1991–4 was carried out. Of 693 articles, twelve (or 2 per cent) criticized MBA education, and eighteen examined the relationship between the business community and MBAs. From a perusal of some twenty of these articles, as well as AACSB and business school publications, it was discovered that almost all American business schools had business advisory boards or committees. They relied on alumni and outside executives to advise students and administrators, to network, and to lecture. Yet very few of the schools actively seek continual input from the diversity of managers (as opposed to recruiting officials) engaged in business to improve courses and programmes. Even fewer see internships or apprenticeships as a crucial part of the curriculum.

Although American business schools are changing their curricula, the stakeholders of business education in the United States – students, business leaders, administrators, faculty, and corporate shareholders – are not demanding radical changes to American business education. In the Porter/McKibbin survey in 1988, most executives stated that they plan to continue to hire MBAs. Only some 14 per cent of executives believe the MBA degree will become less important in the future. According to the AACSB, 'hiring activity remains brisk', although recruitment patterns and staffing needs are changing dramatically (AACSB Newsline, Summer 1993: 16–17). In 1988 at least, there was 'no forceful push for systemic curriculum change emanating from business schools themselves'. This 'inertia persists even though the business community registers serious reservations about some aspects of the current curriculum' (Porter and McKibbin 1988: 79, 81).

This 'inertia' also persists because students still believe the MBA is a passport to high-visibility business jobs. Yet these same MBA students seem to believe that the degree is less useful in preparing graduates for 'an eventual position of significant managerial leadership' (Porter and McKibbin 1988: 113–14).

Business leaders do not seem to be the main force for reforming business education; they remain willing to abdicate executive training to academia. For example, when surveying several reports on competitiveness from 1985 to the present day, all were found to have training sections, but ones in which the focus was on retraining workers, not on retraining management.[2] Business leaders have not, apparently, paid much attention to how management training and attitudes affect productivity.

To Porter and McKibbin, the managerial and corporate world has not yet examined 'what role it wants to play, and is willing to play, in affecting – and perhaps stimulating and improving – the course of business school research and education' (Porter and McKibbin 1988: 335–6). Although business executives say they want to improve business education, they have been relatively uninvolved in developing these new approaches described above (Porter and McKibbin 1988: 181–91, 193–4). For example, the Accreditation Project Task Force of the AACSB had sixteen members, three of whom came from outside academia. One was the Vice-President – Taxation of the American Institute of Certified Public Accountants; one was the Controller of the Research and Development Staff of Monsanto Company; and the third was a Partner in Arthur Young, a prominent accounting firm. Although the AACSB wanted 'to ensure wide representation and participation in developing new accreditation standards', business participation seemed limited (AACSB Newsline, April 1989, April 1990, April 1991). The AACSB did try to obtain corporate perspectives by holding several open hearings and sponsoring an 'invitational corporate forum in New York in order to provide feedback to the task force on expected changes in the business environment' (AACSB Newsline, April 1991: 3). As of the writing of this chapter, however, managers do not appear to have seized this opportunity to help reshape business education. No evidence could be found to support the view that business executives have volunteered to serve as peer reviewers for new accreditations, although they have been invited to do so (AACSB Newsline, Winter 1993: 12). Corporations have, however, provided grants to assist in implementing new accreditations (AACSB Newsline, Summer 1992: 10).

Finally, business inertia about business education may also stem from confusion about future hiring needs. According to Porter and McKibbin,

> many firms were not making effective strategic decisions about what types of student products they really needed. . . . Hence, they seemed neither to have a clear rationale for choosing the particular set of schools at which to recruit . . . nor reliable information about which schools were producing which kinds of graduates.
>
> (Porter and McKibbin 1988: 335–6)

If this is true, business is a relatively uneducated consumer of the business education product.

Conditions affecting demand for MBAs

New market conditions will inspire greater numbers of executives to become more involved in the production of future business leaders. These conditions include a plateau in demand for new MBAs; a decrease in demand for mid-level managers with MBAs; increased competition from new providers of business education; and greater government involvement in business education as a result of concerns about 'competitiveness'.

For example, a greater number of executives are weighing potential return on investment when they hire MBAs. An MBA from a top school today is generally compensated with a job paying from $40,000 to as much as $80,000. Not surprisingly, given their ever-rising price tags, corporations are hiring talented engineering or liberal arts graduates.

Demand for middle-level managers and senior managers may decline in the future, because corporations have learned they do not need these managers. In the period 1987–92, 5.6 million American workers with three or more years of seniority lost their jobs permanently. By January 1992, more than a third were still looking for work (Competitiveness Policy Council 1993: 13). Many of the laid-off executives were MBAs. Other companies have learned from these lay-offs. As the number of grey flannel suits on Wall Street and Main Street declines, the MBA may no longer be the credential of choice for American business leaders.

Graduate business schools are not the only institutions offering advanced training in management. A growing number of the most prestigious companies such as Motorola (Motorola University) and General Motors (GMI Engineering and Management Institute) now have their own educational facilities to train their employees. And many American companies rely on outside vendors which essentially compete with business schools, such as The Center for Creative Leadership, the Brookings Institution, or the American Management Association.

Perhaps most importantly, members of Congress, concerned about the nation's 'competitiveness', have written legislation to encourage American graduate business schools and American business to work together more effectively in the new global economy. In 1988, Congress created twenty-five Centers for International Business Education and Research (CIBERS) under the Omnibus Trade and Competitiveness Act of 1988 'to increase and promote the nation's capacity for international understanding and economic enterprise'. The CIBERS programme 'links the manpower and information needs of U.S. business with the international education, language training and research capacities of universities across the U.S.' (Centers for International Business Education and Research 1994: 3, 6, 13–14). Although there have been no studies of the effectiveness of the CIBERS, a 1992 survey of 1,275 business schools found that American business schools 'fall further behind the reality of the global economy for which they allegedly are to prepare managers'. The report noted that internationalization of business education 'won't advance significantly in the short term', as a result of lagging interest and reduced funding (AACSB Newsline, Spring 1993: 10).

The survey, AACSB's most comprehensive, compared business schools in the United States and those in Africa, the Middle East, North and South America, Europe, and Asia. It found that the non-United States' schools have made greater progress in internationalization. Generally, these schools have targeted a higher level of expertise in their international education and 'more attention is paid by the institution to internationalizing the faculty'. According to Kerry Cooper, Director of the Center for International Business Studies at Texas A&M University, the study 'provides empirical evidence for a perverse aspect of business education' that the United States is not educating its future business school faculty to train effective managers in the international economy (AACSB Newsline, Winter 1993: 10–11). If companies and the federal government recognize economic interdependence, why do not these schools?

CONCLUSION

American business schools have made major changes in recent years to their curricula, administration, and faculty. Yet these changes are, the author believes, incremental. In most business schools, the basic philosophy remains that a person can teach management without actual management practice and without the guidance of experienced managers. But change is inevitable. Terry Maris, Dean of the College of Business Administration at Ohio Northern University, recently noted, as business leaders re-engineer the corporation, 'maybe the time has come for us to consider reinventing the business school' (AACSB Newsline, Summer 1993: 17).

Mark Twain once said, 'I have never let my schooling interfere with my education.' Twain (no stranger to economic success) would have been shocked by the lack of real-world experience in business education. The virtual reality of the classroom can never replicate experience in the school of hard knocks.

To understand the evolution of this strange species, the American graduate school of business, further insights must be gained into the relationship of American business and these schools. Why do firms continue to rely on managers educated by a process that removes them from the real world? Why do managers not get more involved in business education? These are questions that deserve further study, or these academic animals may go the way of the dinosaur.

NOTES

1 A 1959 study of 428 top executives in 1950 found that a majority had gone to

college. Of the group with graduate degrees, nineteen (approximately 4 per cent) had degrees in business administration (Newcomer 1955: 68–9). The number of executives with MBAs increased significantly by 1964. A study of sixty-six business leaders found that 17 per cent had MBAs (Bond *et al.* 1965: 65). A 1979 Harvard study, 'Success of a Strategy', found that, by 1977, over 20 per cent of the top three officers of each of the Fortune 500 manufacturing companies were graduates of the Harvard Business School. Ten years later, 225 of the chief executive officers at the top 1,000 corporations had MBAs. ('A Portrait of the Boss', *Business Week*, 21 October 1988, 28; and 'Success of a Strategy', Harvard University, Graduate School of Business, Unpublished paper 1975).

2 The reports surveyed included: The President's Commission on Industrial Competitiveness (1985), and Competitiveness Policy Council (1993, 1994). However, in a survey of international business leaders, government officials, and academics published in late 1992, the United States ranked twentieth in management development, tenth in corporate performance, eighth in business efficiency, and first in entrepreneurship, giving it an overall management rank of ninth in the top twenty economies of the world. American management was criticized for its short-term orientation, its implementation of strategies, its lack of intercultural experience and understanding, its management of a diverse workforce, its quality control, its corporate credibility, and its productivity. But despite these criticisms, American managers have not paid great attention to how managers are trained (World Economic Forum 1992: 81, 518–51).

REFERENCES

Aaronson, S. (1992a) 'Review of *The Manchester Experiment* and *Lehigh University*', *Business History Review* 334–5.

—— (1992b) 'Serving America's Business? Graduate Business Schools and American Business, 1945–60', *Business History* 34(1): 160–82.

American Assembly of Collegiate Schools of Business (1993) 'Achieving Quality and Continuous Improvement through Self-Evaluation and Peer Review: Standards for Accreditation, Business Administration and accounting', St Louis: AACSB.

—— (1992) 'Crisis and Survival', St Louis: AACSB.

—— (1993) 'Membership Directory', St Louis: AACSB.

—— (1989–94), 'Newsline', St Louis: AACSB.

Bond, F., Leabo, D., and Swinyard, A. (1965) *Preparation for Business Leadership*, Ann Arbor, MI: University of Michigan Press.

Business Week (1988) 'A Portrait of the Boss', 21 October 1988.

—— (1990) 'Is Research in the Ivory Tower, "Fuzzy, Irrelevant, Pretentious"?', 29 October 1990, 52–8.

Centers for International Business Education and Research (1994) *Centers for International Business Education and Research*, Washington, DC.

Chandler, A.D., Jr (1962) *Strategy and Structure: Chapters in the History of the American Industrial Enterprise*, Cambridge, MA: MIT Press.

—— (1992) 'Managerial Enterprise and Competitive Capabilities', *Business History* 34(1): 11–39.

Competitiveness Policy Council (1993) *A Competitiveness Strategy for America, 2nd Report to the President and Congress*, Washington, DC: GPO.

—— (1994) *Promoting Long-Term Prosperity, Third Report to the President and Congress*, Washington, DC: GPO.

Edelstein, R.J. (n.d.) 'The American MBA: Educational Traditions, Quality Issues and New Directions', unpublished speech.

Krugman, P. (1994) 'Competitiveness: A Dangerous Obsession', *Foreign Affairs* 73(2): 28–4.

Lewis, Michael (1994) Review of *Snapshots From Hell: The Making of an MBA* in *The New York Times Book Review* 8 May.

Linder, J.C. and Smith, H.J. (1992) 'The Complex Case of Management Education', *Harvard Business Review* September/October: 16–33.

Locke, Robert (1989) *Management and Higher Education since 1940*, Cambridge: Cambridge University Press.

Lubin School of Business (1994) *Catalogue*, New York: Pace University.

Newcomer, M. (1955) *The Big Business Executive*, New York: Columbia University Press.

Porter, L.W. and McKibbin, L.E. (1988) *Management Education and Development*, New York: McGraw-Hill.

President's Commission on Industrial Competitiveness (1985) *Global Competition: The New Reality*, Washington, DC: GPO.

Robinson, P. (1994) *Snapshots from Hell: The Making of an MBA*, New York: Warner Books.

Schlossman, S. and Sedlak, M. (1988) 'The Age of Reform in American Management Education', Los Angeles: Graduate Management Admissions Council.

Sheridan, J.H. (1993) 'A New Breed of M.B.A.', *Industry Week* 4 April: 11–16.

Stern School of Business (1994) *Bulletin 1993–1994*, New York: New York University.

University of Maryland (2/1994) 'Dean's List', College Park, MD: University of Maryland.

—— (1993) *Maryland, the MBA and MS Programs*, College Park, MD: University of Maryland.

—— (Spring 1994) 'The Maryland MBA', College Park, MD: University of Maryland.

World Economic Forum (1992) *The World Competitiveness Report 1992*, Geneva: World Economic Forum (12th edn).

INTERVIEWS

Milton R. Blood, Director of Accreditation, AACSB, 7 July 1994.

Professor Alfred D. Chandler, Jr, Professor Emeritus, Harvard Business School, 1 October 1989.

Richard Edelstein, Director of Professional Development and International Affairs, AACSB, 7 July 1994.

Mary Jo Gust, Information/System Administrator, AACSB, 1 December 1994.

Charles Hickman, Director of Projects and Services, AACSB, 1 December 1994.

12

MANAGING MANAGEMENT TEAMS

A challenge for management education

Ove Bjarnar and Hallgeir Gammelsæter

INTRODUCTION

Though it can be argued that the nature of leadership or management skills is not clearly established (Yukl 1989), nor standardized to the extent that it can be compared with professions such as law, accounting, or medicine (Whitley 1988), the belief that management can be taught seems to be alive and well in many Western countries. In this chapter, this belief is questioned, not so much because of the difficulty of defining what management is, but rather in the light of what seems to be management's present challenge. The concern is that top management will come to be more the mastery of teamwork in heterogeneous teams and less an individual hero-activity. In relation to education, the question is whether management education today prepares students for this challenge.

Academic preoccupation with executives in organizations has resulted in a lot of perspectives and debates. These include such questions as whether leadership is different from management; whether the focus of interest should be on the psychological traits of managers or on the situational characteristics of the manager's position; whether management (or leadership) in organizations is substantially important or only marginal; whether leadership is merely an attributional phenomenon or not; and so forth (see Yukl 1989 for an overview). Though the scope of this chapter is too narrow to include any further treatment of these debates, it is nevertheless necessary to define what is understood by the terms 'management' and 'management education'.

The kind of management that is of interest here is strategic management at the top of organizations. The assumption is that in organizations there are some people who make – at least, are expected to make – strategic decisions on behalf of the organization. These are the decision makers. The internal and external stakeholders in the organization expect top managers to confront, process, and decide on the most important matters for that organization; to make and implement decisions that enhance that organization's ability to develop and prosper.

It is generally understood that management education means the kind of higher education that applies science to management problems – what Locke has called 'the new paradigm in American management studies' (Locke 1994: 156). More specifically, this means the kind of business or management education that in Western countries today is predominantly a pre-experience postgraduate education taking place in business schools. Certainly, business education in different countries often has, as this book illustrates, its own national imprint. National traditions and structures do differ. In spite of this, however, there seems to be no doubt that the new paradigm – or the American model – has had an immense influence on business education in many European countries, including Norway (Engwall and Gunnarsson 1994).

This chapter is divided into four parts. In the first part, it is proposed that, in order to meet the demands and challenges of the future, organizations will have to build, maintain, and renew top management teams consisting of managers with different specialist backgrounds. Consequently, managers in strategic positions must be both 'teamworkers' and specialists. In the second part, it is argued that management education is built on two basic assumptions – the belief in the individual hero–leader, and the belief that leaders can be educated by introducing them to a broad range of management subjects. These two basic assumptions constitute what is called here the 'hero–generalist paradigm' of management education. In the third part, some barriers to the breaking of this paradigm, as well as some processes that seem to threaten it, are highlighted. Finally, the arguments are summed up and the question asked: 'What implications do they have for further research?'

TOP MANAGEMENT AS A HETEROGENEOUS TEAM APPROACH

Professions in top management positions

Although no management profession has yet established itself (Whitley 1988), it can be argued that specific professions have dominated executive positions in the large enterprises of many countries. Fligstein (1985, 1987) documents that in the United States managers who had a background in financing, marketing, and accounting gained a foothold in American business from the 1920s and onwards. Gradually, these managers replaced more operational managers, who had a background in manufacturing, in the most prominent positions in large enterprises. A similar development has taken place in Britain (Armstrong 1987) and in Scandinavia. In Norway, business-educated managers rose to the highest positions in many of the largest firms during the 1980s (Amdam 1993; Gammelsæter 1990). In Sweden, a similar development is documented by Engwall *et al.* in their contribution to this book.

At least two different theoretical perspectives purport to explain the pattern described above. One strategic contingency perspective (Hickson *et al.* 1971) assumes that those professions that most effectively reduce the organization's uncertainty over time will rise to the key positions. Who reigns is therefore largely determined by developments outside the enterprise itself. In this way, the rise of the accounting profession as a dominating management profession can be explained by the prerequisites for the development of diversification strategies and the multidivisional form of organization. As Chandler (1962) pointed out, the basis for the invention of the diversification strategy and the multidivisional form was changes in markets and government regulations. New production technologies and improvements in infrastructure, such as the development of a coast-to-coast railway system, laid the ground for mass production and modern marketing. The companies that were able to profit from the situation, integrated vertically and horizontally – often by acquisition – and grew into large enterprises. The integration strategy threatened competition in many industries. As a result, around the turn of the century a law was passed that prohibited the creation of monopolies. Subsequently, the large enterprises invested their surplus financial resources in other industries, thereby creating multibusiness enterprises. This diversification strategy later led to the invention of the multidivisional form – a pattern of organization that was controlled by business-educated managers rather than engineers 'because decisions of allocation between dissimilar operations could only be made on a common abstract – and therefore financial – basis' (Armstrong 1984: 104). To put it crudely, engineers were not fit to run more than one business. When the enterprises became multibusiness, it was the accountants who possessed the knowledge and ability to act strategically.

In contrast to the strategic-contingency explanation, Armstrong (1985) argues that different 'organizational professions' compete for controlling the enterprise, and that the result of this competition is not simply based on which profession is the more effective in controlling strategic contingencies. Professions develop control strategies based on generalizations of their techniques and knowledge, and seek actively to define an enterprise's responses to uncertainties and crises in order to capitalize on the situation. This 'power perspective' places rivalry between professions at the forefront, and thus explains both the pattern of who holds key positions and the choices of strategies and structures, as an outcome of the professions' ability to implement their particular point of view in the organization (Fligstein 1985, 1987). This perspective also makes possible the incorporation of institutional explanations, in the sense that the resources professions can draw on in their contention for positions may lie in historically derived national cultures, political institutions and systems, national education systems, metamorphic processes, and so on.

Some very different implications follow from the strategic contingency and the power perspectives, respectively. The first implies a universal pattern of development irrespective of cultures, institutions, and political systems, only mediated by the level of industrialization. The American pattern is assumed to model the effective development, or process of, modernization. Observations like those that German management is dominated by engineers and that qualified accountants in the Western sense are rare in Japanese enterprises, are incongruent with this perspective (Armstrong 1985). The power perspective is arguably more robust for cross-cultural comparison. The assumption that there are many ways to reach the same goal is implied, and there is no a priori contention that one pattern is more effective and powerful than others. Making cross-cultural comparisons forces one to look for nation-specific or typological patterns.

The two perspectives do not necessarily exclude each other. On the one hand, to the extent that the business world gets smaller – resulting, for instance, from the development of global telecommunications and the extension of supernational federations, like the European Union – the same strategic contingencies may apply to more organizations and cause metamorphic processes that ignore national borders. On the other hand, national traditions and cultures, very likely expressed through the competition between professions, may still play a part in the development of management hierarchies. Such national sources may stimulate innovations as contingencies change, and some nations may therefore operate as forerunners in global developments. The 'new paradigm' that has been sweeping over Europe in the last two or three decades may, for instance, be conceptualized as an innovation that partly sprang from the American tradition of higher education and elitist values, and partly as an answer to economic demand (Locke 1994).

Today, the time seems to be ripe for asking whether any profession will be able to dominate the key positions in business in the future, and if so which profession will this be? Do developments in global competition give rise to a redefinition of the modern American management ideal which seems to have stimulated the current domination of business graduates among managers?

The case for management teams

It is believed that in a business world that is becoming smaller but still more complex, multifaceted, and dynamic, no profession alone will either possess or be able to convince us that it possesses the answers to the contingencies that face an organization. It is suggested that it is the companies which are able to operate effectively, with heterogeneous top management teams, that

230

will be the winners of future competitions. Top management, like project management, will have to trust the joint efforts of multiprofessional and multifunctional teams rather than try to live up to the 'heroes' and 'oracles' of American business history. The start of the progress towards team management at the top has already been witnessed (Ancona and Nadler 1989). In many companies, the shift from individual management to team management has been difficult and perhaps premature (Casey 1985). The shift will be even more difficult when it transpires that successful teams must probably also be heterogeneous.

Why will heterogeneous top management teams be more important in the future? One obvious reason is the creation of synergy – to increase coordination across functions, capabilities, and activities so that the performance of the whole is greater than the sum of its parts. Another is the contention, to some extent supported in studies, that a lot of cognitive simplification processes operate in decision making, and that one way to diminish the negative effects of this is the composing of decision-making bodies in which different views are considered (Schwenk 1984; Hambrick and Mason 1984).

Why are synergy and rational decision making more important now than they were before? Ancona and Nadler (1989) argue that there are two contextual factors that influence the necessity for top management teams. One is the environmental context mentioned above. When the complexity and instability of external demands increase, so do the demands on top management. The other is the structural context. When coordination requirements within an enterprise itself increase, the pressure on the top manager grows accordingly. The increase of both internal and external demands means that top management has to manage a lot of processes – strategic, financial, organizational, political, and so forth – simultaneously. A recent trend in many large and middle-sized enterprises in the United States, as well as in Europe (O'Toole and Bennis 1992), Norway included (Reve 1994), is that of creating confederational structures. Monolithic structures are unfashionable, probably because the pressure for innovation is growing in many industries. Thus, even IBM has learned that centralization is 'the death-blow of corporate innovation' and has created numerous semi-autonomous business units and thousands of business-alliance relationships around the world (O'Toole and Bennis 1992: 76).

What requirements for management do these developments create? At first sight, it might appear that the top management requirement of the modern enterprise is that of general or relational managers, 'leaders of leaders' (O'Toole and Bennis 1992: 88), who spend much of their time on the career development of the many leaders of the enterprise. If this is true, it may be equally true that the modern top manager will not be a general manager *qua* education, but a general manager *qua* internal career development, as seems to be the case in Japan (Nagaoka 1994). Because

231

competition is increasingly based on knowledge-intensive innovation, the general top manager is required to have a feel for the expertise as well. Some research also shows that innovation is positively correlated with heterogeneity and the level of education in the top management team (Bantel and Jackson 1989). Increasing instability in the external context would also require greater capacity for strategic change. Keck and Tushman (1993), based on data on the cement industry of the United States from 1900 to 1986, found that heterogeneity in the top management team is characteristic of organizations that survive dramatic organizational shifts. In addition, Wiersema and Bantel (1992) found that educational heterogeneity in the management team was positively related to strategic change.

Is the team approach another management fad? On the contrary, it is believed that the building and maintaining of heterogeneous teams will reduce the chance of companies falling prey to management fads that more often than not turn out to be a waste of time and money (Nohria and Berkley 1994). The heterogeneous team can draw on expert knowledge from many fields and mobilize the necessary professional scepticism to new managerial ideas. This is not to say that new management ideas will be dismissed as fads, void of any important message or knowledge. The point is that management teams with heterogeneous educational specializations will most likely be better equipped to look for critical competencies in such modern ideas than will either a homogeneous team or an isolated professional top manager, especially if most of these are MBAs or have an equivalent educational background. Thus there is agreement with Henry Minzberg who asserts that:

> Perhaps the biggest problem in management today is the superficiality of management people who in many cases don't know their businesses or even some who do but act in a superficial way by being detached from very complex problems. . . . I think there is something intrinsic to the conventional MBA that breeds a certain superficiality.
>
> (in Gosling 1994: 98)

What then is team management? It has already been argued that the nature of management skills is not clearly established, and this of course also applies to team management. Still, there seem to be some features that more or less characterize the ideal team. These include common objectives, commitment, work with process issues, listening, consensus decisions, mutual accountability, openness, trust, conflict resolution, and complementary capabilities (Casey 1985; Katzenbach and Douglas 1993). In contrast, top management teams are most likely to differ from other teams in certain respects – for instance, in the extent and way in which they are influenced by external forces and uncertainty, deriving from the complexity of their tasks; in their higher visibility and the political intent of their job; and in the requirement that one individual must ultimately play the role of chief executive and somehow decide on the rewards of the other team members (Ancona and Nadler 1989). It can be argued that it is exactly this high level of uncertainty and need for problem solving that require a team approach to top management (Critchley and Casey 1984).

It is one thing to accept the general idea that teams have certain advantages over individual models, it is quite another to organize and operate *heterogeneous* teams. Heterogeneity implies difference and disagreement, which in our culture at least is far more difficult to manage than is similarity and agreement. But bad experiences with teams do not mean that as a result teams cannot function. Indeed, malfunctioning teams might tell us a lot of things. One is that teamwork, especially in heterogeneous teams, opposes or challenges some very basic values and norms inherent in our traditions and culture. A relevant question here is whether these values and norms are maintained and reproduced in management education in such a way that the latter in fact counteracts our ability to meet the present management challenge (Locke 1994).

THE HERO–GENERALIST PARADIGM

In this section, two of the basic assumptions which, it is believed, make up the paradigm that underpins modern postgraduate management education will be highlighted. One is the assumption that management is an individual activity – namely, the 'hero assumption'. The other is the assumption that management is a subject, or a sample of interrelated subjects, and that education based on a mix of these subjects qualifies the postgraduate student to become a professional general manager. This will be called the 'grand theory assumption'. These assumptions will be clarified briefly below, and, by using some empirical Norwegian data, the way in which management education in Norway belongs to this paradigm will be illustrated.

The hero assumption

Over twenty years ago, Mintzberg (1973) argued that there was a great deal of folklore about what managers do. One myth, he argued, was that, 'The manager is a reflective, systematic planner.' The assumptions inherent in this phrase are many, but it may be argued that they all possess the essence of the traditional understanding of management. Applied to the historic understanding of top management, these assumptions are even more valid. First, management is about the manager in the singular – assuming that management is an individual activity. The viewpoint that individualism is particularly strong in Anglo-Saxon countries is supported by Hofstedes' (1985) empirical work on the relationship between organizational and national value systems. Second, management is reflection – assuming that the manager has the necessary information, the knowledge to make use of this information, and the cognitive capacity to process it. Third, management is acting systematically – assuming that the manager makes use of a general system of principles in decision making. Finally, management is planning – assuming that the manager has foresight and is able to prepare himself (he is male, of course) and his organization for possible events in the future. In sum, the historic picture of management is that of the male, enlightened, and calculative 'hero–leader' (Barnes and Krieger 1986).

The concept of folklore used by Mintzberg suggests that the understanding of management is built on beliefs rather than facts. Moreover, it has always been known that the real-life manager (referring to mundane and not religious leaders) is not perfectly reflective, systematic, or filled with foresight. Without that knowledge, the idea of educating managers would not have come up in the first place. The folklore refers to the ideals that we want our managers to live up to. So, in order to narrow the gap between the ideal and real life, the development of scientific knowledge is tried, and applied to managers. The ambition has been to educate managers who can live up to management ideals.

The grand theory assumption

Certainly, much effort has been put into the task of establishing a management science. What more correctly may be termed the field of management science has grown into a tree with many branches. The great variety in foci and perspectives, 'the management jungle' (Koontz 1961), and the subsequent lack of integrated principles, have led many to ask whether management is a science (Freedman 1992). It may be described as a 'tree' rather than a 'jungle' because the 'branches' have a common sap or life-blood – the shared inspiration of different schools – which springs from the folklore and ideals described above. Thus, even though some scholars are occupied with the behavioural aspects of management, and others with the strategic planning aspects, management information systems, decision making, accounting, organizational development, innovation, human resource planning, and the health and well-being of the individual manager, are all rooted in the same tradition. And deeply embedded in this tradition is the ideal of establishing a grand theory which integrates insights from the many schools that concern themselves with different management themes.

The hero–generalist paradigm

In Figure 12.1, the two dimensions – 'object of education' and 'type of knowledge' – have been combined in order to suggest possible paradigms of management education. The object of education can be individuals or teams (or a mixture). It has been argued above that in management

234

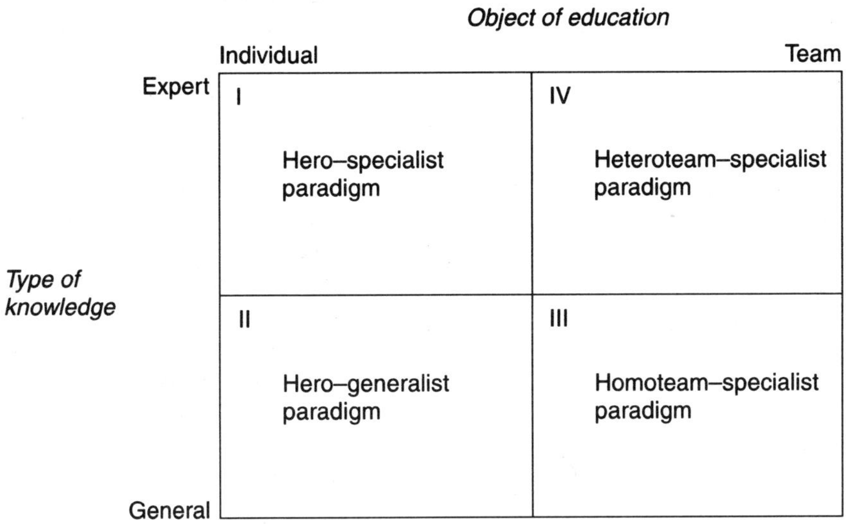

Object of education

Figure 12.1 The combination of type of knowledge and object of
education and the resulting paradigms

education it is the individual who is the object of training. When teamwork
is used as part of the training, it is generally in order to improve the training
of the individual. From business, however, we know that teams can be the
object of training (Björk 1987; MacErlean 1993).

The type of knowledge intentionally transmitted to others may be expert
knowledge, general knowledge, or a mixture of these. 'Expert knowledge'
means the deep knowledge that is attained when studying one or a few
related subjects for a long time. Expert knowledge is often certified – not
only collegiately but by government authorities. This means that the student
must manage certain defined skills in order to qualify as a professional.
'General knowledge' is gained through the study of many subjects,
sacrificing depth for breadth. This type of knowledge is not certified in
the same way as expert knowledge. Although university degrees are
delivered, these do not qualify the graduate exclusively for specific jobs.

In spite of the claim to improve practical skills, management science has
not been standardized around discrete areas of knowledge which help to
resolve discrete sets of problems (Whitley 1988). As management science
has proliferated into a plethora of subjects, postgraduate management
education generally provides the students with brief insights into many
management subjects, although some specialization also occurs. While such
management education is generally certified by a university degree –
namely, the MBA in the United States, or the nearly equivalent *siviløkonom*

235

in the Scandinavian countries – this is not required by the authorities as a necessary qualification to practise as a manager. Government certification is also unlikely because of the difficulty of standardizing what are highly interdependent and situation-specific managerial skills (Whitley 1988). Thus, it is argued here that management education is very much a general type of knowledge.

If these suggestions about management education are correct, the paradigm of present management education falls into quadrant II of Figure 12.1. This paradigm is based on transmitting general management knowledge to individuals to improve their managerial skills, and management education based on this 'hero–generalist paradigm' produces individual generalists.

As indicated in Figure 12.1, there are alternatives to the hero–generalist paradigm. One is the 'heteroteam–specialist paradigm' (quadrant IV). The argument put forward in this chapter is that in future many companies will want to put together heterogeneous top management teams because external and internal contexts are increasingly becoming more complex, dynamic, and knowledge intensive. If higher education is to ease the task of creating such management teams, it is proposed that education is based more on the heteroteam–specialist paradigm. This means that specialist education should also infuse the students with team-values, and a respect for different kinds of expert knowledge.

When claiming to produce management recruits, if management education actually continues to produce generalists, it leaves those who want to put together a heterogeneous top management team in their company to recruit specialists from outside the business schools. After all, generalists put together in teams make more or less homogeneous teams (quadrant III). So, if applying a team approach while sticking to the generalist assumption, management education will at best produce generalists who can make up heterogeneous teams together with specialists from other faculties. This may be fine, but management education will not thereby qualify its graduates for management any more than will other forms of higher education.

Some Norwegian data are used below to illustrate the fact that the hero–generalist paradigm is alive and well in Norwegian education policy and seems to underpin management education in Norway. Policy documents also indicate that, historically, business schools have gradually shifted focus from specialization towards ever broader curricula, while maintaining the idea that the individual manager can be educated.

The hero–generalist paradigm in a Norwegian context

There are three governmental policy reports that concern management education in Norway in the last fifteen years. The first was published by the

Lederopplæringsrådet (Norwegian Council for Management Training and Education) in 1981, at the government's request. The other two were undertaken by government-appointed committees – the Hermansen Committee (1982) and the Gjærum Committee (1992) respectively. Further research is needed to decide how influential these documents have been – for instance, in designing public policies concerning curricula for the business schools. However, representatives of the business schools sat on both the governmental committees and it is reasonable to believe that these reports express viewpoints which existed within the schools themselves. The reports may therefore be very useful to check the extent of hero–generalist reasoning in policy making.

The Hermansen Committee was set up by government to work out plans for the future expansion of business education in Norway. According to its report, the Committee foresaw a future of accelerating changes facing business. This led the Committee to consider the development of higher technical education as an important vehicle for competitiveness in Norwegian business. Another concern, however, was to develop the capability of future managers to interpret problems and possibilities arising from the increasingly complex relations between technology, economy, and administration. This was referred to as 'integral competence' (Innstilling 1982: 26). By suggesting that business school graduates should develop integral competence, the Committee implied that the business school graduate was able to 'substitute' for the technician (Innstilling 1982: 26). Thus, instead of developing an idea of how technicians and business graduates could complement each other in top management teams, the idea of individual integral competence was adopted and elaborated instead. It was this idea that was to be implanted in business students – an approach that can be subsumed under the hero–generalist paradigm.

The report of the Gjærum Committee can also be placed firmly within a generalist and individualist paradigm. In this more recent report, basic perspectives of management education in Norway are explicitly stated. The four-year programme in business administration is claimed to provide management education for middle and top management in both business and the public services (Utredning 1992: 21). Management is understood as 'a profession', and the composition of the curriculum is looked upon as the cornerstone in the creation of a management education: 'the programme has to be oriented towards educating generalists, nevertheless containing some possibilities for specialization' (Utredning 1992: 21). The Committee points out that the backbone of the curriculum should be micro-economic subjects. But the extent to which different subjects, like organization theory, should be represented is left entirely to each school to decide (Utredning 1992: 21).

The Gjærum Committee reveals feelings of great optimism concerning the ability of the *siviløkonom* to be successful in almost any kind of organization. Business administration is also believed to be highly relevant in managing hospitals, churches, and voluntary organizations (Utredning 1992: 13). It is argued that education in business administration will enable students to develop certain skills; to conduct analyses of highly different characters; to communicate and cooperate; and to make (the right) decisions. Because of the variety of situations the postgraduates will face, it is further argued that the programme be theoretically oriented for the most part. The reason for this is that as the postgraduates will have to qualify for management positions through practice, it is seen as the task of business schools to concentrate on developing theoretical skills such as the 'ability to handle problem identification processes and analyze them critically' (Utredning 1992: 25).

The primary concern of the report from the Council for Management Training and Education was management training through in-house programmes in business and public services. Some recommendations concerning management education were also put forward, however. Among other themes, the question of expert versus general knowledge across a variety of subjects was treated. It was argued that, in a society characterized by increasing complexity, managers must be able to interpret a complex set of intra-organizational processes and interorganizational relations in a broader political sense and in relation to developments in the markets (NOU 1981: 7–9). This ability to 'weight contradictory interests and establish mechanisms for effective coordination' was emphasized and related to 'the relationship between generality and specialization in management training' (NOU 1981: 7). It was argued that management education would benefit from a much stronger focus on organization theory, social science, and policy making.

Another central theme in the report was the manager's role. A picture of great complexity was depicted, relating management to a variety of challenges. On this basis, the report was critical of the conception of the postgraduate programme as *the* form of management education; 'The "siviløkonom" is almost automatically defined as a manager . . . we expect, however, that kind of thinking to lose foothold in the future' (NOU 1981: 32). The viewpoint put forward was that management education should be integrated in all of higher education in order to obtain the internalization of such attitudes that would enable managers to deal with complex and multifaceted social relations and situations.

As far as can be seen, the report suggested a much sounder combination of expert and generalist knowledge than did the two governmental committees. However, the prophecy that business administration would lose its hegemony in educating managers *qua* education, seems far from being realized. On the contrary, the broad curriculum model is still considered the answer to the present challenges of management education, at least within the educational system itself. This means that the hero–generalist paradigm is still very persistent.

DEVELOPMENTS IN MANAGEMENT CHALLENGES AND MANAGEMENT EDUCATION – DIVERGING OR CONVERGING PROCESSES?

It has been argued above that management education is biased towards individualism and generalism, while modern enterprises increasingly face demands that require top management models based on team management and heterogeneous expert knowledge. Provided that this perspective is correct, is it likely that the dominance of the hero–generalist paradigm will wither, or are the barriers to change too strong? In Norway, at least three barriers to change can be identified. These are the historical processes of the 'academization' and 'professionalization' of business administration, and the 'structure of higher education'.

Early Norwegian business education had a practical focus. Managers often combined business experience with lower national or foreign business education. This was the tradition when the Norwegian School of Economics and Business Administration (NSEBA) was founded in Bergen in 1936. At that time, the ambition was to build an academic institution based on German traditions of business administration (Amdam and Norstrøm 1994). After the Second World War, the academic development of the school was strengthened. At the same time, the number of Norwegian students graduating from foreign business schools increased (Rasmussen and Wold 1992). This growth was used as an argument for extending the capacity of NSEBA and for certifying the *siviløkonom* education at the Norwegian School of Management (NSM) in 1985 (Amdam and Norstrøm 1994). NSM, established in Oslo in 1943, had not focused on academia until the 1970s, when investigations into operational research began. During the 1980s, NSM continued its development towards becoming an academic institution. The academization process in the Norwegian business schools was related to the development of management research in the United States. After the Second World War, the American influence over Norwegian management education became obvious (Amdam 1993). Thus, Norwegian management education as well as Norwegian management research are both very much influenced by American developments.

What then was the content of the process of academization? Locke (1994) has argued that a new paradigm emerged in American management studies after the Second World War, and that this consisted of the application of science to management problems. Inherent in this paradigm was the conception of motivation as an individual force. To gather support for this argument, a database search was done on three academic journals based in the United States – *Journal of Management, Academy of Management Journal,* and *Academy of Management Review* (Table 12.1). This showed that in the period from 1974 to 1993, only thirty-three articles or responses to articles were identified by the concepts 'team' or 'group' – singular or plural – in combination with either the words 'executive' and 'top management' or 'top leadership'. A search was made of 15,577 articles in a full-text bibliographic database; this revealed that an overwhelming proportion of the articles that focus on management teams are of recent date. According to Table 12.1, only two of the articles emanated from the period before 1985, two-thirds were published in the last half of the 1980s, and one-third has been published in the last five years. An equivalent test on the quasi-academic Norwegian journal – *Praktisk økonomi og ledelse* – published by the Norwegian Society of Business Graduates, resulted in no finds at all. The outcome of these checks supports the contention that in management science, management is conceived of as an individual activity. Though methodological questions may be raised about the checks themselves, the results rather strongly indicate that American management scholars have not been preoccupied with the idea that top managers work in groups or teams. To the extent that the academization process in Norwegian business schools has been inspired by the new paradigm of the United States, it seems reasonable to argue that academization has fostered rather than challenged the hero assumption and that this academic tradition will very probably counteract any business school attempt to break the bias towards individualism.

Another historically derived counterforce would probably be found in the growing professionalization of business graduates and the corresponding spread and influence of these graduates. Membership of The Norwegian Society of Business Graduates grew steadily in the postwar decades, and substantially during the 1980s (Stokke 1989). As already mentioned, from the 1980s, business graduates outnumbered engineers as top managers in large Norwegian companies. In 1983, four of the seven largest Norwegian enterprises had business graduates as CEOs (Svendsen 1985) and business graduates also dominated the management teams. Examples abound. In the Norwegian insurance company UNI Storebrand, four out of five of the

Table 12.1 Number of articles or responses to articles focusing on top management team(s)* in three US-based academic journals on management in the period 1974–94

	1974–84	1985–9	1990–4	Total
Academy of Management Journal	2	14	7	23
Academy of Management Review	0	3	1	4
Journal of Management	0	4	2	6
Total	2	21	10	33

Note: *Includes the text strings 'top management group(s)', 'executive team(s)', 'executive group(s)', 'top leadership team(s)', and 'top leadership group(s)'

Source: Management Contents, Dialog Information Services Inc.

executive group of managers were business graduates, while in the oil company Statoil, five out of seven members of the executive team were business graduates from NSEBA (Amdam 1993).

A third barrier to this paradigm shift derives from the fact that business schools have often developed traditions and identities that are different from those of university faculties. In Norway this has materialized in the fact that the business schools are organized outside the universities. This structural characteristic, it is believed, enforces the understanding that management education is different from university education, especially in the way it is less specialist oriented, and works to legitimize the identity of business education as management education. It may further shield business education from the competing approaches found, for instance, in university faculties of social sciences and humanities. Thus, management education – particularly its generalist imprint – is tightly knit to the present structure of higher education.

Apart from the changing demands facing business enterprises, what are the challenges to the present hero–generalist paradigm? First, one pressure for change has directly emanated from the Japanese business or Pacific Rim challenge. Whether this challenge has been met by appropriate efforts to change is debatable. According to some American writers, it has not (Nohria and Berkley 1994; Hayes and Pisano 1994). The relevant question is whether this can be done without the assistance of higher education, or more specifically whether it can be done within the hero–generalist paradigm. In Japan, organization-specific skills that cannot be learned in business schools seem to substitute for the management techniques that Norwegian students learn at business schools. Nevertheless, Japanese managers are among the most highly educated in the world (Locke 1994).

Second, debates about basic tenets within management science and education may cause some redirection. One such debate concerns the core of management – the belief in management as strategic planning. Titles like 'Why Strategic Management is Bankrupt' (Hurst 1986) and 'Strategic Management and The Straitjacket' (Bettis 1991) indicate a discontent with the present state of management science and education that points directly to the basic rationalist assumption inherent in much of management science. Hurst (1986: 13), for instance, argues that:

> The problem with the strategic paradigm is the assumption underlying it. The paradigm assumes that businesses are like complex, mechanical clockworks operating in an environment that can be objectively determined by senior managers of the businesses.

The problem is that if this assumption is put aside, the illusion of management science and education will doubtless die. Thus, in the short run, the outcome of debates like this one will not, in all probability, be radical change.

Third, the academization of management disciplines may paradoxically also pose a challenge to the hero–generalist paradigm. Academization was described above as constituting a historical barrier to the breaking of this paradigm because it reproduces cultural beliefs about what management is and how it can be taught and learned. However, it may be speculated that further academization is based not on the premises of management science as a whole but on those of the increasing number of specialist management disciplines. The idea of offering students generalist curricula may crumble as more disciplines compete to legitimate their relevance to management education.

Today, public policy making seems to be stuck in a strait-jacket composed of the historic processes of academization and professionalization and the way management education is structured within the superstructure of higher education. The probable reaction to the challenges that face business is therefore further refinement within the hero–generalist paradigm. At some point, however, historic processes and structures will inevitably break under the pressure of new processes and new structures built on new paradigms will be formed.

WHAT SHOULD BE THE BUSINESS OF BUSINESS SCHOOLS?

The discussion so far is naturally both speculative and tentative but the question raised is important: is today's management education really serving business (and public organizations) as these face the new challenges presented by the twenty-first century? It is believed that the increasing complexity and invariability that many enterprises face, and will face, require new ways of managing which imply smooth cooperation and teamwork between different specialist managers. In contrast to this requirement, management education at present is based on a paradigm combining individualism and generalism, as well as the belief that universal management techniques exist and can be conveyed to the individual through a business school education. As management science has increased its scope historically, and failed to synthesize perspectives and findings into a grand management theory, it is feared that the pendulum in business or management education has swung too far towards broader curricula and generalist knowledge. If the pendulum starts swinging back, however, in what business should the business schools be?

It has been proposed that the future belongs to the heterogeneous team of top specialist managers. The question is: can business schools educate these managers? This appears to be too much to ask. First and foremost, management science is no closer to prescribing either the composition of heterogeneous teams or the universal nature of true teamwork. Moreover, in real life heterogeneity is about more than educational background; it also includes personal traits, tenure, and functional experience (see Hambrick and Mason 1984). Business schools, then, should be confident that much of the team composition and team development are taken care of within the companies themselves. Managerial teams are not believed to be created within business schools, and if they were they would probably turn out to be homogeneous rather than heterogeneous teams. And like other homogeneous teams they would all too easily fall prey to cognitive fallacies like 'group-think', 'prior hypothesis bias', 'reasoning by analogy', and so forth (Schwenk 1984). Perhaps that would not be the case if management education gave up the illusion of the educated manager and if the companies stopped 'parachuting graduates who know nothing of the business into middle management levels', to borrow phrasing from Henry Mintzberg (in Gosling 1994).

If business schools gave up management education and left the team composition to the companies and consultants, what would be left? The feeling is that business schools should revert to conveying true expert knowledge and educating experts in such disciplines as marketing, accounting, strategic planning, organization theory and behaviour, and management information systems – everything, in fact, but the general business administration mix in the guise of management education. In addition, business schools should find methods which would prepare students for working together with other and different experts – in other words, they should include some social training. In accordance with the report from the Council of Management Training and Education, referred to above, it is suggested that such training should not be confined to the business schools but be a part of all higher education.

Further research is needed on the development of management education in different countries and regions. It is believed that such research should focus not only on the development of schools and curricula, but on the recruitment patterns of business graduates and the demographic background of managers. What is the educational background of managers and how do they feel about the relevance of their own education some years after graduating from business school? In this context, the technician should not be ignored; research on connections between technical education and management careers is still important. One obvious implication is to search for historical cases where, *de facto*, successful teams, even heterogeneous teams, can be observed. One example of this is Gammelsæter (1991), which related historical, strategic, and structural change in three Norwegian enterprises to changes in the top management teams.

REFERENCES

Amdam, R.P. (1993) *For egen regning: BI og den økonomisk-administrative utdanningen 1943–1993*, Oslo: Universitetsforlaget.

—— and Norstrøm, C.J. (1994) 'Business Administration in Norway 1936–1990', in L. Engwall and E. Gunnarson (eds) *Management Studies in an Academic Context*, Uppsala: Acta Universitatis Upsaliensis, Studia Oeconemia Negotiorum 35.

Ancona, D.G. and Nadler, D.A. (1989) 'Top Hats and Executive Tales: Designing the Senior Team', *Sloan Management Review* 31(1): 19–29.

Armstrong, P. (1984) 'Competition between the Organizational Professions and the Evolution of Management Control Strategies', in K. Thompson (ed.) *Work, Employment and Unemployment: Perspectives on Work and Society*, Milton Keynes: Open University Press.

—— (1985) 'Changing Management Control Strategies: The Role of Competition Between Accountancy and other Organizational Professions', *Accounting, Organizations and Society* 10(2): 129–48.

—— (1987) 'The Rise of Accounting Controls in British Capitalist Enterprises', *Accounting, Organizations and Society* 12(5): 415–36.

Bantel, K.A. and Jackson, S.E. (1989) 'Top Management and Innovations in Banking: Does the Composition of the Top Team Make a Difference?', *Strategic Management Journal* 10: 107–24.

Barnes, L. and Krieger, M.P. (1986) 'The Hidden Side of Organizational Leadership', *Sloan Management Review* Autumn: 15–25.

Bettis, R.A. (1991) 'Strategic Management and The Straitjacket: An Editorial Essay', *Organization Science* 2(3): 315–19.

Björk, S. (1987) 'Ett hjul svetsar dem samman', *Ledarskap* 4: 14–19.

Casey, D. (1985) 'When a Team is not a Team?', *Personnel Management* 17(1): 26–9.

Chandler, A.D., Jr (1962) *Strategy and Structure: Chapters in the History of the American Industrial Enterprise*, Cambridge, MA: MIT Press.

Critchley, B. and D. Casey (1984) 'Second Thoughts on Team Building', *Management Education and Development* 15(2): 163–75.

Engwall, L. and Gunnarsson, E. (eds) (1994) *Management Studies in an Academic Context*, Uppsala: Acta Universitatis Upsaliensis, Studia Oeconomia Negotiorum 35.

Fligstein, N. (1985) 'The Spread of the Multidivisional Form Among Large Firms, 1919–1979', *American Sociological Review* 48 (June): 147–60.

—— (1987) 'The Interorganizational Power Struggle: Rise of Finance Personnel to Top Leadership in Large Corporations, 1919–1979', *American Sociological Review* 57 (February): 44–58.

Freedman, D.H. (1992) 'Is Management Still A Science?', *Harvard Business Review* 70(6): 26–33, 36–8.

Gammelsæter, H. (1990) 'Toppledere i norsk industri: fra sivilingeniører til siviløkonomer', *Norsk Harvard* 1: 90–2.

—— (1991) *Organisasjonsendring gjennom generasjoner av ledere*, Molde: Møreforsking, Rapport 9114.

Gosling, J. (1994) 'Interview with Henry Mintzberg (McGill University) and Sheila Forbes (Reed Elsevier)', *Management Learning* 25(1): 95–104.

Hambrick, D.C. and Mason, P.A. (1984) 'Upper Echelons: The Organization as a Reflection of Its Top Managers', *Academy of Management Studies* 9(2): 193–206.

Hayes, R.H. and Pisano, G.P. (1994) 'Beyond World Class. The New Manufacturing Strategy', *Harvard Business Review* 72(1): 77–86.

Hickson, D.J., Hinings, C.R., Lee, C.A., Schneck, R.E., and Pennings, J.M. (1971) 'A Strategic Contingencies' Theory of Intraorganizational Power', *Administrative Science Quarterly* 16 (June): 216–29.

Hofstede, G. (1985) 'The Interaction Between National and Organizational Value Systems', *Journal of Management Studies* 22(4): 347–57.

Hurst, D.K. (1986) 'Why Strategic Management Is Bankrupt', *Organizational Dynamics* 15(2): 5–27.

Katzenbach, J.R. and Douglas, K.S. (1993) 'The Discipline of Teams', *Harvard Business Review* March-April: 111–20.

Keck, S.L. and Tushman, M.L. (1993) 'Environmental and Organizational Context and Executive Team Structure', *Academy of Management Journal* 36(6): 1314–44.

Koontz, H. (1961) 'The Management Theory Jungle', *Academy of Management Journal* 4(3): 174–88.

Locke, R. (1994) 'Management Education and Higher Education since 1940', in L. Engwall and E. Gunnarsson (eds) *Management Studies in an Academic Context*, Uppsala: Acta Universitatis Upsaliensis, Studia Oeconomia Negotiorum 35.

MacErlean, N. (1993) 'A Tried and Tested Team', *Accountancy* 112(1200): 36.

Mintzberg, H. (1973) *The Nature of Managerial Work*, New York: Harper and Row.

Nagaoka, K. (1994) 'The Japanese System of Academic Management Education', in L. Engwall and E. Gunnarsson (eds) *Management Studies in an Academic Context*, Uppsala: Acta Universitatis Upsaliensis, Studia Oeconomia Negotiorum 35.

Nohria, N. and Berkley, J.D. (1994) 'Whatever Happened to the Take-Charge Manager?', *Harvard Business Review* 72(1): 128–37.

O'Toole, J. and Bennis, W. (1992) 'Our Federalist Future: The Leadership Imperative', *California Management Review* Summer: 73–90.

Rasmussen, L. and Wold, A. (1992) *Utenlandsstudenter, hvorfor finnes de?*, Oslo: Norwegian School of Management (Master's thesis).

Reve, T. (1994) 'Bedrifter uten grenser', *Næringslivets Ukeavis* 18 March.

Schwenk, C.R. (1984) 'Cognitive Simplification Processes in Strategic Decision-Making', *Strategic Management Journal* 5(2): 111–28.

Stokke, B. (1989) *Vekst og virke. Norske siviløkonomer gjennom 50 år*, Oslo: Norske Siviløkonomers Forening.

Svendsen, A.S. (1985) 'Verden tilhører oss siviløkonomer?', in J. Arndt *et al.* (eds) *Tjenester for hvermann: NHHs tredje oppgave*, Bergen: Norges Handelshøyskole.

Whitley, R. (1988) 'The Management Science and Managerial Skills', *Organization Studies* 9(1): 47–68.

Wiersema, M.F. and Bantel, K.A. (1992) 'Top Management Team Demography and Corporate Strategic Change', *Academy of Management Journal* 35(1): 9–121.

Yukl, Gary A. (1989) 'Managerial Leadership: A Review of Theory and Research', *Journal of Management* 15(2): 251–89.

POLICY DOCUMENTS

Innstilling (The Hermansen Committee) (1982) *Innstilling fra arbeidsgruppen for høgre økonomisk/administrativ utdanning*, Kultur- og vitenskapsdepartementet.

NOU 1981: *Ledelse, samarbeid og administrasjon-samfunnsutvikling og opplæringsbehov*, Oslo–Bergen–Tromsø, No. 22.

Utredning (1992) (The Gjærum Committee) *Økonomisk-administrativ utdanning fram til siviløkonomgrad*, Kirke-, utdannings- og forskningsdepartementet.

13

BETWEEN ACADEMIA AND BUSINESS

New challenges for today's modern business schools

Peter Lorange

INTRODUCTION

There are a number of significant external changes facing today's modern business schools. Some of them are fundamental and will call for rapid, but typically reactive, adjustments by the leading business schools to stay on top; other developments will offer an opportunity to follow new proactive avenues for value creation. In this chapter, first what are seen as the major changes in the external context for business schools will be discussed, then potential ways that business schools could respond in order to create value will be reviewed. Specifically, what is seen as an emerging need for a closer relationship between business schools and business corporations will be dealt with. Indeed, it may be that there is an interesting 'blurring' of the boundaries here between the traditional concept of the business school in a classical sense and what is increasingly seen as its major client – the modern learning organization. In this context, the question of how this growing trend can lead to new and greater academic value creation will be particularly critical, as will be discussed. Finally, some of the internal organizational issues and leadership challenges facing today's business schools will be considered in light of the above scenarios.

NEW COMPETITIVE PATTERNS AND A GREATER NEED FOR COOPERATION WITH KEY CLIENTS

More and more, today's leading firms are being seen as 'brain-driven' organizations. Thus, even though a firm may possess large physical assets and routinely undertake huge investments in fixed plants, research and development, market development, and so forth, the overall key success factor seems to boil down to how capable the people in the organization are – in terms of such aspects as spotting business opportunities and mobilizing their own human resource talents – to go after these opportunities. Thus, an increasingly important function of the corporation will be to address the issue of recruiting and developing the firm's human capital. A higher emphasis on finding the best people to join the firm has been in vogue for a long time, of course. However, that means there must also be a correspondingly greater effort made to create a so-called 'learning organization', where individuals can continuously find ways to develop and, in addition, some sort of organizational learning takes place. Such a benefit is particularly apt to result when individuals work in teams to execute certain types of tasks. It is therefore apparent that a more deliberate attempt to enhance the value of a firm's human capital is the driving force behind the learning organization.

The greatest significance of this development is that it has opened up a large number of new opportunities for modern business schools. For one thing, the role of life-long learning becomes relatively much more important. While in the past, executives were given the option to attend courses because it was a 'nice thing to do', or as a reward, being able to select outside courses and send executives on them is now typically part of a much more systematic corporate-wide plan. The result has been an impressive change in executive programmes, with a gradual shift from the classical curriculum offered by business schools – where the bulk of the focus was on undergraduate, MBA, and doctoral programmes – to a much greater emphasis on intensive life-long learning courses with clear take-home value.

Another important change is the realization by companies that they have to incorporate organizational learning more systematically. This means that *teams* made up of selected members of the same organization learn together, often through 'in-company' programmes developed for a given organization. Typically, such programmes are tailor-made for the particular organization in question, so that the learning experience can be applied to a specific context. Not surprisingly, the result has been a growth in the in-company programme segment of many business schools, thereby further accelerating the swing of the pendulum away from curricular activities based on classical undergraduate and MBA programmes.

Many companies have concluded that they are capable of handling these in-company learning activities by themselves. Frequently, they set up their own 'schools' and, in this sense, have indeed become new competitors for the business schools. This very real new source of competition can be particularly complicated when faculty members of business schools are freely available to serve as consultants for the emerging 'in-company schools'. A number of consultancies specializing in developing and delivering in-company learning support have also suddenly appeared on the scene. They too represent a new group that is challenging the classical business school, which has resulted in an intensified competitive climate. Hence, a more thorough examination of these various changes in the competitive patterns facing today's business schools is intended, as they certainly have a direct relationship to the potential ways that the classical schools should (or must) respond.

Even though the market for business school services is shifting – from the classical undergraduate and MBA programmes towards more emphasis on executive development and in-company programmes, a particular business school could, of course, elect *not* to compete in these new areas of potential activity. Instead, it could continue to concentrate on undergraduate and MBA programmes. In this case, other traditional business schools would continue to be the predominant competition. Presumably, these schools would still follow long-established pedagogical patterns where the focus is typically on functional and/or disciplinary paradigms.

However, the business schools that choose to pursue only these 'classical' activities are likely to find their resources more and more constrained. Most societies today, it should be kept in mind, are facing very strict budgetary limitations, which inevitably affect the amount of resources they can allocate to the public sector. In addition, there is inevitably greater and greater competition for whatever resources are destined for these public sector budgets. The university sector in general, and perhaps business schools in particular, will not necessarily emerge from this tightening-up process as automatic 'winners'. A more realistic scenario for many of them, therefore, would be one where the value creation must take place under ever-increasing resource constraints. Clearly then, competition among the classical business schools that continue to offer only traditional value-creating segments can be expected to become tougher than ever. Indeed, some business schools may even be forced to leave the arena altogether. Others may have to consolidate, merge, or develop alliances, in order to achieve a more cost-efficient division of labour. As the boundaries between countries continue to become more open, cross-national competition can also be expected to grow stronger, thereby creating additional shake-outs and realignments among the business schools in the classical segment. In all likelihood, however, a new balance among competing classical institutions will be reached after these shake-outs are over.

The emerging segment of activities, namely the growing interest in executive programmes and in-company courses, will now be considered. The competition here is typically more mixed. For business schools, however, a major feature for success is being able to mobilize internal faculty resources that are sufficiently attuned to the specific challenges and problems that a potential client company faces. The research activities necessary for faculty to be relevant in such company-specific contexts may often differ substantially from the outcome of classical disciplinary paradigm-based research. Typically, cross-functional research on general management issues, often more process oriented in nature and based on a clinical design, can be more valuable for delivering life-long learning activities. In particular, research on various types of implementation seems to be well suited for supporting in-company and life-long executive learning programmes.

The classical business school, structured around functional departments, may therefore find that its ability to focus effectively on emerging eclectic, cross-functional business research issues is severely hindered. To overcome this handicap, it is essential that faculty members from various disciplines be aligned in a tailor-made manner, so that the mix of faculty skills offered provides what is really needed. Further, such an eclectic faculty-based competence mix must 'blend' together – that is, function as a unified team, not merely as a group of individual faculty members randomly serving on a programme together. Here the traditional lack of cross-functional faculty cooperation that is typically seen in business schools will certainly be a hindrance. Understandably, a faculty member will tend to have a strong vested interest in continuing research and teaching within established, traditional, discipline-driven areas of competence. It is therefore no wonder that many faculty members in business schools have been relatively sceptical about becoming involved in life-long learning and in-company programme activities. They see, perhaps justifiably, that this trend could lead to greater 'competition' with – and indeed even a threat to – the more classical functional paradigm-based research and teaching. In addition, they may assume – perhaps intentionally, perhaps not – that this development could affect the internal political balance within their school, which might also be perceived as threatening.

The question, then, is whether or not the classical business school has a clear, realistic ability to respond to these new opportunities. It is, after all, hardly surprising that a number of new actors have entered the emerging ranks of competitors. Management consulting companies, for example, are obviously natural players. They come into the arena already interested in understanding the specific problems that a given company must handle. Management consulting companies typically are expected to use the latest analytically based problem-solving approaches to various strategic issues being faced by firms. Increasingly, however, they are realizing that these 'answers' often only offer a 'beginning' – with little long-term added value for firms when considered in strict isolation. Proposed solutions are valuable only if they are followed up with an implementation programme. And a major aspect of implementation needs to focus on mobilizing the human resources effectively, enabling them to pursue the new strategic opportunities that have been identified. In-company programmes for learning and motivating change will often be recommended at this stage. Not surprisingly, it should be a natural step for consulting firms to expand into delivering this type of activity, thereby providing a more complete 'package'. Accordingly, it can be observed that more and more consulting firms are broadening their business base, evolving from basic problem-solving services towards more fully fledged implementation and support efforts, which indeed encompass executive teaching. Leading consulting firms and leading business schools are thus beginning to focus on the *same* new market, but they are approaching it from two different directions. The result will surely mean tougher competition within the emerging in-company executive education segment.

As already touched upon, some individual faculty members of leading business schools may also – perhaps paradoxically – constitute another new source of competition. They may want to fill the gap that is created by the inadequate adaptive capabilities of their particular school, by 'taking on this business privately'. With the current intensive competition for the best professional brains, it should be kept in mind that business schools are likely to become less and less able to attract good, new faculty members, because they cannot compete on salary. Many leading well-qualified people are inevitably turning instead to business or to the consulting profession. Thus, highly talented faculty members in business schools may begin to see themselves as being underpaid, particularly compared with professionals in other types of institutions. This discrepancy may accelerate the motivation of faculty members to broaden their activities in order to supplement their income – not only through classical problem-oriented consultancy, but also by undertaking more 'easy to reach' executive education teaching on their own. Perhaps some faculty members even perceive that it is 'all right' to go after these emerging business opportunities privately, given their institution's reluctance to adapt. For many business schools, this arrangement also provides a convenient amelioration of the salary pressures that they would have to face otherwise. However, after a more thorough exploration of the consequences of allowing faculty members to compete with their own schools, the answers are truly alarming and indeed unacceptable. If the business school is paying for a major part of its faculty members' professional development – providing research funding, and so on – how can it afford to have those individuals pursuing major value-creating benefits on their own? In light of today's scarce resources, few institutions can allow this kind of activity to happen as a normal *modus operandi*. Accepting this practice will probably eventually bring decay to the high-quality business schools!

Many firms have, as noted, developed their own in-company training facilities. Some of the activities of such centres will undoubtedly focus on certain ventures that business schools cannot (and should not) pursue, given the tailor-made emphasis that will often be needed, and also keeping in mind the fact that large masses of executives will typically have to go through rather standardized training courses. It is, however, also true that such in-company centres tend to be under heavy scrutiny in order to justify themselves as cost beneficial. Hence, they can easily be tempted to start expanding their curricula towards the higher end of the market, the segment which should more naturally be served by the business school. If such a centre can draw on business school faculty members easily, it may be particularly apt to want to create a 'monopoly' of all in-company training. Such a development – while perhaps an attractive cost benefit at a first glance – is not necessarily going to be best for the company in the long term, however. In-breeding and a failure to incorporate the latest cutting-edge research may result – that is, it will not attain as high a quality level as might have occurred otherwise. Despite this warning, it can still be expected that a considerable amount of the high-end in-company training activities will become off limits for business schools, owing to a combination of these various economic and institutional reasons.

All in all it can be concluded that, while there is a new and interesting market opening up for business schools (i.e. the growing area of in-company programmes and life-long learning activities), a large number of new players are also entering the competition. In this heterogeneous competitive arena, it may be difficult for business schools to succeed. Competition on price does indeed become a relevant issue. It may be hard for the typical business school to differentiate itself sufficiently so that it can justify the higher prices for the services being offered, especially when compared with competitors that often have much lower overheads. This discrepancy is further exacerbated when a school's most critical strategic asset – its own faculty – represents a key part of the competition. How can a progressive business school respond to such a situation? Is there a sufficiently viable competitive niche that a leading business school can carve out and develop in a sustainable way? An appraisal of the realistic response options that are available will now be examined.

THE MODERN BUSINESS SCHOOL'S RESPONSE OPTIONS

It is believed that leading business schools *can* respond to these competitive shifts – *both* reactively *and* proactively. The key to any response, it is argued, predominantly depends on developing closer cooperative efforts with business. This thesis may not seem logical at first, particularly in light of the fact that, as has already been seen, the business enterprises themselves are emerging as one of the major competitors to business schools. It will be argued, however, that there is still ample room for cooperation and thus for a true win–win value-creating result, despite the fact that there will always be some competition from in-company executive education activities run by the companies themselves.

At the heart of the competitive response for the leading business schools lies a need to develop a cutting-edge profile of new knowledge, which will be the decisive force behind the competitive new executive development programmes being offered. Undertaking research to establish this cutting-edge knowledge will be the key to a school's ability to be competitive. It goes without saying that such research must focus heavily on specific critical agenda items facing today's leading firms. Examples of potential areas of research might include such issues as:

• finding ways to grow new business – say, by enhancing the capability of searching for truly attractive, new, global business opportunities;
• developing the skills to rapidly mobilize the organizational resources for pursuing such opportunities;
• seeking strategic alliances with other organizations as one way to enhance the capability of benefiting from new opportunities;
• gaining the know-how for strengthening the capability of carrying out effective implementation in a timely and cost-beneficial manner.

Implicit in this sort of a research agenda will be the need to address important cross-cultural issues, human resource development challenges relating to teamwork, ways for individual executives to perform effectively in today's more complex and flatter organizations, and ways that these executives can comfortably function with numerous ambiguous constraints: namely, to be happy 'wearing multiple hats', and so forth.

A strategy, consisting of three main pillars, will be proposed that will enable a leading business school to cope with these challenges:

1 the development of a 'partnership' network with a number of leading business corporations;
2 the institutionalization of an individual faculty member planning effort which would link his or her research, development, and teaching assignments in an explicit manner, including the provision of the necessary institutional support – assuming, of course, that this investment will lead to a development of knowledge on the part of the faculty member which will benefit the school;
3 the delineation of knowledge cells, whereby individual faculty members and faculty teams deliver products founded on recently developed, research-based teaching activities.

Each of these recommendations will now be examined in more detail, at the same time demonstrating how a holistic strategy of cooperation between business and academia can emerge if both sides jointly emphasize all three pillars.

1 Development of a business partnership network

Every company has its own strategic agenda, obviously. Individual faculty members, in turn, will gain knowledge about key strategic issues through their research, dialogue, and teaching activities *vis-à-vis* specific organizations. It goes without saying, then, that when there is some continuity – like a pattern of interaction between a firm and a professor – both sides will be able to understand each other more easily. Representatives from the corporation can influence the choice of research items that those in academia will pursue, as well as heighten academia's understanding of the latest key issues. Academia, meanwhile, will be able to articulate its research findings *vis-à-vis* business, thereby having a real and valuable impact. Thus, a two-way interactive, iterative dialogue will promote and increase a relevant value creation which is mutually beneficial.

This kind of network relationship can have several dimensions. Through annual 'membership' fees, the school can receive sufficient unrestricted resources to carry out a certain amount of state-of-the-art research, which can then be fed back to the companies in workshop briefings. During these workshops, leading executives and academicians can learn and benefit from each other in various ways: state-of-the-art research can be presented and disseminated; companies can determine whether or not they have 'benchmark' capabilities in relation to other companies on current issues; leading practices can be incorporated into ongoing research; and so on.

In-company training activities can also proceed more effectively when partnership firms are involved. Because the business school has gained know-how about the key strategic priorities of a partner firm – developed over time through numerous interactions, such as workshops and research activities – the faculty team is able to design a tailor-made, relevant in-company programme for the particular partner firm. It can incorporate into that programme all its learning about state-of-the-art issues and ideas, while making the appropriate adjustments on presentation and discussion necessary for that firm.

This kind of network – where there is an active long-term commitment between leading firms and the business school faculty team – can thus represent a major dimension of value creation. It can lead to substantial innovation, by encouraging and promoting more realistic research, and then by incorporating those research results into the daily operations of important learning organizations.

2 Planning for individual faculty members

As argued above, each faculty member's research and teaching activities can be significantly shaped by what is learned from the network exchange between firms that are working closely with the school and its faculty members. Faculty members need to see this kind of 'interference' as beneficial, creating positive long-term development opportunities. In order for it to be workable and successful, it will require a certain amount of commitment on the part of faculty. On the positive side, the faculty member will gain access to state-of-the-art practitioner viewpoints, added resources for research, an insight into relevant teaching materials that can be developed, as well as the opportunity to have an impact on the future direction of leading organizations through teaching key executives in in-company programmes. The potential downside, of course, is that a faculty member may be 'pulled' in too many directions by the 'day-to-day' pressures that can stem from an active network relationship: there may be requests for new applications, problem solving, interventions, discussions on specific sub-issues with individual executives on an *ad hoc* basis, 'crisis' situations requiring additional teaching activities, demand for new case development which could take time away from more basic research and writing, and so on. In short, it may be difficult for a faculty member to maintain a holistic agenda, with enough emphasis on the longer-term, more basic side of his or her research plan. How can the business school support a faculty member in developing an individual plan which preserves a long-term holistic dimension, and 'protects' the member from being 'torn apart' by a myriad of short-term pressures resulting from the relationship?

The solution is to institute an individual faculty member planning effort, on an annual basis. Here the faculty member should outline his or her long-term rationale and objectives. The emphasis should be put on major contributions that the faculty member believes can feasibly be provided. Needless to say, such a plan will be 'based' on the ongoing experience that the faculty member has already achieved. Application of this experience will thus shape the plan for active participation in a business network. In other words, the main emphasis is put on what contribution the faculty member intends to make. The key to success here is to keep in mind and to practise the dictum: 'strategy means choice'.

Each individual faculty member should review the plan with the dean of the faculty as well as with the director of research for the school, so that the member can *both* benefit from substantive feedback, including yearly follow-up on how well results are being achieved relative to the evolving plan, *and* also receive the resources essential for research support. These resources are not necessarily confined to monetary needs, but to ensuring that there is a sufficient amount of time available to do the research. In addition, there will need to be an explicit link between teaching assignments and each faculty member's research plans. It may not be realistic to expect significantly lighter teaching loads or extended sabbatical leaves – certainly not on a large scale in today's typical business school scenario where resources are tight. Rather, the ability to make time available for research is more reasonably managed by assigning teaching responsi-bilities to each member of the faculty team in such a way that blocks of time can be set aside for research. It is also extremely important that the faculty member is 'protected' from being intruded on by various *ad hoc* crisis assignments when he or she is engaged in research work. A more structured batching of teaching versus research efforts is therefore needed.

Several overall implications can be drawn from this discussion.

- Faculty members should design an explicit plan, which will be followed up on a yearly basis to determine progress and any relative shift in the research emphasis in light of experience gained.
- There should be more purposeful interaction between the academic leadership of the school and each faculty member regarding the substantive research issues that the member is pursuing, so that he or she will receive real support and input, if necessary, should there be a temporary stalemate in research progress.
- There should be a more relevant link between an individual faculty member's plans and the resource support that the school gives, not only in terms of money for research, but, even more importantly, in terms of providing sufficient time for research. Careful planning of the teaching load and batching teaching time, relative to research, must take place.
- A holistic planning activity within the school is essential, so as to make sure that cutting-edge research, teaching, and interaction with leading businesses can go on as a positive symbiosis, without compromising the research agenda of each individual faculty member.
- If the school lacks well-thought-out planning, the danger is indeed real that the intensity of the interaction in a business partnership network and inevitable *ad hoc* pressures will interfere with an individual faculty member's basic research.

3 Development of faculty-based knowledge cells

It goes without saying that successful delivery of in-company programme activities must be carefully tailor-made to meet the client company's specific needs. Also, it is essential that the school can put together a faculty team which has the know-how and combined breadth and depth of experience to deliver what is needed. It follows that more and more effort will go into the design of in-company programme activities, and that the programme management time will also increase correspondingly. More faculty resources will therefore have to be channelled into preparation and the steps leading up to delivery, relative to the actual classroom performance. The result is that faculty capacity will be utilized in dimensions other than teaching in the traditional classroom setting. Clearly, then, the business school must receive a compensation for the resources it uses for all of these preparatory activities, in order to have a financially viable result. In addition, it is possible that more faculty members will need to be hired, in order for the school to cope with a capacity squeeze.

Needless to say, it can range from being difficult to impossible in practice to achieve a viable cost–benefit equation for how much time must be spent relative to the amount a school can realistically charge a given customer. Consequently, it is important to find ways of being more 'productive' – in the delivery of first-class in-company programme offerings, that is. One solution is to delineate the specific knowledge components that each member is able to deliver, as a result of the member's research-based teaching capabilities. It is most important, however, that these knowledge cells include not only individual members but also *teams* of faculty members who regularly work together as information clusters. In this way, it will quickly become apparent to those designing new programmes which groups of faculty members, building on past experience and individual know-how, can most realistically be expected to deliver a particular programme, thereby requiring that only a minimum of specific new activities be tailor-made.

The change in working mode for the faculty of a modern business school that uses a knowledge cell/knowledge cluster approach is, of course, dramatic. Rather than each faculty member having individual courses, he or she works with teams of other faculty members, some of whom they will inevitably know better than others. The faculty member, as part of a number of teams, will thus contribute in some way to several programmes. The challenge is being able to mobilize delivery of a programme based on the most appropriate knowledge cells/knowledge clusters. Clearly, the effectiveness of a faculty team, in terms of delivering high-quality research-based teaching, will probably increase through such an approach. But if this approach fails to be more productive, then working successfully with business could be affected, in that the faculty team will become too expensive relative to the designated resources. Thus, having an intensive interaction with firms would not be viable from an economic point of view, unless a knowledge cell approach were followed.

It goes without saying that keeping track of the levels of expertise amongst the faculty in the various knowledge cells and clusters will require extra planning. Moreover, those who are leading the school will have a major resource allocation task in terms of mobilizing the knowledge cells and knowledge clusters in a more purposeful way, so that they can meet the various needs that the in-company executive teaching programmes require. Undoubtedly, the whole issue of work assignments takes on a different role in the progressive company-related business school. To succeed, there needs to be both maturity and understanding on the part of all faculty members – on a greater scale, indeed, than has historically been the accepted norm in classical business schools.

CONCLUSION

There are strong reasons for believing that the competitive arena for business schools is changing: new competition is arising, but at the same time many new opportunities are becoming available – all stemming from a progressively greater emphasis on in-house education and more training efforts in the emergent learning organizations. The modern business school can seize this opportunity and thus find a way to develop truly outstanding new, state-of-the-art, value-creating, academic breakthroughs. A key factor in making this change will be the establishment of a close long-term relationship with a select number of leading corporations, coupled with more purposeful individual research and teaching planning, as well as finding feasible ways for faculty teams to deliver programmes on a cost-effective basis by using a knowledge cell/cluster approach.

It will, ultimately, be largely up to the faculty members themselves to determine whether or not a shift in emphasis towards greater cooperation and a closer relationship with business is desirable and viable. Regarding viability, it should be kept in mind that the limited resources available in today's society may even force more cooperation with business, particularly if the alternative means no further development for progressive business schools. In terms of desirability, it will depend on whether or not faculty members feel that they are receiving sufficient stimulus from working on real-life issues and problems stemming from business, rather than focusing only on more axiomatic functionally based research activities. It is hard to predict what will be the outcome in this respect: some faculty teams will be strongly motivated by working with business in this academic value-creating way; others will find that this approach is too radical a deviation from the classical academic values that they are comfortable with. It is important to remember that there is no right or wrong answer to this issue. The key thing is to have ongoing purposeful discussions, and to outline the *pros* and *cons* for each individual business school. Consideration must be given to resource constraints and opportunities, competitive constraints and opportunities, and, above all, to the constraints and opportunities involved in creating a truly stimulating atmosphere for a faculty team. Only in this way can there be a sound basis for attracting and retaining the best possible faculty members, which is *the* most critical condition for ensuring the long-term viability of a business school.

BIBLIOGRAPHY

Blau, P. (1993) *The Organization of Academic Work*, New York: John Wiley and Sons.

Cowen, S.S. (1995) 'Lessons Learned: Guiding Strategic Change in Higher Education', in R.E. Boyatzis, S.S. Cowen, and D.A. Kolb (eds) *Innovation in Professorial Education: Steps on a Journey from Teaching to Learning*, San Francisco: Jossey-Bass.

Engwall, L. (1992) *Mercury Meets Minerva. Business Administration in Academia: The Swedish Case*, Oxford: Pergamon Press.

Fulmer, R.M. (1994) 'A New Model for How Organizations Learn', *Planning Review* 22(3): 20–4.

—— and Vicere, A.A. (1995) *Executive Education and Leadership Development: The*

State of Practice, University Park, PA: UNICON and The Pennsylvania State Institute for the Study of Organizational Effectiveness.

Ghoshal, S., Arnzen, B., and Brownfield, S. (1992) 'A Learning Alliance Between Business and Business Schools: Executive Education as a Platform for Partnership', *California Management Review* 35(1): 50–67.

Harvard Business School (1991) *Intellectual Innovation at Harvard Business School: a Strategy*, Boston, MA: Harvard Business School Division of Research.

Hogarth, R.M. (1979) *Evaluating Management Education*, Chichester: John Wiley and Sons.

—— and Michaud, C. (1993) *Executive Education in Business Schools: Towards a New Paradigm*, CEDEP Fontainebleu, France.

Lorange, P. (1988) 'On Stimulating Strategic Direction in an Academic Department', in Robert Lamb and Paul Shrivastava (eds) *Advances in Strategic Management*, 5, Greenwich, CT: JAI Press.

—— (1996) 'Developing Learning Partnership', *The Learning Organization* 3(2).

Middlehurst, R. (1993) *Leading Academics*, Buckingham: Open University Press.

O'Reilly, B. (1993) 'How Execs Learn Now', *Fortune International* 127(7): 37–40.

Pellicelli, G. and Tardivo, G. (1993) 'The Evolution of Training Programs in Business Schools: A Profile of the Scuola Di Amministrazione Aziendale of the University of Torino', *Journal of European Business Education* 2(2), 45–55.

Schein, E. (1970) 'The Reluctant Professor: Implications for University Management', *Sloan Management Review* 12(Fall): 35–49.

Sergiovanni, T.J. (1993) *Moral Leadership: Getting to the Heart of School Improvement*, San Francisco: Jossey-Bass.

Vicere, A.A., Taylor, M.W., and Freeman, V.T. (1994) 'Executive Development in Major Corporations: a Ten-Year Study', *The Journal of Management Development* 13(1): 4–22.

INDEX

Aaronson, S.A. 12, 38, 212, 213, 215, 216, 218, 219
Academy of Management Development 108
Academy of Management Journal 239
Academy of Management Review 239
Acton Society 137
Administration Research Foundation (ARF) 26
Aken, J.E. van 75, 90
Aldcroft, D.H. 8, 20, 21
All-Japan Federation of Management Associations (*Zen Nihon Noritsu Renmei*) 103
Allais, M. 62
Amano, I. 97
Ambroz, M. 128
Amdam, R.P. 2, 21, 22, 23, 24, 25, 30, 32, 34, 172, 186, 229, 241; *et al.* 27; and Mordt, G. 28; and Norstrøm, C.J. 10, 22, 239; and Sogner, K. 27, 29, 32, 33
American Assembly of Collegiate Schools of Business (AACSB) 213, 217, 218, 219, 220, 221–2, 224
American Foreign Operation Administration (FOA) 24
American Management Association 223
American model 4, 6, 7–8, 8, 19–20, 27, 33, 212, 224, 228; and changes in education 218–24; and European competition 38; evaluation of 214–15; impact of 40, 41–2; influence of 22–7, 100–2, 173–5; and MBAs 215–18, 223–4; overview 213–14; as pre-eminent 38
American Research and Development (ARD) 43
Americanization 43

Amsterdam School of Business Economics 85
Ancona, D.G. and Nadler, D.A. 231, 233
Andersen, S. 181
Anglo-American Council on Productivity 135
Ann Arbor School of Business Administration 66
Arbeidspsykologisk Institutt (API) 186
Armstrong, P. 228, 229, 230
Ashley, W.J. 99
Askvik, S. 26
Aso, M. 96
AT&T 24
Audu, I. 154

Babson University 219
Balfour Committee 155
Ball, Georges 46
Bantel, K.A. and Jackson, S.E. 232
Barclays Bank International 143
Barnard, C. 173
Barnes, L. and Krieger, M.P. 234
Barnes, W. 20
Barry, B. 20
Barsoux, J.-L. 8
Beigel, R. 97
Benton–Moody Amendment 24
Berelson, B. 66
Berger, P.L. and Luckmann, T. 196
Berle, A.A., Jr and Means, G.C. 202
Bettis, R.A. 241
Björk, S. 235
Blood, M.R. 218, 220
Bocconi University 40
Bodo Graduate School 28
Bolin, E. and Dahlberg, L. 201, 202, 204, 205, 209
Bond, F. *et al.* 225

Bontadini, P. 50
Borgonjon, J. and Vanhonacker, W.R. 2
Bosman, A. 88
Bouma, J.L. 88
Bowie, J.A. 135, 138
BP 134
Brglez, M. 127
British Institute of Management (BIM)
    135
British model 8, 19, 20, 21, 133–4;
    business and culture 134–6; changes
    in 136–8; see also Manchester
    Business School (MBS)
Brookings Institute 223
Brown, R.B. 152, 167
Bundy, M. 64
Burnham, J. 202
business administration 40, 72
business culture 134–6; impact of MBS
    on 145–8
business education 172, 208–9, 212, 224;
    in the 1990s 72–4; changes in 70–6,
    218–21; continuity in 70–6; defined
    73; dichotomies in 76–9; in Europe
    69–70; evaluation of 214–15; and
    explanation/construction dichotomy
    77–8; future of 91–3; growth and
    stagnation 74–6; impediments to
    change in 221–2; institutions 182–4;
    and internal recruitment 181–2;
    overview of 213–14; and penetration
    of top management 200–7; in period
    of industrial democracy 185–6; in
    period of managerialism 186–8; post-
    Taylorist 180–4; purpose of 242–3;
    and restrictive/non-restrictive
    dichotomy 77; as science 69–70, 75–8,
    80–1, 83, 87, 89–90, 92; social force
    196–7; in socio-technical period 184–
    5; supply and demand for 195–7;
    technical force of 196; and theory/
    practice dichotomy 76–7; trends 180;
    see also management education
business schools 41, 246; and business
    partnership network 252–3; classical
    248–9; competitive patterns in 246–51,
    256–7; and cooperation with key
    clients 246–51; and cross-functional
    cooperation 248–9; demand for 248;
    and faculty-based knowledge cells
    255–6; and network building 58–60;
    and planning for individual faculty

members 253–5; and private
    undertakings 247, 250; proposed
    strategy of 252; and research agendas
    252, 253; response options 251–6; see
    also new university business schools
    (NUBS); university business schools
    (UBS)
business studies 73, 74, 75, 89, 90, 93, 99,
    166; prewar development of 97–8
Business Week 214, 216
Byrkjeflot, H. 19, 31, 174
Byrt, W. 3, 9, 19

California University 198, 220
Cannon, T. 148
Canziani, A. and Brovetto, P.R. 39
Carew, A. 191
Carlson, S. 195, 201, 202, 208
Carnegie Commission 195, 215
Carnegie Corporation 12
Carnegie Institute of Technology 25, 47,
    88
Carnegie Mellon University 219, 220
Carroll, T. 46
Case Western University 218
Casey, D. 232
Cassel, G. 200, 208, 209
CEDEP 62–3
Centers for International Business
    Education and Research (CIBERS) 223
Centre de Préparation aux Affaires
    (CPA) 43, 50, 51, 53, 60
Centre de Recherche en Sciences de
    l'Organisation (CEROG) 58
Centre for Foreign Trade (Radenci) 128
Centre for Industrial and Business
    Studies (Warwick University) 58–9
Centro Universitario per
    l'Organizzazione Aziendale (CUOA)
    52
Chandler, A.D., Jr 3, 66, 134, 196, 214–
    15, 229
Channon, D.F. 136
Cheit, E.F. 4, 11, 12, 21, 66, 166
Chester, T.E. 138, 146
Chicago University 47, 62, 219
Christiania Glasmagasin 26–7
Chuo University 99
Civil Communications Section (CCS) 101
Clinton, B. 212
Coleman, D.C. 134
Collins, K. 20

Columbia University 47, 218, 219
Comitato Nazionale per la Produttività
   60
competitiveness 1, 12, 19–20, 146–8
Competitiveness Policy Council 223, 225
Comte, A. 80
Confederation of British Industry (CBI)
   156
Constable, T. and McCormick, R. 147
contrasts of contexts 41, 42, 46, 65
control 82, 174
Converse, P. 66
Cooper, C.L. 158
Cooper, K. 224
Copeland, M.T. 50, 51–2, 66
Cornell University 115
Council for Management Training and
   Education 238, 242
Courtaulds 138
Critchley, B. and Casey, D. 233
Crosland, A. 158
cross-fertilization policies 42–3, 61, 64;
   after Second World War 43, 45–6;
   early attempts 43
'Cult of the Amateur' 134
culture 171
Cundiff, E. 66

Dahlberg, L. 201, 202
Daito, E. 109
Darden School of Management 219
Delft Superior School of Technology 78,
   79, 82
Deming, Dr 101
Derossi, F. 53
d'Estaing, O. Giscard *see* Giscard
   d'Estaing
Deurink, G. 53
DiMaggio, P.J. and Powell, W.W. 197
Ditchley Foundation 169
divisionalization 3
Djurdjevic, M. 127, 129
Dockerlay, J.C. 35
Donovan, W. 46
Doriot, G.F. 43, 45, 61, 62
Dornseifer, B. and Kocka, J. 11
Doshisha University 99
Douma, S.W. 75
Drucker, P.F. 25, 108, 173, 174, 191
Duke University 218
Dunlap Smith, E. 25
Dunning, J.H. 3

Dutch Accountants Association 82
École des Hautes Études Commerciales
   (HEC) 53, 61, 198
Economic Cooperation Administration
   (ECA) 24
Economic Development Administration
   Program (EDA) 47
economics 69, 72, 74, 75–6, 83, 83–5, 84,
   89, 91, 93, 99
Economics, Commercial Science, the
   Journal of National Economy 99
Economist 4
Edelstein, R.J. 213, 218, 219
Edvardsen, R. 28
EIASM 59
Eindhoven 72
Engelen, J.M.L. van 90
engineers 28–9, 31, 172–3, 177, 178, 179,
   188, 189
English Sewing Cotton 138
Engwall, L. 5, 9, 194, 200, 209; *et al.* 12,
   229; and Gunnarsson, E. 3, 6, 9, 228
Enteman, W.F. 175, 187–8, 190, 191
Ermarth, M. 173
Euro-Asian Centre 64
Europe, differences in 40–1; influence of
   America on 38–9, 41–2
European Association of Management
   Training Centres (EAMTC) 53
European Productivity Agency (EPA) 10,
   24, 43, 46, 48
Eurosclerosis 178

Fayol, H. 40
Federation of British Industry (FBI) 156
Federation of Economic Organizations 106
Ferranti 138
FIAT 53
finance 71, 73, 85, 91
flexible firm 179
Flexner, A. 154
Fligstein, N. 195, 228, 229; and
   Byrkjeflot, H. 171
Flipovič, N. 127
Fondation Industrie-Université 53
Ford Foundation 12, 42, 45, 53–4, 67,
   195, 215; cross-fertilization policies
   42–6, 61, 64; European involvement
   of 42; European pioneer stage 49–54;
   European plan 54–60; new look in
   management 46–9; retreat from
   Europe 63–5

FORMEZ 52
Fortune magazine 51
Foundation for Management Education
(FME) 136, 137, 142
Foxwell, E. 98
Franks, Lord 138, 144, 156, 168
Franks Report (1963) 137
Freedman, D.H. 234
French model 7–8, 40
Frisch, R. 22
Fukuda, T. and Seki, H. 99

Gammelsæter, H. 27, 29, 31, 33, 229, 242
Gauslaa, S. 176
Geiger, R.L. 2, 20
Gemelli, A. 48
Gemelli, G. 43, 45, 60
general management 173, 185–6, 187–8,
189–91
General Motors 223
Gennaro, P. 50, 52
Gentlemen and Players 20, 134–5
Georgetown University 219
Georgia Tech 220
Georgia University 220
German model 4–6, 6, 7, 12, 27, 39;
influence of 20–2, 98–100, 173–5
Giddens, A. 197
Gils, M.R. van *et al.* 88
Giscard d'Estaing 43
Gjærum Committee 237
Glaxo 32, 134
globalization 3
Godino, R. 43
Gogh, van 79
Goldner, F.H. and Ritti, R.R. 182
Gordon, R.A. and Howell, J.E. 195
Gordon, S. 53
Goshi, K. 106, 107
Gosling, J. 232
Gothenburg 198–9
Goudriaan, J. 79–81, 86, 87, 89, 90, 93
graduates 212; demand for 199–200;
education of 213–15, 218–21; and
MBAs 215–18, 223–4; supply of 197–9
Green, V.H.H. 154
Greenhouse, S. 38
Grégoire, R. 54, 67
Griffiths, B. and Murray, H. 158, 159
Gulowsen, J. 176
Gundhus, P. 25
Gunnarsson, E. 209

Gust, M.J. 216
Gyll, S. 208

Hafslund Nycomed 29
Hagtvedt, B. and Lafferty, W. 178
Hague, Professor 143
Hall, E.T. 76
Halsey, A.H. 151
Halvorsen, T. 171, 172, 175, 181, 183
Hambrick, D.C. and Mason, P.A. 231,
242
Handelschochschulen 4
Handy, C. 147; *et al.* 2, 12, 19
Hanisch, T.J. and Lange, E. 22, 26, 183
Hara, T. 109
Hartmann, H. 173
Harvard Business School (HBS) 2, 29, 43,
47, 50, 62, 100, 108, 115, 142, 225
Harvard University 198
Hedenström, A. 208
Henley Administrative Staff College 26,
135
Hermansen Committee 237
hero-generalist paradigm 228, 233;
grand theory assumption 234; hero
assumption 233–4; in Norwegian
context 236–8
Heymans, G. 83
Hickman, C. 214, 216, 217, 220, 221
Higher Education and Research Program
47
Hijmans, 79
Hitotsubashi 97
Hitotsubashi 50 Nenshi 98
Hitotsubashi Senmon-bu 100
Hitotsubashi University 100
Hofstede, G. 171, 233
Hökby, B. 201
Hosei University 99
Howell, J.E. 66
human relations 71, 72, 73
human resources 179, 184
Hurst, D.K. 241
Hutton, G. 106

ICI 134, 138
ICPE Ljubljana 115
images of knowledge 41
IMD 2, 115
IMEDE 53
Indiana University 115
industrial administration 188–91;

American or German 173–5; industrial democracy trend 178; institutionalization of 172–3; management and education trends in 180–8; managerial trend 178–80; post-Taylorist trend 176–7; socio-technical trend 177–8; trends and movements (1950–90) 175

Industrial Efficiency (*Sangyo Noritsu*) College 103

INSEAD (France) 2, 8, 43, 46, 53, 58, 59, 60, 61–2, 65–6, 66, 115; and development of the faculty 63; history of 60; links to American business schools 61–2; and networks for industry 60–1; transformation of 63–5

Institut Supérieur de Commerce d'Anvers 98

Institute for Industrial Efficiency (*Sangyo Noritsu Kenkyusho*) 102

Institute for Industrial Milieu Research (IFIM) 184

Institute for International Cooperation (Japan) 102

Institute of Management Consultants (Japan) 103

Institute for Technical Productivity and Research (PROFO) 191

Instituts d'Administration des Entreprises (IAE) 58

International Affairs Program (IPA) 47

International Centre for Banking and Finance (Manchester) 143

International Centre for Public Enterprises (ICPE) Radovljica 127

International Executive Development Centre (IEDC) Brdo 115, 127, 129

International Institute for Management of Technology (Milan) 59

International Labour Organization (ILO) 106

International Teachers Program 58

International University Contact (IUC) 53

internationalization 89

IPSOA (Italy) 46, 47, 48, 56, 60, 63, 65; effect of 52–4; history of 49–52

IRAS (*Industriforbundets Rasjonaliseringsgruppe*) 182

ISIDA 56

Iskra Foreign Trade School 128

ISTUD 52

Italian model 40

Italy, and Ford Foundation 46–54, 56–7

Itami, H. 104

Jagersma, P.K. 89

Jaklič, M. 127

Janssen, Claude 43

Japanese Chamber of Commerce and Industry 106

Japanese Federation of Management Associations (*Nihon Noritsu Renogokai*) 102

Japanese Industrial Association (*Nihon Kogyo Kyokai*) 102

Japanese Management Association (JMA) 101, 102–3, 108

Japanese model 8, 8–9, 12, 20, 33, 96; American influence on 100–2; and diffusion of in-firm training 106–9; foreign influences on 98; German impact on 98–100; new managers 103–5; prewar development 97–8

Japanese Productivity Centre (JPC – *Nihon Seisansei Honbu*) 106–7, 108–9

Japanese Society of Business Economics 99

Japanese Society of Industrial Training 108

Japanese Union of Scientists and Engineers (*Nikka Giren*) 101

Jensen, O.H. and Stromme Svendsen, A. 27, 172, 183

Joele, J. 88

Joint Development Activity (JDA) 143–4

joint management 178, 189

joint stock companies 105

Jorna, R.J. 90

Journal of Management 239

Kaizai Doyukai 108

Kakabadse, A. and Mukhi, S. 158

Kalleberg, R. 25, 182

Karsten, L. and Man, H. de 70, 71

Katz, M. 46

Katzenbach, J.R. and Douglas, K.S. 232

Keck, S.L. and Tushman, M.L. 232

Keeble, S.P. 20, 135, 137, 138

Keio Business School 100

Keio Gijuku 97, 98, 99

Keio University 99

Keizai Doyukai 104–5, 106, 107

Kellog University 115

Kenning Circle 25

Kenning, G. 25
Kerr, C. 154
King, A. 45, 48, 49, 52, 66
Kirkbride, P.S. 3
Kishi, N. 105
Kissinger, H. 63
Klant, J.J. 84
Kogan, M. 158, 159
Kogut, B. 3; and Parkinson, D. 9
Kokugakuin University 99
Koontz, H. 234
Kraljič, P. 111, 119
Krugman, P. 212

Labour Productivity Academy (Japan)
    107, 108
labour representation 177, 178
Lai, L. 31
Lane, E. 3, 8, 19, 20
Lange, E. 22
Larsen, K.A. 28
Latin model 7
Lawrence, P. 19, 27, 72
Laws Stores of Gateshead 139
leaders/leadership 173, 174, 181
learning, life-long 247, 248–9, 251;
    organization 72, 247, 257; team 247
Leggatt, T. 156
Lewis, M. 217
Limperg, Th. 79, 84–5, 87, 89, 93
Linder, J.C. and Smith, H.J. 216
linking-pin organization 72
Locke, R.R. 3, 5, 8, 12, 19, 20, 32, 38, 70,
    71, 77, 87, 134, 135, 214, 227, 230, 233,
    239, 241
Lombardo, I.M. 48
London Business School 2
Lorriman, J. and Kenjo, T. 8, 11, 20
Lubin School of Business 218
Lundberg, S. 177
Lupton, T. 139, 144, 148, 158–9
Lyndall Urwick 135

MacErlean, N. 235
McKenna, J.F. 2
McKinsey, 29
McLelland, G. 139
McNamara, R. 57
Maier, P. 66
Malmenström, G. and Wiedenborg, B.
    201
Man, H. de and Karsten, L. 9

management 82, 166, 227; as cultural
    pattern 41; and culture 171;
    development of 103–9; engineering
    approach to 90–1; new look in 46–9;
    new paradigm in 87; in period of
    industrial democracy 185–6; in period
    of managerialism 186–8; in socio-
    technical period 184–5
Management Academy (Keiei Daigaku)
    107
management accounting 71, 72, 74, 84–5
management by objectives 174
management consulting companies 249–
    50
management education 108, 111–12,
    164–6, 180, 227–8; as biased towards
    individualism and generalism 233–8,
    239; and business 11–14; and business
    performance 30–3, 35; challenges for
    13–14; and competitiveness 1; defined
    73; differences in national systems of
    3–9; diffusion of ideas and models 9–
    11; as diverging/converging process
    239–42; expansion in 2–3; and
    managerial skills 1; origins of
    institutions 11; programmes for 112;
    supply side 113–16, 126; see also
    business education
Management Training Programmes
    (MTPs) 101
managerial gap 46, 111
managerialism 175, 176, 178–80, 186–8,
    190
Manchester Business School (MBS) 133;
    adapting to circumstances 142–5;
    Experiment 138–45; and internal
    conflict 142–5
Manchester School of Management &
    Administration (Mansma) 138
Mant, O. 143
March, J.G. 88
Maris, T. 224
marketing 71, 73, 74, 114
Markgren, B. 209
Marshall Aid 24, 70, 106, 176, 181, 184
Marxism 105
Maryland University 214, 218
Masuji, Y. 102
Mayer, J. 128–9
MBA programmes 2, 4, 7, 8, 19, 20, 30,
    63, 66, 73, 93, 112, 115, 126–7, 142,
    150–1, 164, 166, 167–8, 247; criticism

of 215–18; demand for 116–19, 223–4;
evaluation of 119–25
Meiji University 99
Melandri, P. 64
Mendés-France 61
method, time and measurement (MTM)
programme 184
Meyer, J.W. and Scott, W.R. 197
Micheletti, G. 53
Michigan Business School 218, 219, 220
Miller, R. 51, 66
Ministry of International Trade and
Industry (MITI) 106
Mintzberg, H. 232, 233, 234
MIT 59
Mitsui Busan 98
Morello, G. 48, 50, 51, 56
Morito, T. 104
Moroi, K. 104
Morris, J. 139, 143
Motorola University 223
Muysken, J. and Schreuder, H. 83, 84

Nagaoka, K. 231
Nakayama, I. 107
National Economic Development
Council (NEDC) 137, 156
National Economic Development Office
(NEDO) 157–8
National Management Council 50
national systems, differences in 3–9; and
foreign influences on 19–21, 30
Nestlé school 53
Netherlands model 7, 69–70; American
influence on 69–70, 87–9, 92;
continuity and change in 70–6; early
views of 79–86; and future of
academic business education 91–3;
persistent dichotomies in 76–9
New Education Law (Japan) 100
new university business schools (NUBS)
152, 153, 159–60, 161, 163, 164; see
also university business schools
New York University 219
Newcomer, M. 225
Nielsen, W.A. 53, 64
Nihon Kindai Kyoiku 100 Nenshi 101,
107, 108
Nihon Sangyo Kunren Kyokai 101, 106,
108
Nihon Seisansei Honbu 107, 108
Nihon University 99

Nijenrode 73
Nikkeiren 104, 106, 108
Nind, P.F. 136
Nioche, J.P. 19, 65
Nishizawa, T. 98, 109, 147
Noda, K. 104
Nohria, N. and Berkley, J.D. 232, 241
Nordby, P.A. 25
Noritsu-do 102
North European Management Institute
(NEMI) 29, 187
Northwestern University 220
Norwegian Council for Management
Training and Education 237
Norwegian Institute for Human
Resource Management (NIPA) 187
Norwegian Institute for Leadership and
Administration (NILA) 187
Norwegian Institute of Technology
(NTH) 21, 23, 25, 26, 29, 183–5
Norwegian model, American influence
on 22–7, 29–30, 31–2, 33–4, 173–5; and
business performance 30–3, 35;
change from engineers to business
school graduates 28–9, 31; and change
in industrial recruitment 28–9, 31; and
expansion of business schools 27–30;
German influence on 20–2, 33, 173–5;
and government control 34–5; history
of 172–3; and industrial democracy
178, 185–6; and internal recruitment
181–2; and international collaboration
32–3; and managerialism 178–80, 186–
8; and post-Taylorism 176–7; and
socio-technical period 177–8, 184–5;
training and educational institutions
182–4; trends and movements 175
Norwegian Productivity Institute (NPI)
24–5, 26, 191
Norwegian School of Economics and
Business Administration (NSEBA) 21–
4, 25, 26, 27, 30, 183, 185, 239, 241
Norwegian School of Management
(NSM) 23, 28, 29–30, 172, 186, 239
Norwegian Society of Business
Graduates 240
Nouschi, M. 53
Nycomed 32, 33, 34
Nyegaard & Co. 29, 32

OEEC 24
Ohio Northern University 224

Ohlsson, F. 201, 204
Oien, F. 23, 24, 35
Okamoto, H. 104, 105
Okazaki-Ward, L. 103, 106, 107, 108
old university business schools (OUBS)
  152, 155–9, 163, 164, 166, 168
Olivetti, A. 50, 53, 54
OLUF programme 187
Omnibus Trade and Competitiveness
  Act (1988) 223
on-the-job training 20
operations research 71, 72, 73
Organization for Economic Cooper-
  ation and Development (OECD) 40–1,
  59
organizations 83–5
O'Toole, J. and Bennis, W. 231
Otsuka, B. 105
Ouchi, H. 99
overhead value analysis 72
owner–entrepreneurs 174, 177, 181, 189

Papěz, T. 127
Parker, R.H. 10
Pennsylvania University 155
personal capitalism 134
personnel management 71
Pfeffer, J. and Salancik, G.R. 208
Philips 71
Pierson, F.C. 195
Pittsburgh University 220
Platt, J.W. 136
Polak, N.J. 85, 86
polytechnics 146, 151–2, 159–60, 172
'Pool of American Professors in Business
  Administration' project 54–5
Porter, L.W. and McKibbin, L.E. 158, 195,
  214, 215, 216–17, 218, 220, 221–2
Porter, M.E. 20
positivism 39, 90–1
post-Taylorism 175, 176–7, 178, 179, 188;
  education and management in 180–4
Praktisk okonomi og ledelse 240
Princeton Review – Student Access
  Guide to the Best Business Schools 214
production 71, 72
psychology 90
PTT Railways 71
Purg, D. 114

Quality Control (QC) 101
Radovljica University 115, 127

Ragin, C. 41
Rasmussen, L. and Wold, A. 28
Redlich, F. 194–5
research, and 'publish or perish' 74, 89;
  type of 162–3
Reve, T. 231
Ricossa, S. 53
Ringer, F. 175
Robbins Report (1963) 158
Robinson, M. 47–8
Robinson, P. 217
Rogers, J. 158
Rojec, M. and Svetličič, M. 113
Rolls-Royce 143
Rose Report (1970) 157–8
Rossum, W. van 77
Rotterdam Superior School of
  Commerce 69, 81, 82, 85
Royal Agricultural College (Sweden) 199
Royal College of Forestry (Sweden) 199
Royal Institute of Technology (Sweden)
  199

Saito, T. 109
Sakamoto, F. 99, 106, 108
Sanno Management School 103
Sasaki, S. 109
Savoy Group 137, 147
Scandinavian model 6, 7
Schaetzel, R. 63
Schein, E.H. 76
Schjander, N. 182
Schlossman, S., et al. 42, 47; and Sedlak,
  M. 215
Schmalenbach, E. 22, 85, 99
Schrueder, H. 75–6
Schwenk, C.R. 231, 242
Scott, W.G. and Hart, D.K. 190
Searle, J. 154
Sebesta, L. 41
Sejersted, F. 181
Senjur, M. 113
Servan-Schreiber, J.J. 46, 57
Shell 71, 134
Sheridan, J.H. 216, 217, 218, 219, 221
Shiryo 99
Simon, H.A. 38, 52, 88
Skinner, W. 216
Sloan, A.P. 173, 174
Slovene Institute of Management 128
Slovenia 111–12, 126–7; and demand for
  MBA education 116–19; economy of

112–13; genesis/characteristics of management education in 113–16; and transition process 119–25
Society for Social Policy 99
sociology 90
Solomon, J.J. 48, 66
Solstrand courses 185
Solstrand programme 26
Southern Methodist University 220
Standard Oil 24
Stanford 47, 62
Stanford Business School 217
Stanford University 219, 220
Stappen, J. van 98
Starreveld, R.W. 82
Statoil 241
Steiro, J.R. 24
Stern School of Business 214, 218
Stockholm School of Economics 58, 198, 200
Stokke, B. 240
Stone, S. 49–50
Sugiyama, C. and Nishizawa, T. 99
Svendsen, A.S. 240
Svetličič, M. 123, 128
Swedish model 194–5, 208–9; and academic business education 195–7; and demand for graduates 199–200; and penetration of top management 200–7; supply of graduates 197–9
Swidler, A. 175
systems approach 71, 72, 87

Talset, T. 34
Tavčar, M. 127
Taylor, F. 71, 102
Taylor Society 102
Taylorism 177
Tazaki, S. 98
team management 227–8, 242–3; and business schools 242–3; and case for 230–3; challenges and education 239–42; defined 232–3; and hero-generalist paradigm 233–8; and top management 228–30
Technical Assistance Programme 70
technological gap 41
Tennessee College of Business Administration 219
Teresi, S. 60
Texas University 218
theory of the firm 40

Thorbecke, 78
Thorsud, E. 184
Times Higher Education Supplement 151
Toba, K. 105
Tokyo Higher Commercial School 97
Tokyo Imperial University 97, 98, 99
Tokyo University of Commerce 99–100, 104
top management 242–3; and case for management teams 230–3; as heterogenous team 228–33; penetration of 200–7; professions in 228–30; three roads to the top 203–7
Towle, J.W. 66
training 164–6; Civil Communications Section (CCS) 101; in-house 96, 101, 106–9, 147, 247, 248, 250–1, 256–7; institutions 182–4; for management see MBA programmes; Management Training Programmes (MTP) 101; on-the-job 111, 134; Training Within Industry (TWI) 101; vocational 99
Training Within Industry (TWI) 101, 176
Treaty of Rome 54, 65
Truscott, B. 154
Turin school 53
Turin Unione Industriale 51
Turner, G. 133

Ueda, T. 99, 105
Ueno, Y. 102, 103, 109
UNI Storebrand 31, 33, 35, 240
Unilever 71, 134
university business schools (UBS) 150–2, 166–8; education or training 164–6; funding 167; models of university purpose 153–5; new 159–60; old 155–9; research design 152–3; research findings 160–6; teaching in 163–4; type of research in 162–3; see also business schools; new university business schools (NUBS)
University Grants Committee (UGC) 136, 140
University Order (Japan, 1918) 97
Uppsala University 197
Uri, P. 61
U.S. News and World Report 214
Utnes, G. 176

Valletta, V. 50

Veblen, T. 194
Virginia University 219
Volmer, J.G.H. 79, 81
Volvo 184
Vries, J. de 82

Waaler, R. 26, 185
Wakimura, Y. 104
Wallenberg family 198
Wallerstedt, E. 209
Warner, M. 9
Warwick University 58–9
Waseda University 99
Waterman, M. 66
Wedervang, I. 22
Weiner, M.J. 155
Wharton Business School (Philadelphia)
    4, 155, 198, 218, 219
Wheatcroft, M. 138, 155
Whitley, R. 3, 11, 92, 209, 227, 228, 235,
    236; et al. 3

Wiersema, M.F. and Bantel, K.A. 232
Wight Bakke, E. 26
Williams, C.M. 50
Williams, Professor 138, 146
Wilson, J.F. 20, 134, 135, 136, 138, 139,
    142, 144, 146
Woodall, J. 2
World Economic Forum 225

Yale School of Management 220
Yamashita, S. 104, 105
Yasumuro, K. 20
Yonekawa, S. 98; et al. 101, 103
Yttri, G. 191
Yukl, G.A. 227

Zaibatsu 103
Zwaan, A.H. van der 79; and van
    Engelen, J.M.H. 90
Zysman, J. 11